MW00490526

A DICTIONARY
OF VICTORIAN
LONDON

A DICTIONARY OF VICTORIAN LONDON

An A–Z of the Great Metropolis

Lee Jackson

Anthem Press

Anthem Press
An imprint of Wimbledon Publishing Company
www.anthempress.com

This edition first published in UK and USA 2006
by ANTHEM PRESS
75-76 Blackfriars Road, London SE1 8HA, UK
or PO Box 9779, London SW19 7ZG, UK
and
244 Madison Ave. #116, New York, NY 10016, USA

British Library Cataloguing in Publication Data
A catalogue record for this book is available from the
British Library.

Library of Congress Cataloging in Publication Data
A catalog record for this book has been requested.

1 3 5 7 9 10 8 6 4 2

ISBN 1 84331 230 1 (Hbk)

Printed in Singapore

The Editor

Lee Jackson is the author of the acclaimed Decimus Webb series of Victorian murder mysteries, including *A Metropolitan Murder*, *The Welfare of the Dead* and *The Last Pleasure Garden*. He is fascinated by the social history of the Victorian city and maintains the popular website *www.victorianlondon.org*, devoted to exploring the minutiae of daily life in 'The Great Metropolis'. He lives in Stoke Newington, London, with his partner Joanne and their daughter Clara.

LIST OF ILLUSTRATIONS

Preface

The noblest prospect in the world, it has been well said, is
London viewed from the suburbs on a clear winter's evening.
The stars are shining in the heavens, but there is another
firmament spread out below, with its millions of bright lights
glittering at our feet. Line after line sparkles, like the trails
left by meteors, cutting and crossing one another till they are
lost in the haze of the distance. Over the whole there hangs a
lurid cloud, bright as if the monster city were in flames, and
looking afar off like the sea by night, made phosphorescent
by the million creatures dwelling within it.

Henry Mayhew, *'Labour and the Poor'*
(in the *Morning Chronicle*), 1849

In describing Victorian London, it is tempting to evoke its
great contrasts: rich vs poor; East End vs West End; the eerie
beauty of 'London viewed from the suburbs' vs the ugly reality
of the city's 'cholera districts' and 'rookeries'; London as both
'The Great Metropolis' and Disraeli's 'Modern Babylon'; a
great imperial capital, but also a 'monster city'. A world city, in
fact, whose 'million creatures' would become five million by the
end of Victoria's reign.

But the aim of this book is not to address such grand themes,
even though it may help to illuminate them. Rather, it is
intended to reveal the minutiae of daily life in the Victorian
metropolis; *how life was lived*, through the voices of the people
who were there, and the documents they left behind, whether
diaries, memoirs, court reports, advertisements, guidebooks,
statistics, or indignant letters to *The Times*.

I hope many of the topics covered will be surprising: from plaster-of-paris pornography hawked on the streets, to the world's first gas-powered traffic light; and I hope modern readers will sympathise with the pedestrians plagued by prams, and infuriated by the postal service, even if our forebears had slightly higher standards ('*I believe the inhabitants of London are under the impression that Letters posted for delivery within the metropolitan district commonly reach their destination within, at the outside, three hours of the time of postage.*'). I have, wherever possible, tried to include forgotten metropolitan places – from the Regent's Park Diorama to the Tower Subway ('*it is not advisable for any but the very briefest of Her Majesty's lieges to attempt the passage in high-heeled boots, or with a hat to which he attaches any particular value*') – and familiar activities that seem entirely inappropriate to Victorian sensibilities, not least the 1870s rollerskating craze that saw rinks built all over London. Inevitably, much has been omitted. Sadly, for instance, a recently discovered article from *The Lady's Realm* of 1897, entitled *The Pets of Celebrities*, showcasing the work of one Thomas Fall, animal photographer to the aristocracy ('*I may say that my success in taking the portraits of Her Royal Highness with her pets was greatly due to her kind assistance and consideration.*') will now never reach a wider public.

The reader may wonder why a *Dictionary* of Victorian London? Why not an 'anthology' or 'encyclopedia'? The answer is quite simple: the title is a tribute to a book first produced in 1879, namely *Dickens's Dictionary Of London*, compiled by Charles Culliford Dickens, the great novelist's son. Somewhat overshadowed by his father (who at one point disparagingly wrote of his son's 'indescribable lassitude of character'), the *Dictionary of London*, written in A-Z format, is this author's favourite Victorian guide-book. It includes, unusually for such a work, the occasional joke, not least the advice: "Sight-seeing, in the opinion of many experienced travellers, is best avoided altogether." You will, therefore, find some of its wisdom herein – from entries on *Chops and Steaks* to *Circulating Libraries*.

In short, read through this book, or open it at random, and I think you will stumble upon something fascinating on every page. Whether it is anxious advice given to tourists that would almost stand today (*'Carry no more money about you than is necessary for the day's expenses. Look after your watch and chain, and take care of your pockets at the entrance to theatres, exhibitions, churches, and in the omnibuses and the streets.'*) or instructions on forfeits for party games, such as 'To Play the Learned Pig' (*'To do this, the gentleman must first put himself as nearly as possible in the attitude of one. He must go on all fours, and he is then to answer questions that may be put to him either by the company or by somebody who may volunteer as his master, to show his attainments.'*), I cannot imagine you will ever think about Victorian London in quite the same way again.

Lee Jackson

A is for Advertising

This 1887 cartoon from *Punch* satirises the 'advertising nuisance', showing everything from gory fly-posters for the latest theatrical sensations, to a man in an elephant costume (advertising a circus troupe) startling a cab-horse.

ACROBATS

Acrobats and jugglers (then popularly called tumblers) frequently occupied pitches at convenient corners. A troupe visiting our neighbourhood comprised an elderly man, a youth and a girl, possibly all of a family. They spread a carpet, opened a box of properties, threw off their coats and appeared in regulation acrobatic dress. A basin for the reception of coppers was not forgotten at one corner of the carpet. The old man performed feats of strength and dexterity, the others aiding as supernumeraries. His chief act – and it was one common to most of the street tumblers – was to support and balance a pole about ten feet long perpendicularly in a waistband, and allow the youth to climb to the top and there go through several tricks. To keep the balance he had to watch the pole narrowly, hands on hips, as it shifted, but I never witnessed a failure. Then he would take both boy and girl on his shoulders, where they would posture and disport in various ways. He would fasten a cup to his forehead by a band, and, throwing a gilded ball high in the air, catch it in the cup every time. And keep half a dozen balls rotating, and so on. This, with crowded traffic of all kinds circulating within a few feet, required nerve and self-possession. I don't know how many pitches they made in a day, but the old man must have been a tough one to stand the racket.

Alfred Rosling-Bennett, *London and Londoners
in the 1850s and 1860s*, 1924

ADELAIDE GALLERY, THE

The Adelaide Gallery, which was situated at the northern, or St. Martin's Church, end of the Lowther Arcade (where as a child I used to eat buns at Miss Ehrhardt the confectioner's, and buy toys of John Binge, who combined toy-selling in the daytime with theatrical singing at night, and who was called

"The Singing Mouse," owing to the smallness of his sweet tenor voice), was started as a science "show." Its principal attractions were Perkins's steam-gun, which discharged a shower of bullets, but was never adopted in serious warfare; and the gymnotus, or electrical eel, a creature which emitted shocks on its back being touched. Parents and persons in charge of youth were great patrons of the Adelaide Gallery, which flourished until a rival institution appeared in the shape of the Polytechnic, in Upper Regent Street, which speedily and completely took the wind out of the sails of the original establishment.

Edmund Yates, *His Recollections and Experiences*, 1885

ADVERTISING VANS

Sir – I am a banker. Like most of my profession, I have my town-house in Belgravia, and my villa at Roehampton, and I ride daily to my counting-house in the city. I am a fat man and am recommended horse-exercise.

The Strand, always a crowded thoroughfare, became disagreeably so when omnibuses were permitted to ply there. The wood pavement next assisted in making it nearly impassable; and now a third plague has arisen which promises to block it up altogether . . . the advertising-vans.

Leaving Belgrave-square at 11 o'clock, I found the Strand blocked up just beyond Messrs. Coutts's, in consequence of two wretched animals, attached to an immense French diligence, used as a means of making M. Philippe's merits known to the public, having slipped up on the wood pavement. The driver, a sensible phlegmatic man, appeared in no hurry to set them on their legs again, conceiving, with justice, that his employer's object was better attained by remaining where he was. . . . Retreat was out of the question, from the incredible influence of omnibuses which had congregated in my rear.

At length, however, the way was cleared, and I proceeded as far as Temple-bar ... I found the pass in the procession of two more of these accursed vehicles, which had got locked together – one was devoted to the promulgation of the merits of Holloway's ointment in curing diseased legs, and the other was adorned with sketches of a hideous monster called the "human tripod, or young easel."

My cob ... could not stand the horrid sight. He tried to turn round, was poled by a "buss" close astern, fell, and deposited me under the wheels of a dray which, fortunately, at the time was motionless, as, indeed, it had been for three-quarters of an hour previously.

Being active, though corpulent, I escaped unhurt; but I really think, Sir, that when we reflect on the severity with which applewomen are coerced – when the strong arm of the law sternly silences the early sweep, and stills the bell of the dustman, and the tinkle of the muffin-boy – the powers which watch over the lives and interests of Her Majesty's subjects ought to deal promptly and vigorously with such nuisances as these.

letter to *The Times*, 1846

ADVICE TO TOURISTS

In walking through the streets, avoid lingering in crowded thoroughfares, and keep on the right-hand side of the footway.

Never enter into conversation with men who wish to show you the way, offer to sell "smuggled cigars" or invite you to take a glass of ale or play a game at skittles.

If in doubt about the direction of any street or building, inquire at a respectable shop or of the nearest policeman.

Monday is the workman's holiday; Saturday the most aristocratic day for the Opera, Crystal Palace, &c.

Consult the Post Office Directory for addresses of friends who do not live in lodgings.

Do not relieve street-beggars, and avoid bye-ways and poor neighbourhoods after dark.

Carry no more money about you than is necessary for the day's expenses. Look after your watch and chain, and take care of your pockets at the entrance to theatres, exhibitions, churches, and in the omnibuses and the streets.

Routledge's Popular Guide to London, [c.1873]

ANGLING

The angling season begins in London with the very first disappearance of frost and the first blush of blue sky in the heavens; and, with comparatively few exceptions, Sundays and holidays are the only days of sport. The young angler begins his career in the Surrey Canal, the Grand Junction Canal, or the New River, which ever happens to be nearest to the place of his abode. His first apparatus is a willow-wand, bought at the basketmaker's for a penny, and a roach-line for fivepence more. A sixpenny outfit satisfies his modest ambition; and thus equipped he sallies forth to feed – not the fishes – them he invariably frightens away – but himself, with the delusive hope of catching them. The blue-bottles have not yet left their winter quarters, and "gentles" or maggots are not yet to be had; so he has recourse to kneaded bread or paste, hoping to beguile his prey with a vegetable diet. In order that the fishes may be duly apprised of the entertainment prepared for them, he crams his trousers-pockets with gravel, which he industriously scatters upon his float as it sails down the stream, doubtless impressed with the notion that the whole finny tribe within hearing will swarm beneath the stony shower to take their choice of the descending blessings, and finding his bait among them, give it the preference, and swallow it as a matter of course. The theory seems a very plausible one; but we cannot say that in practice, though witnessing it a thousand times, we ever saw it succeed. For the sake of something like an estimate of the amount of success among the juvenile anglers of this class, we lately watched the operations of a group of nearly thirty of them for two hours, but failed in deriving any data for a calculation, as not a fin appeared above water the whole time. With the exception of a few "stunnin' bites," and one "rippin' walloper," which was proclaimed to have carried off a boy's hook, there was no indication of sport beyond that afforded by the party themselves.

Charles Manby Smith, *Curiosities of London Life*, 1853

ANONYMITY

It is strange with how little notice, good, bad, or indifferent, a man may live and die in London. He awakens no sympathy in the breast of any single person; his existence is a matter of interest to no one save himself; he cannot be said to be forgotten when he dies, for no one remembered him when he was alive. There is a numerous class of people in this great metropolis who seem not to possess a single friend, and whom nobody appears to care for. Urged by imperative necessity in the first instance, they have resorted to London in search of employment, and the means of subsistence. It is hard, we know, to break the ties which bind us to our homes and friends, and harder still to efface the thousand recollections of happy days and old times, which have been slumbering in our bosoms for years, and only rush upon the mind, to bring before it associations connected with the friends we have left, the scenes we have beheld too probably for the last time, and the hopes we once cherished, but may entertain no more. These men, however, happily for themselves, have long forgotten such thoughts.

Charles Dickens, *Sketches by Boz*, 1836

Londoners have been forced to sacrifice the best qualities of their human nature, to bring to pass all the marvels of civilization which crowd their city; that a hundred powers which slumbered within them have remained inactive, have been suppressed in order that a few might be developed more fully and multiply through union with those of others … The brutal indifference, the unfeeling isolation of each in his private interest becomes the more repellent and ofference the more these individuals are crowded together, within a limited space … The dissolution of mankind into monads of which each one has a separate principle and a separate purpose, the world of atoms, is here carried to its upmost extreme.

Friedrich Engels, *The Condition of the Working Class in England*, 1845

APOLLONICON, THE

The Apollonicon, 101, St. Martin's Lane, is a grand mechanical musical instrument. By its mechanical, or self-acting powers, it is capable of performing any piece of music which may be arranged on it with a grandeur and precision unequalled by any instrument hitherto produced, of a similar description. Any piece of music may likewise be played on it by one or six performers at the same time. This exhibition is open daily, from

1 to 4 o'clock; but an eminent professor is engaged to play on Saturdays, during the winter season; admission, 1s.

> *Mogg's New Picture of London and Visitor's*
> *Guide to its Sights*, 1844

A CHAMBER-ORGAN of vast power, supplied with both keys and barrels, was built by Messrs. Flight and Robson of 101, St. Martin's-lane, and first exhibited by them at their manufactory in 1817 ... "The Apollonicon," says a contemporary description, "is either self-acting, by means of machinery, or may be played on by keys. The music, when the organ is worked by machinery, is pinned on three cylinders or barrels, each acting on a different division of the instrument; and these, in their revolution, not only admit air to the pipes, but actually regulate and work the stops, forming, by an instantaneous action, all the necessary combinations. The key-boards are five in number; the central and largest comprising five octaves, and the smaller ones, of which two are placed on each side the larger, two octaves each. To the central key-board are attached a swell and some compound pedals, enabling the performer to produce all the changes and variety of effect that the music may require. There is also a key-board, comprising two octaves of other pedals, operating on the largest pipes of the instrument.

> John Timbs, *Curiosities of London*, 1867

ASTLEY'S AMPHITHEATRE

Astley's Amphitheatre, near Westminster Bridge, was first established by the late Mr. Philip Astley in 1767, and was then an open area. In 1780, it was converted into a covered amphitheatre, consisting of boxes, gallery and pit. It was twice destroyed by fire; in August 1794, and in September 1803; it was rebuilt in about six months after, and first opened in April 1804. A third fire, attended with fatal consequences, occurred here on the 8th of June, 1841, when the theatre was again destroyed. The dreadful shock sustained by its talented proprietor, the late Mr. Ducrow, from this conflagration, which terminated in the death of one of his oldest servants, and destruction of the whole of his theatrical property, induced a state of insanity, from which he never recovered, and finally sunk on the 27th of January 1842. An elegant Theatre, upon an enlarged scale, and of increased splendour, the decorations being of crimson and gold, has been erected by Mr. Batty, a celebrated equestrian performer.

Mogg's New Picture of London and Visitor's Guide
to its Sights, 1844

B is for Bloomerism

WOMAN'S EMANCIPATION.

(Being a Letter addressed to Mr. Punch, with a Drawing, by a strong-minded American Woman.)

In 1851 *Punch* vigorously mocked the American reformer, Amelia Bloomer, and her ideas for women's trousers, designed to alleviate the difficulty of moving in layers of petticoated skirts. Women in bloomer costumes were repeatedly cartooned apeing the habits of men.

BALLOON ASCENTS

In the opposite direction to that in which the wind was insensibly wafting the balloon, lay the leviathan Metropolis, with a dense canopy of smoke hanging over it, and reminding one of the fog of vapour that is often seen steaming up from the fields at early morning. It was impossible to tell where the monster city began or ended, for the buildings stretched not only to the horizon on either side, but far away into the distance, where, owing to the coming shades of evening and the dense fumes from the million chimneys, the town seemed to blend into the sky, so that there was no distinguishing earth from heaven. The multitude of roofs that extended back from the foreground was positively like a dingy red sea, heaving in bricken billows, and the seeming waves rising up one after the other till the eye grew wearied with following them. Here and there we could distinguish little bare green patches of parks, and occasionally make out the tiny circular enclosures of the principal squares, though, from the height, these appeared scarcely bigger than wafers. Further, the fog of smoke that over-shadowed the giant town was pierced with a thousand steeples and pin-like factory-chimneys.

That little building, no bigger than one of the small china houses that are used for burning pastilles in, is Buckingham Palace—with St. James's Park, dwindled to the size of a card-table, stretched out before it. Yonder is Bethlehem Hospital, with its dome, now about the same dimensions as a bell.

Then the little mites of men, crossing the bridges, seemed to have no more motion in them than the animalcules in cheese; while the streets appeared more like cracks in the soil than highways, and the tiny steamers on the river were only to be distinguished by the thin black thread of smoke trailing after them.

Indeed, it was a most wonderful sight to behold that vast bricken mass of churches and hospitals, banks and prisons, palaces and workhouses, docks and refuges for the destitute, parks and squares, and courts and alleys, which make up

London ... to take, as it were, an angel's view of that huge town where, perhaps, there is more virtue and more iniquity, more wealth and more want, brought together into one dense focus than in any other part of the earth ...

Henry Mayhew in the *Illustrated London News*, 1852

BATHING

BATHS. Those who luxuriate in bathing will find ample means for their gratification in the various baths with which the metropolis abounds; of which, after a statement of the usual charges, a catalogue is subjoined. List of prices: - Cold bath, 1s.; warm bath, 3s. 6d.; sea water, 3s.6d.; warm sea water, 7s. 6d.

Bagnio Court, Newgate Street; Chapel Place, Oxford Street, shower and warm; Cold Bath Fields; Coram Street, warm and cold; Culverwells, New Bond Street; George Street, Adelphi, sea water; Great Marlborough Street, chlorine, vapour, and warm, or hot air; Harley Street, warm and shower; Hewitt's, Old Hummums, Covent Garden; King Street, Westminster; Lambeth, near the Marsh Gate; Leicester Square, warm, vapour, salt, cold, and shower; Lothbury, Founder's Court, shampooing, vapour, hot air, sea water, &c.; New Road, near Fitzroy Square, cold, warm, and shower; Peerless Pool, City Road; St. Mary Axe, warm and cold; Strand Lane, near Somerset House, cold; Suffolk Place, Pall Mall East; and St. Chad's Well, Gray's Inn Lane Road.

*Mogg's New Picture of London and Visitor's
Guide to its Sights*, 1844

Bath-rooms were much rarer than they have been for the last few decades. Lack of cleanliness must not be too rashly inferred, however. Tubs and portable baths were quite the rule, and the universally-fitted copper provided plenty of hot water. The daily bath, hot or cold, was not so practised, either for children or adults, but matters were very much better than they had been, by all accounts, forty or fifty years earlier. There were a few public baths and wash-houses already established in the 1850s. . . . It was not, I think, before the 1870s that London saw its first Turkish Bath, the one still extant in Jermyn Street. Real Turkish masseurs from Constantinople were at first employed, but they advertised the novelty but indifferently by succumbing very readily to the climate. Several died, and ultimately all were replaced by men to whom Golden Horn conditions were not so essential.

Alfred Rosling-Bennett, *London and Londoners in the 1850s and 1860s*, 1924

Upon the south-east side of Westminster Bridge Road are the Lambeth Baths, more famous for its Temperance Meetings and social assemblies of working people than even for its sanitary appliances. When the water has been drawn out of the spacious bath, the place serves for a lecture and concert-room. Here all kinds of simple amusement, in the way of songs, chorused by the people, newspaper readings, social discussion and temperance meetings, are held regularly through the winter.

Herbert Fry, *London*, 1889

BAZAARS

The Soho Bazaar stands at the head of its class. It was founded many years ago by a gentleman of some notoriety, and has been uniformly a well-managed concern. It occupies several houses on the north-west corner of Soho Square, and consists of stalls or open counters ranged on both sides of aisles or passages, on two separate floors of the building. These stalls are rented by females, who pay, we believe, something between two and three shillings per day for each. The articles sold at these stalls are almost exclusively pertaining to the dress and personal decoration of ladies and children; such as millinery, lace, gloves, jewellery, &c., and, in the height of 'the season,' the long array of carriages drawn up near the building testifies to the extent of the visits paid by the highborn and the wealthy to this place. Some of the rules of the establishment are very stringent. A plain and modest style of dress, on the part of the young females who serve at the stalls, is invariably insisted on, a matron being at hand to superintend the whole; every stall must have its wares displayed by a particular hour in the morning, under penalty of a fine from the renter; the rent is paid day by day, and if the renter be ill, she has to pay for the services of a substitute, the substitute being such an one as is approved by the principals of the establishment. Nothing can be plainer or more simple than the exterior of this bazaar, but it has all the features of a well-ordered institution.

The Pantheon Bazaar is a place of more show and pretensions. It was originally a theatre, one of the most fashionable in London; but having met with the discomfitures which have befallen so many of our theatres, it remained untenanted for many years, and was at length entirely remodelled and converted into a bazaar. When we have passed through the entrance porch in Oxford Street, we find ourselves in a vestibule, containing a few sculptures, and from thence a flight of steps lead up to a range of rooms occupied as a picture gallery. These pictures, which are in most cases of rather moderate merit, are placed here for sale, the proprietors of the bazaar receiving a commission or percentage on any picture which may find a purchaser. From these rooms an entrance is obtained to the gallery, or upper-floor of the toy-bazaar, one of the most tasteful places of the kind in London. We look down upon the ground story, from this open gallery, and find it arranged with counters in a very systematical order, loaded with uncountable trinkets. On one counter are articles of millinery; on another lace; on a third gloves and hosiery; on others cutlery, jewellery, toys, children's dresses, children's books, sheets of music, albums and pocket-books, porcelain ornaments, cut-glass ornaments, alabaster figures, artificial flowers, feathers, and a host of other things, principally of a light and ornamental character. Each counter is attended by a young female, as at the Soho Bazaar. On one side of the toy-bazaar is an aviary, supplied with birds for sale in cages; and adjacent to it is a conservatory where plants are displayed in neat array.

Charles Knight, *Knight's London*, 1842

BEAUTICIANS

FACE Ablutionist and Beautifier
Also MANICURE, to LADIES ONLY
MISS SPODE (a Physician's daughter) is a Specialist in the above Arts. Her preparations are eminently successful in restoring and rejuvenating the Skin of the Face, Neck, Arms and Hands.
She is able to greatly benefit those suffering from Acne (Blackheads).
Also skilled in MASSAGE, particularly for the Head for Neuralgic Pains.
She receives at her residence from 10 a.m. to 6 p.m. daily. Saturdays, 10 a.m. to 2 p.m. Visits paid to Clients in the evening. Country Orders receive prompt attention.
SPECIALITY LIST SENT POST FREE
MISS SPODE 60 (late 37) Drayton Gardens, South Kensington, S.W.

advertisement in Baroness Staffe,
The Lady's Dressing Room, 1893

BEGGARS

Of the beggars there are many distinct species. (1.) The naval and the military beggars; as turnpike sailors and "raw" veterans. (2.) Distressed operative beggars; as pretended starved-out manufacturers, or sham frozen-out gardeners, or tricky hand-loom weavers, &c. (3.) Respectable beggars; as sham broken-down tradesmen, poor ushers or distressed authors, clean family beggars, with children in very white pinafores and their faces cleanly washed, and the ashamed beggars, who pretend to hide their faces with a written petition. (4.) Disaster beggars; as shipwrecked mariners, or blown-up miners, or burnt-out tradesmen, and lucifer droppers. (5.) Bodily afflicted beggars; such as those having real or pretended sores or swollen legs, or being crippled or deformed, maimed, or paralyzed, or else being blind, or deaf, or dumb, or subject to fits, or in a decline and appearing with bandages round the head, or playing the "shallow cove," i.e., appearing half-clad in the streets. (6.) Famished beggars; as those who chalk on the pavement, "I am starving," or else remain stationary, and hold up a piece of paper before their face similarly inscribed. (7.) Foreign beggars, who stop you in the street, and request to know if you can speak French; or destitute Poles, Indians, or Lascars, or Negroes. (8.) Petty trading beggars; as tract sellers, lucifer match sellers, boot lace venders, &c. (9.) Musical beggars; or those who play on some musical instrument, as a cloak for begging – as scraping fiddlers, hurdy-gurdy and clarionet players. (10.) Dependents of beggars; as screevers or the writers of "slums" (letters) and "fakements" (petitions), and referees, or those who give characters to professional beggars.

Henry Mayhew and John Binny, *The Criminal Prisons of London*, 1862

MENDICITY SOCIETY, Office, 13, RED LION SQUARE. The society gives meals and money, supplies mill and other work to applicants, investigates begging-letter cases, and apprehends vagrants and impostors. Each meal consists of ten ounces of bread, and one pint of good soup, or a quarter of a pound of cheese. The affairs of the Society are administered by a Board of forty-eight managers. The Mendicity Society's tickets, given to a street beggar, will procure for him, if really necessitous, food and work. They are a touch-stone to impostures: the beggar by profession throws them aside. This meritorious Society deserves every encouragement. Tickets are furnished to subscribers.

Peter Cunningham, *Hand-Book of London*, 1850

Sir, – At a time when our sympathies are so strongly excited on behalf of the suffering poor, every attempt at imposture ought to be exposed.

Yesterday, in walking up Idol-lane, I saw a girl lying on the pavement weeping over and gathering up a quantity of matches which lay scattered beside her. In the hurry of business I passed on, and my heart reproached me afterwards for not having administered to her relief when two or three pence would have repaired the damage. To-day, in Cullum-street, a girl was in the same situation with a pair of common varnished prints in frames, through one of which was a hole, as if her hand had accidentally fallen through. She appeared in the greatest grief, and I gave her 6*d*.; when in the act of raising her head to return thanks, I discovered the match girl of yesterday. I charged her with it, which she stoutly denied; and my suspicions being strongly raised, I watched her. In Lime-street (so little a distance as that) I saw her deliberately throw herself down with the same pictures, and enact the same scene over again. On threatening to give her in charge of the police, after a good deal of blustering, she admitted the trick and promised if I would let her go this time she would never do so any more; and seeing no policeman at hand, I let her off, first recovering my 6*d*. I am told this is a stale device, but as it is new to me it may be so to some others of your readers.

I am, Sir, your obedient servant,
11, Mincing-lane, Jan.12.   W.C.

letter to The Times, 1850

BERMONDSEY LEATHER MARKET

Through the leather market into the skin market. Here was another square, with a broad piazza flanking every side of it. Business was brisk enough here in all conscience. The square was chokeful of terrible-looking vehicles – terrible because not only the tires and fellows, but the very spokes of the wheels, were plastered with a red-brown substance, in which were matted scraps of hair and fragments of wool, dreadfully suggestive of slaughter and the shambles; as were the carters with their streaked hands, their speckled woollen leggings, and their oozy wooden shoes; as were the carters' whips, with the brass about their handles all lacquered red; as were the horses in the terrible carts – animals of high mettle and with sleek coats, who snorted and shook their heads as they sniffed the reek of the wet hides, much liking it.

Worming in and out among the carts was a swarm of busy men – buyers and sellers, and blue-smocked porters – while under the piazza were stacks of hides of Spanish, and Dutch, and English beasts, each to be distinguished by the length, or the breadth, or the width of the horns still attached to a bit of skull and hanging about the fronts of the stacks as though still vicious and daring you to approach. Besides these were heaps of innocent-looking calves' skins, and the skins of sheep and lambs, still so warm-looking and comfortable that one might imagine them new sheep-coats just come home, rather than cast-off garments, of no further use but to the fell-monger and the tanner. In addition to these there were several piles of hides that had been exported from foreign parts, and that had been salted that they might come to market wholesome.

James Greenwood, *Unsentimental Journeys*, 1867

BETTING

They are posted up in the dates of, and latest betting, upon all important sporting matters, and discuss the probable results of "coming events" as learnedly and vaguely as any of the professional sporting prophets. They are great in slang, always speaking of the features of the human face in the technical phraseology of the ring – according to which the nose is the beak or conk, the eyes ogles or peepers, the teeth ivories, and the mouth the kisser or tater-trap. They are ready to settle all matters of opinion by offering to lay or take long odds upon the question. They have a great deal of the "make-believe" sort of imagination in their composition, complacently speaking of "lumping it on" or "going a raker" when they have backed their fancy for five shillings, and regarding themselves as daring speculators when they have "put the pot" on to the amount of a sovereign. And while the events on the results of which their speculations depend are in abeyance, they confidentially inform everybody whom they can get to listen to them that if they "land the pot," it is their intention to "jack up work" and go on the turf; which they believe to be their proper sphere. Meantime they have their hair cut short, and, when off work, wear fancy caps and mufflers, and suits of the latest sporting cut; in which they assume the swaggering walk of the minor sporting celebrities whom they are occasionally permitted to associate with and "treat." As they get older the majority of these young fellows become more sensible. They give up the more dangerous of their sporting practices, abandon the idea of going on the turf, and confining their gambling transactions to a draw in a shilling workshop sweepstake for the Derby, or wagering half-a-crown on the English representative in any international sporting contest; while to younger young fellows they leave the expensive honour of "standing" drink for the East-end Antelope, or purchasing tickets for the benefit of the Whitechapel Slogger.

Thomas Wright, *Some Habits and Customs of the Working Classes,* 1867

BICYCLING

Mr. Stanton, the well-known bicyclist, engaged to ride fifty miles against Mr. Markham, at Cremorne Gardens, on Saturday, and allowed his opponent fifteen minutes' start. Stanton caught Markham in the forty-third round, and at the thirty-fifth mile the latter gave up. Stanton, however, kept up his speed and completed the distance in 3h. 13min. 30sec. A bicycle-race of 106 miles, between Stanton and Keen, the former receiving half an hour's start, for £50, will take place on Monday next, at Lillie-bridge.

Penny Illustrated Paper, 1874

IN writing my reminiscences of police duty in Hyde Park, I feel I should not perhaps be altogether completing my undertaking to omit if only a few remarks on the subject of the bicycling season, or rather the bicycle craze, as it was more appropriately termed, and which undoubtedly it proved to be; for, like the proverbial donkey's gallop, it was short and sweet. One brief season – and it vanished as quickly as it sprang up! As a matter of fact, I was somewhat undecided about referring to the event at all.

However, for the little while it did exist it certainly caused no small talk, and looked at one time to even vie with the Row in popularity.

The Ring Road, from the Achilles Statue, Hyde Park Corner, to the Magazine, was the selected track, – a nice level straight run of about a mile – and soon after ten o'clock in the morning, cyclists – chiefly ladies – made their appearance from all directions, and by eleven o'clock that portion of the roadway was simply thronged with them; for carriage traffic or equestrians it was almost impossible to get through, at all events dangerous to attempt, consequently they were advised to proceed by other routes. At every crossing constables were posted to assist foot passengers over the roadway – no easy matter to accomplish, either for the policeman himself or for those he was escorting. To pass safely through those rapid, silent wheels – no putting one's hand up and promptly stopping them like the ordinary carriage, traffic – it was a case of getting over the best way one possibly could.

I was fortunate enough to escape without getting knocked down myself, but I believe it was more by luck than judgment – judgment was out of the question, for in getting out of the way of one you were in that of another – it was sheer dodging to and fro. My post was at the crossing directly opposite the Achilles Statue, the turning point of the track, and the cutting and twisting and incessant tinkling of bells around you kept one in a state of fever heat. I have done duty on every conceivable crossing on the Row and carriage-way in the Park, and positively assert I would a thousand times rather do four hours of that duty in the busiest of the season than the one hour and a half or two hours amid those enthusiastic cyclists; and when twelve o'clock came – the limit of the time extended to bicycles in the Park then – and they began to disperse, it was a great relief to be able to breathe freely once again, at least, that is expressing my feelings on the matter.

Edward Owen, *Hyde Park, Select Narratives, Annual Event, etc, during twenty years' Police Service in Hyde Park*, 1906

BILLIARD ROOMS

A casual visit to some of these billiard-rooms is not uninteresting. We will instance one in the Upper Street, Islington, the street which is popularly supposed to be attended with more danger to young men than any other in London. The entrance is through an unimposing public-house door, from which a passage conducts to a long, narrow, low-pitched billiard-room, which after 8' o'clock at night is filled with smoke and reeking of whisky, and tenanted by a lot of aimless men of all ages, with nothing to do until from 8 to 9 o'clock the next morning, and most of them intent upon enjoyment in the meantime. Some of them put clean collars on in the evening instead of the morning, so that they may look nice and fresh in the eyes of the barmaids; others wear rings, and have a dig with them that they hold by the collar so as to display them. Most of them smoke pipes of various patterns, a few cigars, whilst some of the younger ones even descend to cigarettes. Somebody once said that it was a sure sign of the deterioration of a country when its inhabitants took to smoking paper. If that be the case the London suburbs must be going headlong to ruin, for one may everywhere see small boys smoking paper cigarettes.

Anon., *Tempted London: Young Men*, c.1889

BOXING

Sir, – "G.W." in to-day's *Times*, expresses his surprise that no man was found who would assist in the capture of the brute who knocked a woman down. Your correspondent will probably cease to wonder when he reads the following:- About a month ago I was at breakfast with my family at Kensal-green, when I perceived a number of persons passing through the field adjoining my house. I endeavoured to ascertain the cause. With much difficulty I did so. The stream of men and women had come from

Paddington to a prize-fight between two – no, not men – women! One of my family, being incredulous, contrived to look across the fields, and there saw the combatants stripped to the waist and fighting. Men took them there, men backed them, men were the bottle-holders and time-keepers. They fought for about half-an-hour, some say for 5s., some say for a sovereign, and some say they will do it again. I saw the winner led back in triumph by men. After the above, I think your correspondent will cease to wonder at the indifference of a Paddington mob. You, Sir, have already drawn the moral from such things. Perhaps you will permit me to add my matured conviction that some vices and some crimes are too disgraceful for mere punishment of a clean, well-ordered, and well-fed prison. Let us have the whipping-post again, and at the flogging let the crime of "unmanly brutes" be written over their heads.

Aug. 31   C.E.W.

letter to *The Times*, 1852

The old sporting-houses, once the resort of half the black-guardism of the East-end and a good deal of the West, have gone down before the steady bowling of the law. The friendly bouts with the gloves between local "chickens" and "novices," which once were regular Saturday night amusements, are few-and-far between, and dog-fights and ratting matches have to be searched for by the curious as diligently as though they were looking for a policeman in a suburban neighbourhood, and the result is generally the same.

That boxing and ratting, and other forms of the "fancy," still exist as part of the amusement of the lower orders, is perfectly true, but they exist in such a hole-and-corner, out-of-the-way, few-and-far-between style, that they can no longer be classed as among the amusements of those who cannot afford to pay high prices of admission to illegal entertainments.

The noble art of self-defence did undoubtedly linger among the lower orders as a pastime long after it had passed out of

24

favour with the Corinthians, and many of the porters of Billingsgate, Covent Garden, and Smithfield, waterside labourers, costermongers, and street hawkers are to this day famous as "bruisers," and given to indulge their friends at odd times with a display of their prowess on the extreme Q.T., in quiet out-houses and secluded spots where the police are unlikely to mar the harmony of the proceedings. Such meetings, when they do take place, always attract a mob of the lowest riff-raff....

It has been my good or evil fortune, in my desire to know all sorts and conditions of men, to witness some of the latest revivals of glove-fighting; now in drill-sheds, now in top floors of public-houses, and once in the upper floor of a workshop, which nearly gave way with the weight of accumulated blackguardism collected. These, it is only fair to say, were mostly "ramps," or swindles, got up to obtain the gate money, and generally interrupted by circumstances arranged beforehand by those who were going to "cut up" the plunder.

George R. Sims, *How the Poor Live*, 1883

BOXING DAY

I AM rather out of conceit with Christmas boxes. I have been wished the compliments of the season by no less than six individuals this very morning, and for those good wishes I, poor man though I be, with family of my own to work for, have had to pay half-a-crown each. I grow suspicious of every smiling face I meet. I walk with my hands in my pocket, and my eyes cast down. I wonder how it fares with my strong-minded wife at home. I know she will have had a rare battle to fight. She will have had the Postman – and the Dustman – and the Waits – and the Sweep – and the Turncock – and the Lamplighter – and the Grocer's lad – and the Butcher's boy; and if she compounds with them at the rate of a shilling a-piece, she may bless her stars. I feel that I cannot stand much of this kind of work, and that for a merry Christmas and a happy New Year I shall have to pay rather handsomely. Stop at home – tie up your knockers – say you are sick or dead, or a shareholder in the Royal British Bank, still you cannot escape the tender mercies of a London Boxing day. Mind, I have not one word to say of the various good wishes and gifts offered by friends and relatives to each other as pledges of esteem and goodwill. I would be the last to find fault with the customs originating in the warm heart of love, and honoured by the sanction of the whole civilized world. By all means let us reverence them ten-fold. But I have a right to complain that I am compelled to pay for mercenary goodwill, and that on me, or such as me, a tax is levied which does no good in most cases, and frequently does an immense amount of harm. When I read, as I am sure to do, in the police reports of the next day, that, "yesterday, being the day after Boxing day, the time of the magistrates was chiefly occupied with cases of drunkenness," am I not right in wishing that I had kept the money in my own pocket?

J. Ewing Ritchie, *The Night Side of London*, 1858

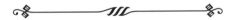

BREAKFASTS

I wish that, in this age so enamoured of statistical information, when we must needs know how many loads of manure go to every acre of turnip-field, and how many jail-birds are thrust into the black hole *per mensem* for fracturing their pannikins, or tearing their convict jackets, that some M'Culloch or Caird would tabulate for me the amount of provisions, solid and liquid, consumed at the breakfasts of London every morning. I want to know how many thousand eggs are daily chipped, how many of those embryo chickens are poached, and how many fried; how many tons of quartern loaves are cut up to make bread-and-butter, thick and thin; how many porkers have been sacrificed to provide the bacon rashers, fat and streaky; what rivers have been drained, what fuel consumed, what mounds of salt employed, what volumes of smoke emitted, to catch and cure the finny haddocks and the Yarmouth bloaters, that grace our morning repast. Say, too, Crosse and Blackwell, what multitudinous demands are matutinally made on thee for pots of anchovy paste and preserved tongue, covered with that circular layer – abominable disc! – of oleaginous nastiness, apparently composed of rancid pomatum, but technically known as clarified butter, and yet not so nasty as that adipose horror that surrounds the truffle bedecked *paté de foie gras.* Say, Elizabeth Lazenby, how many hundred bottles of thy sauce (none of which are genuine unless signed by thee) are in request to give a relish to cold meat, game, and fish. Mysteries upon mysteries are there connected with nine o'clock breakfasts. Queries upon queries suggest themselves to the inquisitive mind. Speculations upon speculations present themselves to him who is observant. Are those eggs we see in the coffee-shop windows, by the side of the lean chop with a curly tail, the teapot with the broken spout, and the boulder-looking kidneys, ever eaten, and if so, what secret do the coffee-shop proprietors possess of keeping them from entire decomposition? For I have watched these eggs for weeks together, and known them by bits of straw and flecks of dirt mucilaginously adhering to their shells, to be the selfsame eggs.

George Augustus Sala, *Twice Round the Clock,* 1859

BRICK LANE

Where Sclater Street crosses Brick Lane, near the Great Eastern Station, is the market of the 'fancy'. Here the streets are blocked with those – coming to buy, or sell, pigeons, canaries, rabbits, fowls, parrots, or guinea pigs, and with them or separately all the appurtenances of bird or pet keeping. Through this crowd the seller of shell-fish pushes his barrow; on the outskirts of it are move-able shooting galleries, and patent Aunt Sallies, while some man standing up in a dog-cart will dispose of racing tips in sealed envelopes to the East End sportsman.

Brick Lane should itself be seen on Saturday night, though it is in almost all its length a gay and crowded scene every evening of the week, unless persistent rain drives both buyers and sellers to seek shelter. But this sight – the 'market street' – is not confined to Brick Lane, nor peculiar to Whitechapel, nor even to the East End. In every poor quarter of London it is to be met with – the flaring lights, the piles of cheap comestibles, and the urgent cries of the sellers. Everywhere, too, there is the same absolute indifference on the part of the buyer to these cries. They seem to be accepted on both sides as necessary, though entirely useless. Not infrequently the goods are sold by a sort of Dutch auction – then the prices named are usually double what the seller, and every bystander, knows to be the market price of the street and day, 'Eightpence?' – 'Sevenpence?' 'Sixpence?' 'Fivepence?' – 'Say Fourpence?' – well, then, 'Threepence halfpenny?' A bystander, probably a woman, nods imperceptibly; the fish or whatever it is passes from the right hand of the seller on which it has been raised to view, on to the square of newspaper, resting in his left hand, is bundled up and quick as thought takes its place in the buyer's basket in exchange for the 3 ½*d*, which finds its place in the seller's apron or on the board beside the fish – and then begins again the same routine, 'Eightpence?' 'Sevenpence?' 'Sixpence' etc.

Charles Booth, *Life and Labour of the People in London*, 1903

BRIXTON FEMALE CONVICT PRISON

The chaplain gives us the following curious statistics as to the education and causes of the degradation of the several women who have been imprisoned at Brixton –

"Of the 664 prisoners admitted into this prison from November 24th, 1853, to December 31st, 1854, there were the following proportions of educated and uneducated people:-

Number that could not read at all	104
Number that could read a few syllables	53
Number that could read imperfectly	192
Total imperfectly-educated	349
Number that could read tolerably, but most of whom had learned in prison or revived what they had learned in youth	315
Moderately-educated	None
Total	664

"Hence it appears," adds the chaplain, "that among 664 prisoners admitted into this prison, there is not one who has received even a moderate amount of education. Among the same number of male prisoners, judging by my past experience, I feel persuaded that there would be many who had received a fair amount of education. This confirms me in the opinion which I expressed last year, that the beneficial effects of education are more apparent among females than men.'

"Of the same 664 prisoners, the minister tells us-

453 trace their ruin to drunkenness or bad company, or both united.

97 ran away from home, or from service.

84 assigned various causes of their fall.

6 appear to have been suddenly tempted into crime.

8 state that they were in want.

16 say they are innocent.

Henry Mayhew and John Binny,

The Criminal Prisons of London, 1862

BURGLARS

I have been meaning to write to you without waiting for New Year's Day; but in all my life I never have been so driven off letter-writing as since the repairs began in this house. There were four months of that confusion, which ended quite romantically, in my having to sleep with loaded pistols at my bedside! the smell of paint making it as much as my life was worth to sleep with closed windows, and the thieves having become aware of the state of the premises. Once they got in and stole some six pounds' worth of things, before they were frightened away by a candlestick falling and making what my Irish maid called 'a devil of a row'. It was rather to be called 'an angel of a row', as it saved further depredation. Another time they climbed up to the drawing-room windows, and found them fastened, for a wonder! Another night I was alarmed by a sound as of a pane of glass cut, and leapt out of bed, and struck a light, and listened, and heard the same sound repeated, and then a great bang, like breaking in some panel. I took one of my loaded pistols, and went downstairs, and then another bang which I perceived was at the front door. 'What do you want?' I asked; 'who are you?' 'It's the policeman, if you please; do you know that your parlour windows are both open?' It was true! I had forgotten to close them, and the policeman had first tried the bell, which made the shivering sound, the wire being detached from the bell, and when he found he could not ring it he had beaten on the door with his stick, the knocker being off while it was getting painted. I could not help laughing at what the man's feelings would have been had he known of the cocked pistol within a few inches of him.

Jane Welsh Carlyle, *Letters*, 1852

C is for Calisthenics

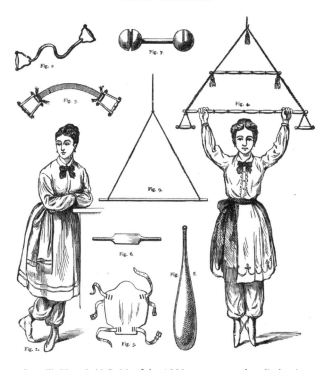

Cassell's Household Guide of the 1880s recommends calisthenics. "Helplessness and inactivity are no longer looked upon as feminine virtues. Lack of exertion leads to irregular muscular action, which, if well directed and regular, invigorates the system."

CABBAGE-DRESSING

One of the greatest evils to be met in the "warren" is the scarcity of water. There is a cistern attached to each alley, and once every week-day the water company allows a limited supply of the precious fluid to run into it. The said supply, to judge from the size of the vessel that holds it, would be unequal to the wants of the inhabitants even supposing that the water was required only for time ordinary purposes of personal ablution and cooking and house scrubbing, but apart from these legitimate uses the inhabitants, or half their number at least, require water for trade purposes. They are costermongers (as we style them, but "general dealers" as they invariably style themselves), and the commodity in which they mainly deal is green stuff – such as cabbages, savoys, and turnip tops. They buy at a cheap rate such stock as is left over from the day's market and will not keep till the next market day. They carry it home – over-night, perhaps – and stow it somewhere (where, one is afraid to hint at almost as regards houses where space is so precious) till the morning. The appearance a bunch of greens would then present may be easily imagined; no one would give a single halfpenny for the flabby yellow things and they must be revived. Every general dealer has a tub that is used for this purpose amongst others, and any one bold enough to look into either of the alleys on a Saturday morning may witness at full blast this process of cabbage dressing. Every coster man or woman is busy over a tub, soaking, trimming, and selecting, batch after batch, until the stuff in the vessel becomes too thick and nauseous to be of further service – a fact lothfully recognized by the green-washers, since no more than that one tubful of water may be obtained. In the evening this precious "green-stuff" is carried on the barrows to the Aylesbury Street or Leather Lane markets, and there disposed of in "lumpin' penn'orths" to economical mothers, who take home the vegetable and boil it for their husband and children. It might be worth inquiry how much disease and death may be traced to this source. "I have known the neighbourhood through several years," said an individual with whom I had some talk on the subject, "and I never yet knew a time when sickness in some shape or another did not exist amongst us. In summer time it is frightful. I have seen as many as thirteen children buried out of the alleys in the course of a single Sunday afternoon."

James Greenwood, *The Wilds of London*, 1874

CABS

There are, probably, in London about 4300 cabs, which daily convey from one part of the Metropolis to another some 50,000 passengers, at a yearly cost to the public of nearly 900,000*l.* These cabs are usually hired by their drivers, at a daily rate of 9*s.* to 12*s.*, from the large cab-owners, and are divided into "two-wheelers" (Hansoms) and "four-wheelers;" the former accommodating two, and the latter four or five persons.

Fares are calculated (1) by "distance," or (2) by "time."

1. DISTANCE FARES – 6*d.* per mile, or part of a mile, for two persons, within a four miles radius of Charing Cross.

1*s.* per mile, or part of a mile, for every mile, or part of a mile, beyond four miles from Charing Cross.

For every additional adult carried, beyond two persons, 6*d.* extra for the whole distance. Two children, under ten years of age, are counted as one adult.

2. TIME FARES (for two persons). – For any time not exceeding one hour, 2*s.*; and for every fifteen minutes, or less than fifteen minutes, over the hour, 6*d.*

1*s.* for every mile, or part of a mile, beyond four miles (radius) from Charing Cross.

The driver is required to drive at a rate not exceeding four miles an hour. If ordered to drive with greater speed, he may claim 6*d.* a mile, or portion of a mile, in addition to his time-fare.

For additional passengers, beyond two persons, the extra fare is 6*d.* each passenger for the whole hiring.

Back-fare cannot be charged.

6*d.* may be charged for every fifteen minutes during which the cab is detained by the hirer. This applies only to engagements by distance.

The driver can be compelled to hire his carriage for a "time fare" between 8 p.m. and 6 a.m.

LUGGAGE. – A reasonable quantity is required to be carried free of charge, except when more than two persons are carried inside, and then 2*d.* may be demanded for every package placed outside.

DISPUTES. – In case of any dispute between driver and hirer, the latter may require the driver to drive to the nearest Metropolitan Police Court, where the complaint will be immediately investigated. If no magistrate be sitting, the hirer may be driven to the nearest Police Station, where the case will be duly entered for the magistrate to decide at his next sitting.

For luggage lost, apply at the chief Police Office, Scotland Yard, Parliament Street.

The Hansom cabs are the most expeditious; but it is customary to reward their drivers with a trifle more than the legal fare.

In London there are 218 cab-stands, 39 of which are within the City precincts.

Cruchley's London in 1865: A Handbook for Strangers, 1865

A CIRCUMSTANCE which has given a very evil name to cab-men in general, on the part of the public, is a class of men, who, though dismissed from their body, are yet much mixed up with it.

These are cabmen who have been deprived of their licenses for drunkenness or bad conduct. The law, in kindness to the licensed cabdriver, allows him, in case of need, to employ an unlicensed substitute for a period not longer than 24 hours, and by this means these discharged men get to drive licensed cabs. This is especially the case with the cabs of what are called long-day men, – for the cab-drivers are divided into several distinct classes, according to the number and character of the hours during which they ply for hire, and there are, consequently, the long-day men; the morning men, who are out from 7 a.m. to 6 p.m.; the long-night men, who are out from 6 p.m. to 10 a.m.; and the short-night men, who are out from 6 p.m. to 6 a.m. The long-day men (and it is they chiefly who are employed by the contractors) leave the stables at 9 or 10 in the morning, and do not return home till 12 or 1, or, in some cases, till 4 or 5, or even later, the next morning. These hours are more than one man can well endure, and he is therefore glad to avail himself of the help of the unlicensed driver towards the end of the day, or while he is at his meals. There is also employment for these discarded men on the stands, and the licensed driver is ordinarily glad to give them the sixpence they expect from each driver for cleaning up the cab and harness, which otherwise he would have to do himself. Their mode of life is correctly sketched in the following extract: – They usually loiter about the watering-houses (as the public-houses are called) of the cab-stands, and pass most of their time in the tap-rooms. They are mostly of intemperate habits, being usually "confirmed sots." Very few of them are married men. They have been what is termed fancy men in their prime, but, to use the words of one of the craft, "got turned up." They seldom sleep in a bed. Some few have a bed-room in some obscure part of the town, but the most of them loll about and doze in the tap-rooms by day, and sleep in cabs by night.

Rev. J. Garwood, *The Million-Peopled City*, 1853

CALISTHENICS

Helplessness and inactivity are no longer looked upon as feminine virtues. Lack of exertion leads to irregular muscular action, which, if well directed and regular, invigorates the system. Exercise is now recognised to be as great a necessity in woman's education as in man's: we are learning that many bodily defects and much of her weak health is attributable to the want of it; more especially in youth, when the frame is growing. Nine women out of twenty have one shoulder larger than the other, many pursuits, such as reading, writing, and drawing, tending towards this; and physical exercise is absolutely necessary to counteract such tendencies, curing as it does many deformities of mind and person, rendering the soft, flexible tissues firm and strong, and making weak, delicate constitutions robust. The advantage of calisthenics to a narrow-chested girl is untold, for bodily-organs unpractised naturally become weak, and general weakness of the whole system follows.

Such exercises must, however, be carried out under a system; irregularly conducted, they do more harm than good. The constitution must be coaxed, not strained; the strength not unduly taxed, no over-fatigue ensuing; for exhaustion makes people look worn and old. The exertion must not be too violent, and the health and physical development of each pupil must be specially studied.

Early morning or evening are the best times to select, but on no account immediately after a meal. The clothing should not be too warm, nor interfere in any way with the action of the limbs.

It is a very usual plan in America and France, where the subject has been carefully studied, to wear a special costume, consisting of a loose blouse, with a sash at the waist, and Turkish trousers; or in place of the blouse, a Garibaldi bodice and skirt; dark blue serge with white or scarlet braid, or unglazed holland with the same sort of trimming, are most in favour, being both strong and light. Grey and red is another favourite mixture.

The boots should be an easy fit, with low heels. Our illustration (Fig. 1) will show that such a dress, while ensuring perfect ease and liberty of action to the wearer, is by no means unbecoming.

Ample space will be required, and good ventilation; a temperature of from 63° to 70°, with an abundant supply of fresh air. The teacher should be careful to give his directions in a clear, distinct voice, and to have the several exercises carried out with military precision. A musical accompaniment will best preserve the necessary rhythms – the time, four or eight beats to a bar; failing this, the pupils should be taught to sing or count in concert, thereby keeping up their interest and zest. A castanet will, failing better means, help to mark the time with or without music.

Cassell's Household Guide, c.1880

CAMPING

Camping Out is a form of entertainment which has lately come into fashion, and is spoken of with much enthusiasm by its devotees, among whom may be numbered a proportion of ladies. It is a little difficult to see the great enjoyment of sleeping in a tent when you can get a bed, or of being exposed to the mists and fogs which are so plentiful on the river at night and in the early morning even in the summer. It is not necessary to give any detailed advice on this subject, as the enthusiast will probably have imbibed the taste for camping from an experienced friend, who will be able to "show him all the ropes." It may be suggested that a good deal of the land on the banks of the river is private property, and that trespassing in private paddocks and gardens, as is too often done, indiscriminate wood-cutting for fires, and similar practices, should be avoided. The owner of one well-known and extremely comfortable camping-ground has been, we regret to say, compelled to close it against campers owing to the ill return so constantly made him for his courtesy. This gentleman is a man of the world, and not at all of a fidgety or touchy disposition; but when it came to cutting down valuable ornamental shrubs, climbing garden walls, stealing fruit and eggs and surreptitiously milking cows at unholy hours, it was felt that the line must be drawn. A lock-island is generally a good place for a camp. Tents should be pitched a little distance from the water, on rising ground if possible, and upon no account under the shadow of overhanging trees. It is well to be provided with a sufficiency of reasonable comforts, but the example of a party who were seen last year at Cookham, with a servant in livery laying the table for dinner, is not one to be followed. Half the fun of camping consists in doing everything for oneself, and in the perfect freedom from all conventional social trammels which such a mode of existence involves. For cooking utensils, the cooking-stoves sold at 93, Wigmore-street, have been well spoken of. An iron tripod, with chain and hook to which to hang the kettle or the saucepan, is very useful. B. Edgington, of Tooley-street, can be recommended for tents of all kinds.

Charles Dickens (Jr.), *Dickens's Dictionary of the Thames*, 1881

CAN-CAN, THE

We observe that an indecent can-can dancer, sufficiently wanton to gain an unenviable notoriety in London, is now indulging in her repulsive pantomime throughout the country. Nothing less severe than the intervention of those in authority seems to affect these brazen creatures, whose prurient perform-ances must be sowing the worst of seed among our youth; but the worst of it is that this disgraceful nuisance is no sooner suppressed in one place than it crops up in another. This pest of can-canism must be stamped out. Will it be considered presumptuous to call the Lord Chamberlain's attention to the fact that certain managers, whose innocent bleatings were heard at the last granting of dancing licenses in London, are apparently again falling into an error with regard to their interpretation of the term dancing license? Licentious dancing is certainly again cropping up at certain notorious houses, and we would advise the Lord Chamberlain to go the round of the fastest theatres and stop the career of managers whom no number of warnings appear to affect.

The Penny Illustrated Paper, 1871

CANDLES

I was an eager devourer of literature from my earliest years, and used to read, stretched on the hearthrug, with my book between my elbows, on which I rested, or at night curled up in a chair, with a candle and the snuffer-tray in close proximity.

The casual mention of the snuffer-tray, an article never seen by modern readers, brings to my mind a thousand and one changes in things, manners, and customs between the present time and the days of my childhood, forty years ago, which will properly find mention in this chapter. In those days, though there was gas in the streets and shops, and wax-candles for the great ones of the earth, those who could not afford such luxuries were compelled to seek their illumination in tallow-candles, which required snuffing – i.e., the removal of their burnt wicks – about every quarter of an hour. "Require no snuffing," was the boast in the advertisement of the Palmer's composite candles, which were the first improvement, and one variety of which was, I remember, burned in a lamp, forced down on a spring into a socket, and liable to shoot out like a rocket. Mention of Palmer's name reminds me that there were no so-called "night-lights," only a long "farthing rush-light," set up in the middle of a huge tin lighthouse perforated with round holes, the reflection of which on the walls and ceiling was ghostly in the extreme; no lucifers, but a round tinder-box, with a flint, and a bit of steel on which to strike it, and a bundle of long sulphur-tipped slips of wood called matches. The lucifer, or Congreve match as it was called, as originally produced, was ignited by friction on sandpaper, and had a very unpleasant smell.

Edmund Yates, *His Recollections and Experiences*, 1885

DAVIES'S BOTANIC WAX CANDLES, 11*d*. per *lb*; Sperm, 2*s* and 2*s* 2*d*; Patent Sperm, 11*d*; British Wax or Sperm, 1*s* 4*d*; German Wax, 1*s* 2*d*; fine Wax, 1*s* 5*d*; Transparent Wax, 1*s* 4*d* and 2*s* 4*d*; best Wax, 2*s* 3*d*; Composite 6½*d*, 7½*d*, 9*d* and 9½*d*; Palmers' 6½*d*; Magnums, 3*d*; Mid-size, 7½*d*; Store Candles, 4½*d* and 5*d*; Waxed-wick Moulds, 6*d*; Yellow Soap, 44*s*, 50*s*, and 54*s* per 112*lbs*; Mottled, 56*s*; Windsor Soap, 1*s* 4*d*; Brown Windsor, 1*s* 9*d*; Rose, 2*s*; Almond, 2*s* 6*d*; Sealing Wax 4*s* 6*d* per *lb*; Argand, Vegetable, Carcel or Colza Oil, 4*s* 6*d* per gallon; Sperm oil, 7*s* 6*d*; Solar, 3*s* 6*d*; Seal 4*s*; for cash at DAVIES'S old established warehouse 83 St Martin's lane, opposite the Westminster County Court.

advertisement from *The Daily News*, 1851

CARS

We hear much now of "street accidents," but what may they become should London be invaded by the "horse-less carriage"?

And then think how it would be if one of them were to bolt. We read of active policemen catching the reins of a runaway, and saving the lives of those sitting helplessly behind it, but who would snatch at the reins of an iron cab over which its driver has lost control? There are "cons" as well as "pros" in the outlook of a street invasion by blind unfeeling motors. It is the use, however, of private ones on country roads that many contemplate their adoption with safe promised enjoyment. A "Tour on Wheels" will bring a decidedly new sensation: no anxiety about uncertain stabling, or sudden lameness; no tiresome carriage of hay or oats ; no breaking of harness in out-of-the-way places. Of course there is the chance of an inside pipe going wrong, or a cog coming off, and then – where are you? Far from an intelligent artificer to repair the damage, or manufactory where you can buy what you want? Again, there is no "loving" of a reservoir ; you must feed it, indeed, but it does not care to be patted. You can't give it a carrot or lump of sugar before you start. Perhaps some ingenious inventor will enable a motor to neigh instead of "toot," but it can never become an affectionate companion who knows your voice and likes to be stroked. There is bloodless satisfaction in steering the best horseless carriage, however swiftly and safely it may carry you where you would go.

The Leisure Hour, 1896

Our legislators have never favoured horseless traffic – witness the way in which they have treated steam-rollers and traction-engines; though it must not be overlooked that badly built houses may be dangerously shaken by heavily moving machinery. Steam, however, is not so likely to furnish the motive power as oil or electricity. One of the most entertaining features of this revived interest in what it is the fashion to call automobility, is the series of laments as to the supersession of the horse expressed in almost exactly the same terms as in Trevithick's day. The railways also were to have wiped out the horses, but have they? There are more horses now than there ever were.

The Leisure Hour, 1896

CATACOMBS, CEMETERY

We go down by a stone staircase, and I am speedily in the centre of a wide avenue, out of which branch other avenues; and on stone shelves on each side of these rest coffins. This is Catacomb B. Catacomb A is away from the chapel, and has long been filled. This present catacomb has room for five thousand bodies, and my companion (who has been custodian of the vaults for the last thirty years) considers it about half full. I am therefore in a village below ground, of some two thousand five hundred dead inhabitants, and I can (not without reproaching myself for the incongruity) compare it to nothing but a huge wine-cellar. The empty vaults are precisely like large bins, and were it not for the constant gleams of daylight from the numerous ventilating shafts, my guide with his candle would seem to be one of those astute cellarmen who invariably appear to return from the darkest corners with a choicer and choicer wine. The never altogether absent daylight destroys this illusion, and I proceed to examine the coffins around me. They are, as a rule, each in a separate compartment, some walled up with stone, others having an iron gate and lock and key, others with small windows in the stone; others, again, are on a sort of public shelf on the top. The private vaults are fitted up, some with iron bars for the coffins to rest on, others with open shelves, so that their entire length can be seen. The price of a whole vault, holding twenty coffins, is, I learn, one hundred and ninety-nine pounds; of one private compartment, fourteen pounds; the cost of interment in a public vault is four guineas; each of these sums being exclusive of burial fees, and an increased rate of charges being demanded when the coffin is of extra size.

Edmund Yates, *The Business of Pleasure*, 1879

CAT'S MEAT

The Cat and Dogs' Meat Dealers, or "carriers," as they call themselves, generally purchase the meat at the horse-slaughterers' yards. There are nearly twenty of these in and around London. There are three or four in Whitechapel, one in Wandsworth, two in Cow-cross – one of these is the largest establishment in London – two in Maiden-lane, and two over the water, about Bermondsey. The proprietors of these yards purchase live and dead horses. They contract for these with most large firms – such as brewers, coal – merchants, and large cab and 'bus yards – giving so much per head for their old live and dead horses through the year. The price they pay is from £2 to 50*s*. the carcase. The horse-slaughterers also have contractors in the country (harness-makers and others), who bring or send up to town for them the live and dead stock of those parts. ... The flesh when boiled is taken from the coppers, laid on the stones, and sprinkled with water to cool it. It is then weighed out in pieces of a hundred, half a hundred, twenty-eight, twenty-one. fourteen, seven, and three pounds and a half weight. These are either taken round in a cart to the "carriers," or else at about five o'clock the carriers begin to call at the yard to purchase it themselves, and continue doing so till twelve o'clock in the day. The price is 14*s*. per *cwt*. in the winter, and 16*s*. in the summer time. The tripe is served out at 12 *lbs*. for 6*d*. All this is sold for cats and dogs. The carriers then take the meat round town, wherever their walk might lie. They sell it out to the public at the rate of 2½*d*. per *lb*., and in small pieces, on skewers, at a farthing, a halfpenny. and a penny each. Some carriers will sell as much as a hundredweight in a day, and about half a hundred-weight is about the average quantity disposed of by the carriers in London. Some sell much cheaper than others. They will frequently knock at the doors of persons whom they have seen served by another on the previous day, and show them that they can let them have a larger quantity of meat for the same money.

Henry Mayhew, *'Labour and the Poor'*
(in the *Morning Chronicle*), 1849

CHILDREN'S GAMES

Some of their games seem to be of a rather spiteful nature. Here is a party playing "Ugly Bear." One boy crawls on the pavement and the rest belabour him with caps attached to lengths of string. Here are others playing "Egg Cap" and "Mondays and Tuesdays." If you are a muff at this you will have to lay your open hand against a wall and allow a boy to shy a ball at it. "King of the Castle" and "No Man Standing" are just red savagery set to rules; "Release" is plain fighting with the anger left out ; whilst "Leading the Blind Horse" is merely an elaborate practical joke, the point of which is to blindfold a trusting innocent and then to maltreat him in any handy way that his defencelessness suggests. Better games than these, though dangerous still, are in progress. Notable among them is tip-cat, but this is perilous only to onlookers.

These urchins who are engaged in throwing pieces of the roadway at other pieces of the roadway are playing "Gully" or "Duck" ; they have just been playing "Castles", a game in which loose stones also play a big shin-shattering part. "Horny Winkle's Horses," in which one set of boys stoops down and makes a bridge of backs against a wall, and other boys ride them to a thrice-repeated chorus of "Charley Knackers-one, two, three!" or, until they collapse, is another boisterous game. In this category come also "Rounders," a game resembling baseball; "Chevy Chace," a form of prisoners base in which one unit of a "side" is captured and held to ransom until a comrade rescues him; "I-spy-I," or hide and seek; "Tom Tiddler's Ground," "Red Rover" and "Puss-puss," which resemble one another in that one player is prominent above all the rest.

In the midst of the prevalent turmoil there are boys at games that might be called "quiet," if only the players would refrain from argument. "Buttons" can be played without any adjuncts at all, or in conjunction with a ball, a peg-top, or a knicker – the last a heavy, leaden disc. There are some curious conventions connected with these games that are religiously observed. You may not, for example, use iron buttons or buttons below the regulation size; and if the peg of your top measures less than an average thumbnail it is a "mounter" and may be thrown over the house by any boy who can get hold of it.

George R. Sims, *Living London*, 1902

CHILDREN, ROBBERY OF

Seven years penal servitude to be followed by an equal term of police surveillance, was meted out to Elizabeth Townsend, at the Surrey Sessions for the systematic plundering of children in the streets. The prisoner resided at Kennington-oval, and it was proved that she was in the habit of making excursions nightly with the purpose of decoying little children into courts and alleys and then stripping them of their clothes or robbing them of whatever else they possessed. She had been several times previously convicted.

Illustrated London News, 1873

CHOLERA

The connection between disease and defective structural and economic arrangements continues to demand the most serious attention. The relationship of cholera, and fever, and crime, to cesspools, imperfect drainage, impure water, overcharged graveyards, and want of ventilation, is a great sanitary question, with which we feel ourselves all the more urgently called upon to deal, to the best of our ability and experience, since it is one on which the medical faculty themselves, strange to say, differ materially.

This is an unfortunate state of things, and shows the necessity for renewed and continued inquiries.

One thing appears beyond all doubt, – and it is on this we work resolutely, however feebly, – that where human beings are crowded together in ill-arranged dwellings; where the drainage is bad and the cesspool lurks; where refuse rots, the air is vitiated, or the water impure and scanty, – there cholera and fever, when evoked, reign and slay.

George Godwin, *Town Swamps and Social Bridges*, 1859

THE CHOLERA AND AUTUMNAL COMPLAINTS.— To oppose cholera, there seems no surer or better means than cleanliness, sobriety, and judicious ventilation. Where there is dirt, that is the place for cholera; where windows and doors are kept most jealously shut, there cholera will find easiest entrance; and people who indulge in intemperate diet during the hot days of autumn are actually courting death. To repeat it, cleanliness, sobriety, and free ventilation almost always defy the pestilence; but, in case of attack, imme- diate recourse should be had to a physician. The faculty say that a large number of lives have been lost, in many seasons, solely from delay in seeking medical assistance. They even assert that, taken early, the cholera is by no means a fatal disorder. The copious use of salt is recommended on very excellent authority.

Isabella Beeton, *Mrs. Beeton's Book of Household Management*, 1861

CHOP HOUSES

Chops and Steaks.—It is only recently that a great superstition as to chops and steaks has been exploded. It was for very many years a popular delusion that west of Fleet-street chops and steak could not be had—or, at all events, could only be had in a very inferior style. The West-end chop or steak, it is true, was for a long time difficult to come at, and, as a rule, exceedingly bad when you got it, although the grill-loving Londoner was even then able to go to Stone's in Panton-street with a tolerable certainty of finding what he wanted. This house, which dates from the beginning of the century, and has been well known to literary London, still holds its own, although grills have of late year grown up round it in all directions. The Inns of Court Hotel, the Criterion, the Gaiety, the Royal Aquarium, the St. James's Hall, the "Holborn," and the "Horseshoe" restaurants, and many of Spiers and Pond's railway refreshment rooms make a specialty of their grills, and the foreign reader of the DICTIONARY who wishes to try this peculiar English form of meal can be recommended to any of these places. The City itself absolutely swarms with chop-houses, and it is only possible here to say that anywhere about Finch-lane and Cornhill the grill business is thoroughly well understood and well done. Between the City proper and the West-end is the "Cheshire Cheese," Wine Office-court, Fleet-street, one of the old fashioned chop houses, specially famous for rump-steak pudding on Saturday afternoons.

Charles Dickens (Jr.), *Dickens's Dictionary of London*, 1879

CHRISTMAS

In anticipation of the liberal expenditure of ready cash – the most interesting consideration of the season to a London trader – and which expenditure every shopkeeper is dutifully anxious to engross as far as possible to himself; a thousand different persuasive devices are already placarded and profusely exhibited. "Christmas presents" forms a monster line in the posters on the walls and in the shop-windows. Infantine appeals in gigantic type cover the hoardings. "Do, Papa, Buy Me" so-and-so; so-and-so being blotted out in a few hours by "The New Patent Wig," so that the appeal remains a perplexing puzzle to affectionate parents, till both are in turn blotted out by a third poster, announcing the sacrifice of 120,000 gipsy cloaks and winter mantles at less than half the cost-price. Cheap Christmas books are a part of every bookseller's display; Christmas fashions fill the drapers' windows, and stand on full-dressed poles in the doorways. There are Christmas lamps, lustres, and candelabra; Christmas diamonds made of paste, and Brumagem jewellery for glittering show, as well as Christmas furniture for parties and routs, to be hired for the season-carving, gilding, hangings, beds; everything which, being wanted but once a year, it may be cheaper to hire than to purchase or to keep on hand. ...

But these and such as these are very minor and subordinate preparations. Eating and drinking, after all, are the chief and paramount obligations of the Christmas season. As the month grows older, the great gastronomic anniversary is heralded at every turn by signs more abundant and less equivocal. Among the dealers in eatables, one and all of whom are now putting in their sickles for the harvest, the grocer, who is independent of the weather, leads off the dance. Long before the holly and the mistletoe have come to town, he has received his stock of Christmas fruit, on the sale of which, it may be, the profit or loss of the whole year's trading is depending.

Charles Manby Smith, *Curiosities of London Life*, 1853

CHRISTMAS CLUBS

It is with a feeling doubtless somewhat analogous to that of the angler, that the London shopkeeper from time to time regards the moneyless crowds who throng in gaping admiration around the tempting display he makes in his window. His admirers and the fish, however, are in different circumstances: the one won't bite if they have no mind; the others can't bite if they should have all the mind in the world. Yet the shopkeeper manages better than the angler; for while the fish are deaf to the charming of the latter, charm he never so wisely, the former is able, at a certain season of the year, to convert the moneyless gazers into ready-money customers. This he does by the force of logic. "You are thinking of Christmas," says he – "yes, you are; and you long to have a plum-pudding for that day – don't deny it. Well, but you can't have it, think as much as you will; it is impossible as you manage at present. But I'll tell you how to get the better of the impossibility. In twenty weeks we shall have Christmas here: now if, instead of spending every week all you earn, you will hand me over sixpence or a shilling out of your wages, I'll take care of it for you, since you can't take care of it for yourself; and you shall have the full value out of my shop any time in Christmas-week, and be as merry as you like, and none the poorer."

This logic is irresistible. Tomkins banks his sixpence for a plum-pudding and the etceteras with Mr. Allspice the grocer; and this identical pudding he enjoys the pleasure of eating half-a-dozen times over in imagination before the next instalment is due. He at length becomes so fond of the flavour, that he actually – we know, for we have seen him do it – he actually, to use his own expression, "goes in for a goose" besides with Mr. Pluck the poulterer. Having once passed the Rubicon, of course he cannot go back; the weekly sixpences must be paid come what will; it would be disgraceful to be a defaulter.

Charles Manby Smith, *Curiosities of London Life*, 1853

CIRCULATING LIBRARIES

Libraries (Circulating). —The two principal circulating libraries for ordinary light literature, are W. H. SMITH and SON'S, Strand, with depots for exchange of Books at all their Railway Bookstalls, and MUDIE'S, Oxford-street. Terms for W. H. Smith and Son's :— 1. Subscribers can only change their books at the depot where their names are registered. A Subscriber may exchange once a day; the Clerk in charge will obtain from London any work in the Library which a Subscriber may desire to have. Novels exchanged only in unbroken and complete Sets. London Subscribers transferring their Subscriptions to a country depot, will be entitled only to the number of volumes which the country terms assign to the amount they subscribe; similarly, Country Subscriptions transferred to Town become subject to the London regulations. Terms —

I. For Subscribers obtaining their Books from a London Terminus, or 186, Strand:

	Six Months	Twelve Months
1 Vol. at a time	£0 12s 0	£1 1s 0
2 Vols. at a time	£0 17s 6	£1 11s 0
4 Vols. at a time	£1 3s 0	£2 2s 0
8 Vols. at a time	£1 15s 0	£3 3s 0
15 Vols. at a time	£3 0s 0	£5 5s 0

II. From a Country Bookstall

	Six Months	Twelve Months
1 Vol. at a time	£0 12s 0	£1 1s 0
2 Vols. at a time	£0 17s 6	£1 11s 0
3 Vol. at a time	£1 3s 0	£2 2s 6
4 Vols. at a time	£1 8s 0	£2 10s 0
6 Vols. at a time	£1 15s 0	£3 3s 0
12 Vols. at a time	£3 0s 0	£5 5s 0

Charles Dickens (Jr.), *Dickens's Dictionary of London*, 1879

CLEOPATRA'S NEEDLE

Cleopatra's Needle stands on the Victoria Embankment, left hand of the river. This famous monolith of red granite, from Alexandria, originally stood at Heliopolis, and was presented to this country by Mehemet Ali in 1819. No ministry was bold enough to face the difficulty and expense of transporting it across the Bay of Biscay, and for many years it lay half buried by sand at Alexandria, at the foot of its still erect sister, which, according to some people, is the real original Cleopatra's Needle. In the Alexandrian sand the English obelisk would probably have remained until the end of time (unless, indeed, the British tourist had not carried it away piecemeal in the form of relics) but for the public spirit of Mr. Erasmus Wilson and Mr. John Dixon, the well-known civil engineer. Mr. Wilson put down £10,000 for the expenses of transport, and Mr. John Dixon undertook to deliver the monument in the Thames for that sum on the principle of "no cure, no pay" – no obelisk, no £10,000. A special cylinder boat was designed, in which the needle was encased, and justified Mr. Dixon's expectations by making good weather of it until it became unmanageable and untenantable in a heavy gale in the Bay of Biscay. Abandoned by the steamer which had it in tow, after the sacrifice of six lives in a last gallant attempt to save the Cleopatra, few people doubted that the needle would find its last resting-place at the bottom of the sea. Fortunately a passing steamer succeeded in securing it, and towed it into Ferrol, whence it was safely transferred to its present site. Much ingenuity was shown in the machinery designed for its erection, the difficulties of which will readily be understood when it is stated that the obelisk is over 68 feet in height, and weighs 180 tons. NEAREST Steamboat Piers and Bridges, Waterloo and Charing-cross; Railway Sattions, Charing-cross (Dist. & SE.) Omnibus Routes, Waterloo Bridge and Strand.

Charles Dickens (Jr.), *Dickens's Dictionary of the Thames*, 1881

CLARE MARKET

Clare Market lies hidden behind the western side of Lincoln's-inn, and can be reached either by the turning up from the Strand next to the new law courts, or through the archway in the western side of Lincoln's-inn. It is a market without a market-house; a collection of lanes, where every shop is tenanted by a butcher or greengrocer, and where the roadways are choked with costermongers' carts. To see Clare Market at its best, it is needful to go there on Saturday evening: then the narrow lanes are crowded, then the butchers' shops are ablaze with gas-lights flaring in the air, and the shouting of the salesman and costermonger is at its loudest. Nowhere in London is a poorer population to be found than that which is contained in the quadrangle formed by the Strand, Catherine-street, Long-acre, and Lincoln's-inn and the new law courts. The greater portion of those who are pushing through the crowd to make their purchases for to-morrow's dinner are women, and of them many have children in their arm. Ill-dressed, worn, untidy, and wretched, many of them look, but they joke with their acquaintances, and are keen hands at bargaining. Follow one, and look at the meat stall before which she steps. The shop is filled with strange pieces of coarse, dark-coloured, and unwholesome-looking meat. There is scarce a piece there whose form you recognise as familiar; no legs of mutton, no sirloins of beef, no chops or steaks, or ribs or shoulders. It is meat, and you take it on faith that it is meat of the ox or sheep; but beyond that you can say nothing. The slice of bacon on the next stall is more tempting, and many prefer a rasher of this for their Sunday's dinner to the coarse meat which neither their skill in cooking nor their appliances enable them to render tender and eatable, or satisfactory to the good man who is at present drinking himself to a point of stupidity at the publichouse at the corner, and spending an amount which would make all the difference in cost between the odds and ends of coarse meat and a wholesome joint. It is a relief to turn from the butchers' shops to the costermongers' barrows. Here herrings or mackerel, as the season may be—bought, perhaps, a few hours before at Billingsgate—are selling at marvellously low prices, while the vegetables, equally cheap, look fresh and excellent in quality.

Charles Dickens (Jr.), *Dickens's Dictionary of London*, 1879

CLUBLAND

A man may, if he be so minded, make his club his home; living and lounging luxuriously, and grazing to his heart's content on the abundant club-house literature, and enjoying the conversation of club friends. Soap and towels, combs and hair-brushes, are provided in the lavatories; and there are even some clubs that have bed-rooms in their upper storeys, for the use of members. In those that are deficient in such sleeping accommodation, it is only necessary to have a tooth-brush and an attic in an adjacent bye-street; all the rest can be provided at the club. Thus it is that, in the present generation, has been created a type peculiar thereunto – the club-man. He is all of the club, and clubby. He is full of club matters, club gossip. He dabbles in club intrigues, belongs to certain club cliques, and takes part in club quarrels. No dinners are so good to him as the club dinners; he can read no journals but those he finds in the club newspaper-room; he writes his letters on the club paper, pops them into club envelopes, seals them with the club seal, and despatches them, if they are not intended for postage, by the club messengers. He is rather sorry that there is no club uniform. He would like, when he dies, to be buried in a club coffin, in the club cemetery, and to be followed to the grave by the club, with members of the committee as pall-bearers. As it is, when he has shuffled off this mortal coil, his name appears on a board among the list of "members deceased." That is his epitaph, his hatchment, his oraison funêbre.

The great complaint against clubs is, that they tend towards the germination of selfishness, exclusiveness, and isolation; that they are productive of neglect of home duties in married men, and of irrevocable celibacy in bachelors. Reserving my own private opinion on this knotty point, I may say that it is a subject for sincere congratulation that there are no ladies' clubs. We have been threatened with them sometimes, but they have always been nipped in the bud.

George Augustus Sala, *Twice Round the Clock*, 1859

Not very many years ago ladies' clubs were comparatively unknown; now-a-days, almost every up-to-date London woman belongs to one, butterfly of fashion and working bee alike. Dive into the back streets, or journey eastwards, and you find that the same holds good of the toiling home-worker, the dress-maker, and the factory girl. But what, it may be asked, do the members do at their clubs? What goes on behind the portals of the magnificent Empress, the exclusive Green Park, as well as the humbler doors of a Working Girls' Institute? This is what we are about to investigate; we shall, in fact, follow some of the titled dames, the lecturers and journalists, the tailoresses, and chorus-girls into their citadels, and see what use they make of them.

A coroneted carriage turns into Dover Street, centre of feminine Club-land. Lady A. is going to her club; will it be the Empress, Sandringham, Sesame, Pioneer, or Green Park? They all lie within a stone's throw. The carriage stops at the Empress; Lady A. passes through the heavy swing doors, and is in the most luxurious ladies' club in London. In the hall she finds a visitor waiting for her, non-members being allowed no farther than this without their hostesses. Together they pass on to the Lounge; the band is playing, and "five-o-clocker," as the French drolly style tea, going forward. Footmen with tea-trays move swiftly hither and thither; groups of fashionably attired men and women are standing or sitting about, chatting and listening to the music. The Empress is a favourite rendezvous, and on Sunday evening full to overflowing.

In one of the rooms, which might from its appearance be a salon at Versailles, more groups and more conversation. In another two or three ladies are writing letters, while others turn over papers and glance through magazines. Her visitor having departed, Lady A. joins a couple of acquaintances going upstairs to the corridor for a quiet cigarette.

George R. Sims, *Living London*, 1902

COFFEE SHOPS

COFFEE, &c., IN LONDON. The best cup of coffee to be had in London is at the Cigar Divan, 102, Strand. You pay 1*s*. to enter the Divan, which will entitle you to a cup of coffee and cigar, and the privileges of the room, the newspapers, chess, &c.

Coffee may be had good at Verrey's, corner of Hanover-street, Regent-street, at 6*d.* a cup ; and still better at Croom's, 16, Fleet-street, for only 3*d.* (Ask for a small cup.) For ices, go to Gunter's in Berkeley-square, and Granges in Piccadilly, over against Bond-street, and for cool drinks to Sainsbury's, 177, Strand. The best buns are to be had at Birch's, 15, Cornhill, and at Caldwell's, 42, Strand.

Peter Cunningham, *Hand-Book of London*, 1850

COFFEE STALLS

ON a foggy or a frosty night a London coffee-stall is a pleasant thing for the eye to fall upon. It looks like a little bit of Home come out of doors to comfort the cheerless and the cold. Perhaps it may be somewhat tantalizing to those who cannot purchase of its wares, but even they can linger in its warmth; and those who are hurrying or drifting through the blinded, shuttered streets in the small hours, not caring to eat or drink, get a notion of company from the coffee-stall as they go by, which they do not find in the solitary, suspicious policeman, flashing his bull's-eye into dark entries, trying windows and rattling door-handles, or in the long lines of dimly-gleaming lamps, and abbreviated ranks of the night cabs. Most canvas tenements have an unpleasantly temporary look about them, – are disagreeably suggestive of vagrancy. The gipsy, the Arab, the soldier, the gold-digger, all strike their tents, and wander on – who knows whither? The covered coffee-stall, on the contrary, has, as I have said, a look of home. We know that although its glow may vanish in the garish light of day, it will re-appear next night in the same place, like a night-blowing cereus to shed its perfume. Brightly gleam or cosily twinkle the lamps of the coffee-stall. The round eyes of its cans have no angry heat, but warm welcome in their red glow, which surrounds them with a ring of light, pleasantly reflected in broken radiations from their polished silver-like tin, their burnished gold-like brass. How fragrant is the aroma of the coffee, although it may not have come from Mocha. Tea and cocoa may also be obtained at the coffee-stall, but the beverage from which it derives its name is the specialty which deservedly gives it its fame.

Let those who will talk of chicory, – to many palates a pleasant, and by them demanded adulteration, – and of chicory itself adulterated with turnips, carrots, and Venetian-red, – of horse-beans, burnt crusts, and so on and so on: those who have drunk coffee-stall coffee when cold and weary, or simply feverishly thirsty, will declare that it has a flavour peculiarly its own, – and not mean this altogether as a left-handed compliment. It warms the cockles of the heart, and makes the footsore one inclined to leap like the kids of the dervish who was – well, perhaps, not its discoverer.

What a dairy-like whiteness – at any rate by night – the earthenware of the coffee-stall displays. How, I might go on to say, how richly oleaginous is its cake, how piquantly salt its bread and butter, how delicately cut its sandwiches, how full-flavoured its eggs, however fresh its watercress,– were it not for a fear that I might be supposed to have some covert meaning of satire; whereas I sincerely wish to glorify the hot, brown, cheering beverage, and warm, redly-golden, cosy look of a night coffee-stall.

Richard Rowe, *Life in the London Streets,* 1881

COFFEE TAVERNS

Coffee Taverns.—Five years ago a company, of which Lord Shaftesbury was president, made the first attempt on a large scale to give the lower section of the inhabitants of London a chance of escape from the public-house. The object of this company was to establish attractive places of refreshment in the "more densely peopled parts of London, and elsewhere, to serve as a counter-attraction to the public-house and gin palace." It would appear, from the interesting brochure by Mr. Hepple Hall, that the enterprise for some reason or another did not succeed so well as its promoters expected, and the houses opened under the auspices of the company have since been leased to Mr. McDougall, in whose hands they seem to making satisfactory progress. In 1877 the Coffee Public House Association was organised under the presidency of the Duke of Westminster. The central agency of the association is at 40, Charing-cross. Again, to quote Mr. Hall, "adequate provision for the wants of the population of London alone requires that coffee public-houses should be numbered, not by tens or scores, but by hundreds. It is the business of the association: 1. To ascertain the localities in which Coffee Publics can be most aptly planted, and the character of the structure and fittings best suited to each locality. 2. To investigate the schemes submitted to it by those who desire its help and the claim which each scheme has upon it. 3. To make the necessary advances upon the most expedient terms, and whenever the conditions of success are sufficiently assured" It will be seen that the last-mentioned clause distinguishes this society from any other of its class. It is a promoter and encourager of coffee taverns, not a trader in them. That some such organisation was a necessity of the times may be gathered from the fact that in the United Kingdom the number of houses now open for this business is nearly 3,000, under the control of nearly 80 companies.

Charles Dickens (Jr.), *Dickens's Dictionary of London*, 1879

COLISEUM, THE

I have mentioned the Adelaide Gallery and the Polytechnic Institution, and there were many other exhibition-places eminently respectable and popular in my youthful days, which have since been done away with, and the very names of which are now scarcely heard. Foremost of these was the Coliseum, on the east side of the Regent's Park ... an enormous polygon, a hundred and twenty-six feet in diameter, and over a hundred feet high, built from the designs of Decimus Burton, whose best-known work nowadays is the Marble Arch. ... I remember it well – my father, in partnership with John Braham, once owned it, to his sorrow – with its wonderful panoramas of London by day and London by night, best things of the kind until eclipsed by the "Siege of Paris" in the Champs Elysées; its glyptotheca, full of plaster casts; its Swiss chalet, with a real waterfall, and a melancholy old eagle flopping about its "property" rocks; its stalactite cavern, prepared by Bradwell and Telbin; and its sham ruins near the desolate portico.* (*The gallery from which the vast panoramas of London were inspected was reached by a spiral staircase, and also by the "ascending room," the precursor of the "lifts," "elevators," and "ascenseurs," now to be found in every European and American hotel.) In a small dark tank in the interior of the building I once skated on some artificial ice; and there was a lecture-theatre, in which I found myself, just before the final doom of the establishment (I had come in for shelter from a rain-storm), one of an audience of three listening to an entertainment given by a little gentleman, who was nothing daunted by the paucity of his appreciators, and who sang and danced away as if we had been three thousand... To the Coliseum, some years before its final fall, was added the Cyclorama – an extraordinarily realistic representation of the earthquake of Lisbon. The manner in which the earth heaved and was rent, the buildings toppled over, and the sea rose, was most cleverly contrived, and had a most terrifying effect upon the spectators;

frightful rumblings, proceeding apparently from under your feet, increased the horror, which was anything but diminished by accompanying musical performances on that awful instrument, the apollonicon. Never was better value in fright given for money.

Edmund Yates, *His Recollections and Experiences*, 1885

CONSUMPTION

CONSUMPTION HOSPITAL, Brompton, fronting the Fulham-road, was commenced in 1844, June 11, when Prince Albert laid the first stone; the site was formerly a nursery garden, and the genial, moist air of Brompton has long been recommended for consumptive patients. The Hospital is in the Tudor style, of red brick, with stone finishings; Francis, architect; it was opened in 1846. In 1850 was attached an elegant memorial chapel; and in 1852 was added the western wing of the Hospital, towards which Mdlle. Jenny Lind, when residing at Old Brompton, in July, 1848, munificently presented 1606*l.* 16*s.*, the proceeds of a concert held by her for its aid. This noble act is gracefully commemorated by Mdlle. Lind's bust being placed upon the Hospital staircase: here also is a painted window, of characteristic design, presented by a governor. The Hospital is ventilated by machinery, worked by a steam-engine; and is warmed by water heated by two large Arnott stoves. In the kitchen, steam is used for boiling caldrons of beef-tea, mutton-broth, arrow-root, coffee, chocolate, &c.; and the provisions are wound up a shaft to the respective wards. The patients take exercise in the well-ventilated passages: and the wards are tempered by warm fresh air, which enters at the floor, and escapes by valves in the ceiling. There is a library for the in-patients, and the Rose Charity Fund for convalescents.

The deaths in this new Hospital have never exceeded one in every five in-patients, whereas in the former Hospital they were one in four.

John Timbs, *Curiosities of London*, 1867

COSMORAMA, THE

THE COSMORAMA, though named from the Greek (Kosmos, world; and orama, view, because of the great variety of views), is but an enlargement of the street peep-show; the difference not being in the construction of the apparatus, but in the quality of the pictures exhibited. In the common shows, coarsely-coloured prints are sufficiently good; in the Cosmorama a moderately good oil-painting is employed. The pictures are placed beyond what appear like common windows, but of which the panes are really large convex lenses, fitted to correct the errors of appearance which the nearness of the pictures would else produce. The optical part of the exhibition is thus complete; but as the frame of the picture would be seen, and thus the illusion be destroyed, it is necessary to place between the lens and the view a square wooden frame, which, being painted black, prevents the rays of light passing beyond a certain line, according to its distance from the eye: on looking through the lens, the picture is seen as if through an opening, which adds very much to the effect. Upon the top of the frame is a lamp, which illuminates the picture, while all extraneous light is carefully excluded by the lamp being in a box, open in front and top.

A Cosmorama was long shown at Nos. 207 and 209, Regent-street, where the most effective scenes were views of cities and public buildings. Cosmoramas have also formed part of other exhibitions. – At the Lowther Bazaar, 35, Strand, the

"Magic Cave" (cosmoramic pictures) realized 1500*l*. per annum, at 6*d*. for each admission.

John Timbs, *Curiosities of London*, 1867

CRECHES

In Peter Street, getting towards Tufton Street, there is a quiet-looking house in a row with the others. It has a shop, but the windows are now partially whitened, and nothing now is sold there. On the door is a notification that this is the infant nursery, all information concerning which may be obtained on ringing the bell.

I rang the bell, and a decent-looking woman answered, and in reply to my inquiry, civilly informed me that the matron was from home, but that I was very welcome to look over the establishment. The shop and parlour appeared to be used as a sort of office and living rooms in one. The young woman took me upstairs to the first-floor, where one of the oddest sights it was ever my lot to witness immediately met my view. In the front room, which is a large room, there is a space in the middle railed round like a miniature horse circus, the rail being about eighteen inches high, a netting of string extending from it to the floor. Spread within this ring was first a wool mattress, then an indiarubber sheet, and over all a warm woollen rug. This was where the babies, the tiny things from a month old up to toddling size, disported, and there they were disporting – happy and contented, seemingly, as birds in a nest.

Toddling about the room, which was plentifully furnished with comfortable little chairs, were several other little children, all with clean faces and well-brushed hair, and all wearing an ample pink pinafore with the sleeves tied up with a bit of blue ribbon. There were toys to play with, and pictures on the walls, and a swing, and a magnificent rocking-chair, presented by some kind patron; and somehow the decent little women in charge of them had such a capital way of managing them that they were all as merry as grigs, and in the best of humours one towards the other.

Out of this room you came to one even prettier, for here ranged along the walls were tiny iron cots with white sheets and feather pillows; and this is where the youngsters tired of play were laid to rest of afternoons. There was one so resting now, with an elephant out of Noah's Ark in his chubby hand.

The civil young woman took me a little higher in the house, and showed me a lead flat securely railed in, and on one side of which were growing some blooming scarlet-runners. This was the babies' playground.

James Greenwood, *The Wilds of London*, 1874

CRIME STATISTICS

In 1856 it appears that in all 73,240 persons were taken into custody, of whom 45,941 were males, and 27,209 females; 18,000 of the apprehensions were on account of drunkenness, 8160 for unlawful possession of goods, 7021 for simple larceny, 6763 for common assaults, 2914 for assaults on the police; 4303 women were taken into custody as prostitutes. The period of life most prolific of crime is that between the 20th and 25th years.

The convictions upon trial in 1856 were in the following proportions :- Under 10 years of age, 1; 10 years and under 15 years, 91; 15 years and under 20 years, 610; 20 years and under 25 years, 770; 25 years and under 30 years, 390; 30 years and under 40 years, 410; 40 years and under 50 years, 188; 50 years and under 60 years, 90; 63 years and upwards, 37.

The committals for murder in the year 1856 were 11; they were 12 in 1855, 10 in 1854, 7 in 1853, 11 in 1852, 8 in 1851, 11 in 1850, 19 in 1849, 11 in 1848, and 10 in 1847. Of the larcenies in dwelling-houses last year, only 315 were committed by means of false keys, as many as 2175 through doors being left open, 679 by lifting up a window, or breaking glass, and 31 by entering attic windows from empty houses. Again, 1595 such larcenies were committed by lodgers, 1701 by servants, and as many as 673 by means of false messages. The cases enumerated under the last three heads are such as the police could hardly be expected to prevent. 2371 persons were reported last year to the police as lost, and of these the police restored 1084.

J. Ewing Ritchie, *The Night Side of London*, 1858

CROSSING-SWEEPERS

"My luck seems to be gittin' runned hover – that's ow I lost my leg. I was a-'elpin' a drover in the Mile End Road. I'd gone out lookin' arter sumfink to do as fur as Romford, an' he picked me up at the markit there, an' give me a job to 'elp drive some ship to the Cattle Markit – it was in Smiffle then. Well, I'd run on to 'ead 'em back from the Cambridge 'Eath Road, when up come some fellers in a cart, 'alf sprung. The 'oss was goin' as fast as hever it could, but the chap as was drivin' kep' on leatherin' it wi' the hend o' the reins – he 'adn't got no whip. So I shouted to 'em not to run over the ship, an' flung up my harms – but they never took no 'eed. On they come, an' down I went, an' the cart went hover me, an' scrunched my leg like a snail. They carried me to the Lon'on 'Orspital, an' arter a bit, the doctors cut off my leg – they said they couldn't mend it – an' I've been a hippety-hop hever since. I shall be glad, though, when I'm peggin' away on my timber-toe ag'in, for it's lonesome layin' on yer back wi' nuffink to do.

"Sundays is my best days. People ain't in sich a 'urry to git to church as they are to git to their business, an' then they're kinder a-Sundays. There's a sweet-lookin' lady goes hover my crossin', as true as the clock, hevery Sunday, with 'er three little gals, as like their mar as little peas is to a big 'un. They takes it in turns to give me my penny, an' they speaks so pretty to me. I reg'lar look hout for seein' of em. Real gentlefolks they are, I'll go bail, though they ain't dressed nigh so smart as a good many as goes by an' never gives me nuffink."

Richard Rowe, *Life in the London Streets*, 1881

D is for Dance of Death

THE ARSENIC WALTZ.
The new Dance of Death. (Dedicated to the Green Wreath and Dress-Mongers.)

'THE ARSENIC WALTZ : THE NEW DANCE OF
DEATH. (DEDICATED TO THE GREEN WREATH AND
DRESS-MONGERS)'. In February 1862 a letter to *The Times*
pointed out the high level of arsenic poisoning amongst the
makers of artificial leaves, worn in fashionable adornments to
ball-gowns. Arsenic was used to provide a vivid green colour.

DANCING ACADEMIES

Next to the theatres and music-halls, the shilling, sixpenny, and threepenny "hops" of the dancing academies and saloons which abound in manufacturing districts, are the amusements most affected by the younger and more spruce of unmarried working men. And it is at these cheap dancing academies (which, not being connected, as the saloons generally are, with public-houses, are looked upon as exclusive and genteel establishments) that unfortunate working men generally make the acquaintance of those young ladies of the millinery and dressmaking persuasion, who entertain secret hopes of one day marrying a gentleman; but who, unhappily for society in general and the working classes in particular, become the slovenly mismanaging wives of working men.

> Thomas Wright, *Some Habits and Customs of the Working Classes,* 1867

DANCING SALOONS

I entered through a side door, and found myself in a carpeted room, handsomely and tastefully furnished and decorated.

The saloon is nearly as large as Irving Hall, in New York, but lit up in a splendid manner with handsome chandeliers, which depend from the lofty ceiling, the gas jets burning in a deep glow through the shining metal stalactites that ornament the chandeliers. A splendid band of fifty instruments is stationed in the gallery at the further end of the room, and the music is of the best kind. The leader is attired in full evening dress, as is also every fiddler in the band, and the wave of the chef's baton is as graceful as that of Julien, when he was in his prime. Women, dressed in costly silks and satins and velvets, the majority of them wearing rich jewels and gold ornaments, are lounging on the plush sofas in a free and easy way, conversing with men whose dress betoken that they are in respectable society. A number of these are in full evening dress, wearing their overcoats, and a few of them have come from the clubs, a few from dinner parties, and a greater number from the theatres or opera.

They are not ashamed to be seen here by their acquaintances – far from it; they think this is a nice and clever thing to do, and, as no virtuous woman ever enters this place, there is no danger of meeting those who own a sisterly or still dearer tie, and who might cause a blush to redden the cheeks of these charming young men. Across the lower end of the room an iron railing is stretched, and this keeps the vulgar herd from mingling with the elite of the abandoned women who frequent the Argyle. Three-fourths of the ground space is devoted to dancing, and inside this railing sets are formed at a signal from the band above.

The charge for admission below, where I stand with the detective surveying this strange scene, is but a shilling, while the entrance fee to the gallery is two shillings, and this admits, as I am told by a servant, to all the privileges of the place whatever they may be. Even in vice the "horrid spirit of caste" prevails.

> Daniel Joseph Kirwan, *Palace and Hovel:*
> *Phases of London Life*, 1878

DINNER PARTIES

Without wishing to particularise any great dinners given during the London season, it may suffice to give a brief account of the average of the best mounted houses. You order your carriage, which lands you within five minutes of the appointed hour at your host's door, and after passing through the hall lined with servants in and out of livery, you are ushered into the drawing-room. About ten minutes after, dinner is announced, and your hat is taken from you as you descend the stairs to enter the dining-room. To make your appearance in the drawing-room without your hat is unknown, – except, perhaps, in what Theodore Hook used to term the wild, uninhabited parts of London. The uses of an opera-hat are to be commended upon this and all such occasions. A delicate soup and turtle are handed round, – nothing on the tables except flowers and preserved fruits in old Dresden baskets, a bill of fare placed next to every person, a turbot with lobster and Dutch sauces, carved by an able domestic on the side-board, and a portion of red mullet with Cardinal sauce are offered to each guest; cucumber and the essential cruet-stands bringing up the rear. The "flying dishes," as the modern cooks call the oyster or marrow patés, follow the fish. The entrées are carried round, a supreme de volaille aux truffes, a sweetbread au jus, lamb cutlets, with asparagus, peas, a fricandeau d l'oseille; – be careful to avoid what are called flank dishes, which, if placed on the table, are usually cold, and are quite unnecessary. Either venison, roast saddle of mutton, or stewed beef a la jardinière, are then produced, the accessories being salad, beetroot, vegetables, French and English mustard. A Turkey poult, duckling, or green goose, commences the second course, peas and asparagus following in their course; plovers' eggs in aspic jelly, a mayonaise of fowl succeeding; a macédoine of fruit, meringues a la créme, a marasquino jelly, and a chocolate cream, form the sweets. Sardines, salad, beetroot, celery, anchovies, plain butter and cheese, for those who are gothic enough to eat it. Two ices, cherry-water, and pine-apple cream, with the fruit of the season, furnish the dessert. Two servants or more, according to the number of the party, must attend exclusively to the wine; sherry, Madeira, and champagne, must ever be flowing during dinner. Coffee, hot and strong, ought always to be served in the dining-room with liqueurs; if it be carried up stairs, it gets cold, and the chances are ten to one some awkward person upsets a portion of the aromatic beverage into the lap of a lady;

besides, it is unfair to ask a butler and his myrmidons with the trays to steer through a crowded drawing-room, amidst chairs, ottomans, fauteuils, screens, and tables, with gentlemen lounging in every direction.

Anon., *London at Dinner*, 1858

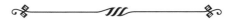

DISEASE

The congregation at the Refuges for the Destitute is indeed a sort of ragged congress of nations—a convocation of squalor and misery—a synopsis of destitution, degradation, and suffering, to be seen perhaps nowhere else. Nor are the returns of the bodily ailments of the wretched inmates of these abodes less instructive as to their miserable modes of life—their continual exposure to the weather—and their want of proper nutriment. The subjoined medical report of the diseases and bodily afflictions to which these poor creatures are liable, tells a tale of suffering which to persons with even the smallest amount of pathological knowledge, must need no comment. The catarrh and influenza, the rheumatism, bronchitis, ague, asthma, lumbago—all speak of many long nights' exposure to the wet and cold; whereas the abscesses—ulcers—the diarrhoea, and the excessive debility from starvation, tell—in a manner that precludes all doubt—of the want of proper sustenance and extreme privation of these, the very poorest of all the poor:—

MEDICAL REPORT FOR 1848–49

Of the persons who applied at the Central Asylum, there were afflicted with:—

Catarrh and influenza 149	Atrophy 3
Incipient fever 52	Dropsy 3
Rheumatism 50	Incised wounds 3

Diarrhoea 60

Cholera 2

Bronchitis 13

Abscesses 15

Ulcers 11

Affections of the head 12

Ague 13

Excessive debility from
  starvation 17

Inflammation of Lungs 2

Asthma 10

Epilepsy 4

Diseased Joints 4

Erysipelas 3

Rupture 3

Cramps and pains in bowels 2

Spitting of blood 4

Lumbago 1

Rheumatic ophthalmia 2

Strumous disease 2

Sprains 1

Fractures 4

Pregnant 30

Henry Mayhew, *'Labour and the Poor'*
(in the *Morning Chronicle*), 1850

DIORAMA, THE

The Diorama, in Park Square, Regent's Park, long an object of
wonder and delight in Paris, was first opened in London,
September 29, 1823. This is a very extraordinary and beautiful
exhibition; it consists of two pictures that are alternately
brought into view by a very ingenious mechanical contrivance;
the interior resembling a theatre, consisting of one tier of boxes
and a pit, being made to revolve upon a centre with the spectators, thus gradually withdraws one picture and introduces
the other to the view. A judicious introduction of the light, and
other contrivances, give increased effect to pictures beautifully
painted, which, by a concentration of talent, completes an
illusion that with perfect justice may be pronounced "the acme
of art".

Mogg's New Picture of London and Visitor's Guide
to its Sights, 1844

THE ORIGINAL DIORAMA, Regent's Park – NOW
EXHIBITING, two highly interesting Pictures, each 70 feet
broad and 50 feet high, representing MOUNT AETNA
in SICILY, DURING an ERUPTION, and the ROYAL
CASTLE of STOLZENFELS on the RHINE, with various
effects. – Admission to both pictures only 1*s*; children under 12
years, half price. Open from 10 til dusk.

advertisement from *Daily News*, 1851

DOCKS

As you pass along *this* quay, the air is pungent with the vast
stores of tobacco. At *that* it overpowers you with the fumes of
rum. Then you are nearly sickened with the stench of hides and
huge bins of horns; and shortly afterwards, the atmosphere is
fragrant with coffee and spice. Nearly everywhere you see
stacks of cork, or else yellow bins of sulphur, or lead-coloured
copper ore. As you enter one warehouse, the flooring is sticky,
as if it had been newly tarred, with the sugar that has leaked
through the tiers of casks; and as you descend into the dark
vaults, you see long lines of lights hanging from the black
arches, and lamps flitting about midway in the air. Here you
sniff the fumes of the wine – and there are acres of hogsheads
of it – together with the peculiar fungous smell of dry-rot.

Along the quay you see, among the crowd, men with their faces
blue with indigo, and gaugers with their long brass tipped rules
dripping with spirit fresh from the casks they have been probing.
Then will come a group of flaxen-haired sailors, chattering
German; and next a black seaman, with a red-cotton handker-
chief twisted turban-like round his head. Presently, a blue-
smocked butcher pushes through the throng, with fresh meat and
a bunch of cabbage in the tray on his shoulder; and shortly afterwards comes a broad straw-hatted mate, carrying green parroquets

in a wooden cage. Here, too, you will see sitting on a bench a sorrowful-looking woman, with new bright cooking-tins at her feet, telling you she is some emigrant preparing for her voyage.

Then the jumble of sounds as you pass along the dock blends in anything but sweet concord. The sailors are singing boisterous nigger-songs from the Yankee ship just entering the dock; the cooper is hammering at the casks on the quay; the chains of the cranes, loosed of their weight, rattle as they fly up again; the ropes splash in the water; some captain shouts his orders through his hands; a goat bleats from a ship in the basin; and empty casks roll along the stones with a hollow drum-like sound. Here the heavy-laden ships have their gunwales down in the water, far below the quay, and you descend to them by ladders, whilst in another basin the craft stand high up out of the dock, so that their green copper-sheeting is almost level with the eye of the passenger, and above his head a long line of bowsprits stretch far over the quay, with spars and planks hanging from them as a temporary gangway to each vessel.

"It is impossible," says Mr. M'Culloch, "to form any accurate estimate of the amount of the trade of the Port of London. But if we include the produce conveyed into and from the Port, as well as the home and foreign markets, it will not," he tells us, "be overrated at the prodigious sum of sixty-five millions sterling per annum."

Henry Mayhew and John Binny, *The Criminal Prisons of London*, 1862

DOG SHOWS

I darted at once into the "Thingumbob," and made my way to the exhibition-room – a public-house parlour of the usual dimensions. In the centre, a couple of tables placed together were surmounted with a roomy cage of wood and wire in several compartments A solitary poodle lay curled up in the bottom of the cage, and his owner, who looked a cross between a bailiff and a stable-keeper, and in whose mouth stuck a short pipe very considerably blacker than his rusty hat, sat contemplating him with perfect satisfaction. In a minute or two, he was joined by another exhibitor, who produced from his pocket a spaniel of King Charles's breed, no bigger than a kitten, and passed it into an upper compartment of the cage. The owner of the poodle had a bull-dog sitting gravely between his knees, and the proprietor of the spaniel had another at his heels. Tokens of recognition, consisting of a species of electric nods, almost too rapid for observation, passed between the candidates, but no speech. Two newcomers anticipated any conversation that might have ensued: they were handicraftsmen – shoemakers I think – and each produced a miniature terrier from his pouch, full grown, but not much bigger than a good-sized rat. They then pulled the bell, and ordered stout from the waiter. Other exhibitors now poured in fast, and nearly every man produced his dog, most of them from the pocket. . . . Bets were rife upon the chances of the prize, and the "favourite" was a black and tan spaniel, about the size of a rabbit, with long broad ears, long silken hair, and no nose to speak of. This was a dog of fortune – had been pupped, to speak figuratively, with a golden spoon in its mouth, having been bred to order for a certain beautiful duchess, to whom, after it competed for, and probably won, the first prize, it would be forwarded on the morrow, to be pillowed henceforth on silk plush, or fondled in the folds of lace or satin; to be dieted on fricassees and cream, to be attended, in case of an attack of the spleen, by a physician who keeps his carriage and to be led forth in park or shrubbery every day for an airing, by a liveried page impressed to melancholy by the awful responsibility of the charge.

Charles Manby Smith, *The Little World of London*, 1857

DONKEY-RIDES

There are, I am assured, but two proprietors who let out donkeys for riding on Clapham Common, Mr. Carter and Mr. Laurence. The former has by far the most important business, and as many as twenty or twenty-five of his donkeys may be seen out on the common. . . . As a rule, the donkeys are bought at the beginning of each season, the female being invariably preferred, firstly, because its jolt is not so objectionable, and secondly, because, being generally in foal at the end of the season, it can be sold with a view to providing asses' milk, for a higher price than it cost. Eighteenpence per day is supposed to suffice for the keep of a donkey; but the income derived from the hire varies considerably, amounting on Good Fridays to £1 and even £1 10s., and falling at times as low as 4s. The ideal average is 10s. per day, and the true average probably a little less. It depends, however, who attends to the business, and one man driving two donkeys can make more out of each than what is derived from a greater number entrusted to the care of small boys. These latter generally receive a shilling per day, and are naturally apt to neglect or miss opportunities of obtaining a fare. If, however, the owners would content themselves with sure but smaller profits, they would find many ladies in the neighbourhood ready to pay 5s. or 6s. per day to secure the exclusive use of a donkey for their children, and would also treat it with kindness. One lady even paid 4s. during all the winter months so that her favourite donkey should not be sold, but reserved for her children to ride again at the earliest dawn of spring.

J.Thomson and Adolphe Smith, *Street Life in London*, 1877

DOSSERS

There is, however, a stratum of society even lower than that of the poor wretches who herd together in noisome courts and foetid, filthy alleys. These are the unfortunate creatures whose only home is the "doss-'ouse," whose only friend the "deppity"* [*"Doss-'ouse" and "Kip-'ouse" are synonymous, and signify a common lodging-house. The deputy is the man who super-intends the establishment.]; who have, perhaps, for years never known what it is to have the shelter of a roof save that of a common lodging-house. There is no bitter cry from these, or at all events they have as yet found no spokesman to echo it in the public ear. Those who wrote – and wrote with power and pathos – of the squalid houses and still more squalid rooms in which the denizens of "horrible London" herd, and breed, and die, said little or nothing about the people who have neither house nor room that they can call their own, and who night after night, week in, week out, for many a weary year, "doss" in the nearest lodging-house, and hardly dare to dream of any other or better accommodation. While they live their principal care is to find the necessary fourpence each night, together with a few coppers more for food, or at all events for drink. When they die they depend upon the kindly feeling of their chums and fellow-dossers for the means of burial, or upon the scantier, if more certain, mercy of the parish sexton and the workhouse hearse.

In the course of some work in connection with one of those grand East-end institutions which undertake the rescue of des-titute gutter-children, I became acquainted, in a practical form, with the class I have described. I came into contact with many boys, of all ages, who had known no other sleeping-place than the lodging-houses, from the time when they could first remember sleeping at all. Every one of these lads spoke with horror and disgust of them, and of the surroundings at present inseparable from them.

Howard J.Goldsmid, *Dottings of a Dosser*, 1886

DRINKING FOUNTAINS

Until the last few years London was ill-provided with public drinking fountains and cattle troughs. This matter is now well looked after by the Metropolitan Drinking Fountain and Cattle Trough Association, which has erected and is now maintaining nearly 800 fountains and troughs, at which an enormous quantity of water is consumed daily. It is estimated that 300,000 people take advantage of the fountains on a summer's day, and a single trough has supplied the wants of 1,800 horses in one period of 24 hours. Several ornamental fountains have been provided by private munificence. Amongst these may be instanced the Baroness Burdett Coutts's beautiful fountains in Victoria-park and Regent's-park the Maharajah of Vizianagram's in Hyde-park; Mrs. Brown's, by Thornycroft, in Hamilton-place, Mr. Wheeler's at the north of Kew-bridge; and Mr. Buxton's at Westminster.

Charles Dickens (Jr.), *Dickens's Dictionary of London*, 1879

DRIVING

London driving is a very different thing to country driving. To begin with, the roadway changes so frequently and unexpectedly. What with macadam rolled and rough, and granite squares, and wood, and asphalt, now in this order, now in that, the horse has to be very careful of his footing where the change comes, and the driver must be on the alert to assist him. Then the cross-roads are so numerous, the stream of traffic so varied, the blocks at the Street corners so many and embarrassing, that the young man from the country requires an effort to keep his head clear. On the country road he has had to pass, perhaps, one vehicle in a quarter of a mile, in London he has to pass a hundred in the same distance. But this does not affect the way he sits in his seat and uses his hands. Under no circumstances, if he had been properly trained, would he hold his hands a foot apart with a rein in each.

If he were to think it out, he would see that it must be better in every way to drive with the left hand and keep the right in reserve for emergencies. Further, that it is better for the horse to draw willingly and steadily than to be constantly reminded that the man at the end of the reins does not know what to do next. For the horse knows instantly who is driving him and the extent of liberty he may take.

Horses go differently with different drivers, and it is always with the quiet light-handed ones that they go fastest and longest. A good horse with a good driver will do fifteen miles a day for five days a week, and keep on at it week after week; but give him a worrying driver and he will soon become obviously incapable of such work. And the driver will get very tired of his work also, for the curious part of driving is that what is best for the horse is best for the man. That hard, dead pull at the reins, that some people are so proud of, not only spoils the horse but wearies the driver's hand and wrist.

W.J. Gordon, (in *The Leisure Hour*), 1896

DUST-HEAP SCAVENGERS

I have been amongst factory-workers and "mill-hands," and market-garden women, and assistants at City establishments, but I never yet met a body of female labourers looking so thoroughly healthy and jolly. Every one was fat, every one was rosy, and laughing and singing as though it were capital fun to grovel among the refuse of the town out in the open air – a Siberian air, bleak and withering. The least likely-looking of the company was a corpulent lady, aged about fifty, and with her jaws bound round with a red rag; but even she was not so poorly but that she puffed away at a hideous little pipe with an appetite, and which, without taking her hands from the sieve, she dexterously shifted to the corner of her mouth so as to admit of her swelling the chorus of a ditty a leather-lunged young Irishwoman was at the time singing. I have since ascertained – and I am thankful for the discovery – that my impressions as to the healthiness of these toilers amongst filth and ashes were not erroneous. I have Dr. Guy's authority for stating that, despite their constant and immediate contact with the most loathsome refuse, they are among the healthiest of our working population. ... I observed that every sifter had near at hand two or three old baskets, and that each time she called out "sarve," and a youth, by tipping into her ready sieve a shovelful from a "raw" heap "sarved" her, she gave the fresh supply a handy twist, so as to spread the material over the entire surface of the sieve, and proceeded to deal with it in a way that I could not readily understand. Resting the outer edge of the great sieve against the heap before her, and its other extreme on her knees, she dived into it with both her hands, and went through a series of evolutions that, for rapidity, were unmatched by any conjurer I ever yet saw. Whatever it was she plucked from the sieve, was tossed over her left shoulder, over her right shoulder, and under either arm, and never failed to find a lodgment in one or other of the baskets. "What is she picking out ?" inquired I of my guide. "She's picking out everything," replied he. "She's picking 'hard-core,' and 'fine-core,' and rags, and bread, and bones, and bits of metal, and cabbage-stumps, and that sort of awful (offal), and bits of iron, and old tin pots, and old boots and shoes, and paper, and wood, likewise broken glass. After that's done, she can get along with the breeze and ashes straightfor'ard." "She retains the scraps you have enumerated as perquisites, I presume ?" I observed. "Oh no, she don't!" replied Mr. Scorch, shaking his head vigorously. "She retains only what's give to her, and that's the wood. She don't retain nothing else – leastways, not if I know it."

James Greenwood, *Unsentimental Journeys*, 1867

E is for Entertainers

A sketch of street life from the *Illustrated London News*, 1850.
Street entertainers of all sorts, from acrobats to musicians, were a
commonplace of daily life in the mid-Victorian metropolis.

EEL-PIE SHOPS

The dressing of an eel-pie shop window is conservative. It is a tradition handed down through many generations to the present day. The eels are shown artistically in lengths on a bed of parsley which is spread over a dish. On either side of the eels cold pies in their pans are laid in tempting profusion but in perfect order. The eel-pie shop varies its menu. You may procure at the same establishment cranberry tarts, and at some of them apple tarts ; also meat pies and meat puddings, and at the Christmas season mince pies.

To see the eel-pie business at its best, to appreciate its poetry, you must watch the process of serving its customers. Behind the counter on a busy night stands the proprietor in his shirt sleeves, a clean white apron preserving his waistcoat and nether garments from damage. Observe with what nimble deftness he lifts the lid of the metal receptacle in front of him, whips out a hot pie, runs a knife round it inside the dish, and turns it out on to a piece of paper for the customer – possibly into the eager outstretched hand.

He is generally assisted by his wife and daughter, who are almost, but not equally, dexterous. There are metal receptacles in front of them also, and the pies are whipped out in such rapid succession that your eyes become dazzled by the quick continuous movement. If you watch long enough it will almost appear to you that a shower of hot pies is being flung up from below by an invisible agency.

George R. Sims, *Living London*, 1902

ELECTRICAL APPLIANCES, MEDICINAL

PULVERMACHER'S Improved Patent GALVANIC CHAIN-BANDS, BELTS, BATTERIES and Accessories have rendered this life-promoting restorative perfectly efficacious and conveniently self-applicable in a mild continuous form, without shocks or unpleasant sensation; and hosts of patients have been by its means restored to health and strength. Reliable evidence in proof of the unparalled efficacy of these self-applicable Electro-Generators in Rheumatism, Gout, Neuralgia, Deafness, Head and Tooth Ache, Paralysis, Liver Complaints, Cramps, Spasms, Nervous Debility, Functional Maladies &c. is given in the pamphlet "Nature's Chief Restorer of Impaired Vital Energy." To ensure against the extortions of the quack fraternity, patients should peruse Pulvermacher's new work entitled "A Sincere Voice of Warning against Quacks &c." Price of Galvanic Appliance, according to Electric Power, from 2*s.* and upwards.

advertisement from *Illustrated London News*, 1873

ELECTRO-DENTISTRY
PAINLESS DENTISTRY.
TEETH! TEETH! TEETH!
Extracted by Electricity, 5*s.*
WITHOUT PAIN.
Inventor of the Improved Electro-Dental Chair.
J.J. ATWOOD, L.D.S., R.C.S
Qualified and Registered Surgeon-Dentist (Late Middlesex and Dental Hospitals, London.)
Scientific Dentistry in all Branches. The Surgeries lighted by Electricity. Reduced Charges on Mondays and Thursdays.
HOURS 10 to 6.
SPECICIALIST: Electro-Dentistry and Tooth Manufacturing Company.
Press Opinion
COURT JOURNAL. February 13th 1891, says: "ELECTRO-DENTISTRY. An improved dental chair was lately exhibited

at the Royal College of Physicians. The patient sits in the chair and grasps two knows, or terminals, whilst the operator stands on a platform covered with crimson felt, the apparatus being entirely out of sight; in fact, it is enclosed in the platform. By a movement of the operator's foot the current passes through the hands and body, finally reaching the face. The operator then takes the forceps with his right hand, and simulateously lifts his foot from off the press, and out comes the tooth or teeth without any pain .... Most patients state that they much prefer a mild current of electricity to nitro-oxide gas. The inventor of this improved electro-dental chair is J.J. Atwood, L.D.S., R.C.S., 242 Oxford Street, Dental Surgeon, late of the Middlesex and Dental Hospitals, London."

advertisement in Baroness Staffe,
The Lady's Dressing Room, 1893

ELECTROPHONES

The most picturesque and entertaining adjunct of Telephone London is the electrophone. There is not a leading theatre, concert-room, or music-hall but has the electrophone transmitters – in shape like cigar-boxes – installed before the footlights, out of sight of the audience. They are at the Royal Opera, Covent Garden; and in many of the principal places of worship a wooden dummy Bible in the pulpit bears the preacher's words, by means of the N.T.C. telephone lines, to thousands of invalid or crippled listeners in bed or chair in their homes or hospitals. It was thus that Queen Victoria, seated at Windsor Castle, heard 2,000 school children in Her Majesty's Theatre, in the Haymarket, cheer her and sing "God Save the Queen" on her last birthday. King Edward was likewise relieved from ennui at Buckingham Palace during his illness, for the brightest music, mirth, and song of London were ever on tap at his side. Queen Alexandra is also a devotee of the electrophone, more especially throughout the opera season. On the other hand, the cruel lot of certain hospital patients, of the blind, and even the deaf – for the microphonic capacity of the electrophone enables all but the stone-deaf to hear – is thus greatly brightened by science. The sadness of the bedridden, the incurable, or the sufferer from contagious disease is enlivened by sacred or secular song and story, and, as a much-to-be-welcomed addition to the alleviations of London's strenuous life, the benefits of the electrophone are innumerable. It may be added that in the imposingly decorated salon in Gerrard Street from time to time fashionable parties assemble and "taste" the whole of London's entertainments in one evening.

Thus, over mammoth aerial and subterranean wire-webs does London, annihilating distance, work and play by the aid of Science.

George R. Sims, *Living London*, 1902

EMBANKMENT, THE

This fine promenade alongside old Father Thames is one of London's most modern improvements. The greatest city in the world was, until some few years ago, so much occupied in amassing riches, that very little was done to make it beautiful. Its river's banks, although presenting an animated appearance with the unlading of ship's cargoes, had been spoken of as an 'eyesore.' When the tide was low, large and unhealthy muddy reaches were left exposed. These became not only the sporting ground of the 'mudlark,' but the hotbed of pestilence and fever; and were at last superceded by the beautiful promenade which you see in our picture.

The idea of an Embankment is no new one. As far back as 1666, after the Great Fire of London, Sir Christopher Wren proposed to raise a spacious embankment to the river. But unfortunately, when the best opportunity presented itself, while London was a heap of ruins and had to be rebuilt, the idea was not adopted. Since that time, until Mr. Bazalgette, the engineer, came forward with his plans, not one of the numerous schemes for this sorely needed improvement had been carried out.

To construct an Embankment such as we now have was a work of no little difficulty: for some distance the river had to be dammed, while the works were in progress; the mud had to be dredged out, excavations made, and a granite wall built on a foundation of Portland cement concrete, thirty-two and a half feet below high-water mark, or fourteen feet below low-water mark. A low-level sewer, a subway, and the District Railway, were also built underground. To go further into details would not interest many of you, but I will jot down a few of the quantities of material used, for those who would like to know. Of granite there were 650,000 cubic feet; brickwork, 80,000 cubic yards; concrete, 140,000 cubic yards; timber, 500,000 cubic feet; York paving, 125,000 superficial feet.

The Embankment is divided into three parts. The first, extending from Westminster to Vauxhall Bridge, is named the Albert, and was opened in November, 1869; the Victoria, from Blackfriars to Westminster, was opened in July, 1870; and the Chelsea, from Chelsea to Battersea, in 1874.

'Uncle Jonathan', *Walks in and Around London*, 1895

ESTATE AGENTS, ADVERTISEMENTS OF

A spade isn't a spade in 1859, but something else ; and with our house-agents, a house is not only a house, but a great many things besides.

A House to Let may be a mansion, a noble mansion, a family mansion, a residence, a desirable residence, a genteel residence, a family residence, a bachelor's residence, a distinguished residence, an elegant house, a substantial house, a detached house, a desirable villa, a semi-detached villa, a villa standing in its own grounds, an Italian villa, a villa-residence, a small villa, a compact detached cottage, a cottage *ornée*, and so on, almost ad infinitum. Rarely do the advertisements bear reference only to a house, a villa, or a cottage: we must call the spade something in addition to its simply agrarian title.

Now, are all these infinitesimal subdivisions of Houses to Let merely intended as ingenious devices to charm the house hirer by variety, in the manner of Mr. Nicoll, with regard to his overcoats, and Messrs. Swan and Edgar with reference to ladies' cloaks and shawls; or do there really exist subtle distinctions, minute, yet decidedly perceptible, between every differently named house? Can it be that the desirable residence has points calculated to satisfy desire in a different degree to the elegant predilections to be gratified by the elegant residence? Can it be that a residence, after all, isn't a house, nor a house a residence? It may be so. People, in the innocence of their hearts, and unaccustomed to letting or hiring houses, may imagine that there can be no very material difference between a villa, a genteel villa, and a compact villa; but in the mind of the astute house-agent, and equally intelligent house-hirer, differences, varieties of size, aspect, and convenience, immediately suggest themselves; and to their experienced eyes there are as many points of distinction between the genteel and the compact, the desirable and the distinguished, as to the visual organs of those learned in horses between a cob and a hack, a racer and a screw; or to the initiated in dog-lore, between a greyhound and a setter.

I do not pretend to any peculiarly nice perception as to things in general. I cannot tell to this day a hawk from a falcon (between the former bird and a handsaw I might be able to guess). It was a long time before I could distinguish between a leveret and a rabbit, or tell very high venison from decomposed shoulder of mutton; and I will not be certain, even now, if I could tell from the odour (being blindfolded) which was pitch and which tar. So, the immense variety of Houses to Let has always been to me a mystery, the subtle distinctions in their nomenclature sources of perplexed speculation.

George Augustus Sala, *Gaslight and Daylight,* 1859

EXHIBITIONS, ORIENTAL

THE CHINESE EXHIBITION. – This very curious collection was opened yesterday to the public, and was crowded for many hours with the masses of people returning from the Great Exhibition at the Crystal Palace. The collection, however, which occupies the space immediately to the west of Albertgate, Knightsbridge, is of itself sufficiently attractive to draw all who feel interest in what relates to China, without any other aid to visit its contents. In addition to the many specimens, both natural and artificial, of the Celestial Empire, there is a Chinese family – a young lady, whose feet are of the most aristocratic proportions of her native country, and who is considered by those most capable of judging a perfect vocalist, according to the Chinese notion, of vocalism; a musical professor of the first rank, and two children, who are precocious in talent, and very amusing; an interpreter, and a lady's maid. This interesting group gave specimens of their powers to a crowded audience, and were very favourably received. The rooms in which the contents of the collection are distributed are well arranged. The arrangements for creature comforts of the visitors, under the management of Mr. Ellis, are equally good, and the place generally affords such accommodation as the public require.

The Times, 1851

London at the present time possesses no public lounging-place so pleasantly picturesque as the Japanese Village erected by a cheery band of Japanese opposite Knightsbridge barracks, and near the top of Sloane-street. In this wintry weather, it is particularly enjoyable to drop into the Japanese Village; to stroll past the bamboo houses and shops, so neatly constructed that many will wish to transplant some of the dainty chalets to town gardens for Summer Houses; to watch the dextrous mechanics artistically working; to be refreshed by five o'clock tea; and to be made to laugh uproariously by the singularly grotesque wrestling and single-stick, dancing and muscial performances of the Japanese company in their little theatre. Mr. Augustus Harris laughed so merrily at the quaintness of the deliberate wrestling that very shortly Mr. Harry Nicholls and Mr. Herbert Campbell will presumably be imitating the strangely comic poses of the Japanese athletes in "Whittington," at Drury-Lane Theatre.

Penny Illustrated Paper, 1885

EXTORTION
A HINT TO THE POLICE

Sir, – Would you, through the medium of your columns, put the timid on their guard against a horrid system of extortion, carried on at dusk by a gang of wretches who infest the passage leading from St. Martin's Church to Bear and Orange streets, Leicester-square? The plan adopted is as follows:-

A smartly dressed, well-looking boy comes up to you, and asks some frivolous question as to the time of closing the National Gallery. He manages to keep you in conversation for some seconds, and walks on by your side as far into the obscurity as may be. On a sudden a man comes up, and asks, "What are you doing with my son?" On this, the boy affects to cry, and hints that the gentlemen got into conversation with him for a grossly immoral purpose. The man then says, "There, you hear what he says; now the only way to get out of it is to give the boy a sovereign, or to the police you go."

Now, Sir, a nervous man is so thrown off his guard by this threatened imputation, that he submits to this or any other infamous demand.

Surely, Sir, the police must be remiss in their duty not to scare away a gang of monsters who loiter at dusk near what are meant to be "public conveniences," but which have become "public nuisances."

The foregoing, Sir, happened to me the other night, and if you would insert the same, others might profit by my experience and loss.

I remain, Sir, &c.,

A VICTIM

letter to *The Times*, 1849

F is for Flogging

'PITY THE POOR GAROTTERS!' *Punch* in 1872 had little
sympathy with those who criticised corporal punishment for
garotters (muggers).

FAMILY BUDGETS

Expenditure of an Income of £500 a year.

Rent, rates, taxes, and cost of locomotion £72 10s 0d
Housekeeping
(provisions, coal, gas, servants' wages, laundry,
and wear-and-tear) £250 0s 0d
Clothing £62 10s 0d
Education £32 10s 0d
Insurance, medical attendance, and savings £62 10s 0d
Incidental expenses £20 0s 0d
[Total] £500 0s 0d

. . . . FROM the housekeeping, taken at £250, for an income of
£500 a year, the following deductions may be taken as a pretty
fair allowance:

Servants' wages. £14 per annum, or £1 3s. 4d. per month, for a
general servant; and £12 per annum, or £1 per month, for
nurse or housemaid £26 0s 0d
Gas £8 0s 0d
Coals and Coke £12 0s 0d
[Total] £46 0s 0d

Leaving a balance of £204 for housekeeping.

Before disposing of this £204, however, there is still another
point to be considered, and that is the summer holiday. In these
modern days a yearly visit to the seaside or to the country is
regarded as one of the necessities of life. Men and women draw
upon their strength until it is almost exhausted, and then trust
to a periodical enjoyment of fresh air, rest, and change to rein-
vigorate them and furnish them with health and energy for
another year's work. But how is it to be paid for? The answer is
evident to all; it must be taken from the half of the income
apportioned to housekeeping.

By this arrangement the amount set aside for housekeeping
could be continued through the year; that is, the expenses

would be supposed to be the same as usual wherever the family might happen to be. Therefore it would be necessary only to deduct from the £204 as much as would pay for travelling expenses and lodgings. For these £20 might well be deemed sufficient. The amount should either be put aside in a lump sum if the income be received yearly or quarterly, or it should be taken from the weekly income and put every week in the Post-Office Savings Bank, there to remain until the occasion for which it is needed shall arrive.

We find, therefore, that after deducting this additional £20 from the £204 we have a balance of £184, or an average sum of £3 10s. per week, for housekeeping. There is a small surplus, but this may be left for security, as it is not well to draw the line too closely.

Cassell's Household Guide, c.1880

I have selected certain typical weeks in the domestic life of a worker of a somewhat lower class than the one just referred to, but who may be taken as a fair representative of a large number of tailors in the West – a sober, respectable man, working quietly at home and receiving occasional assistance from his wife, but unable to obtain a regular supply of work. ... The family consisted of the man and his wife, and four children (all of them too young to be wage-earners). At the beginning of April 1895, following upon a winter of exceptional severity, the man found himself several pounds in debt to landlord, baker, pawnbroker, etc., while several of the children required boots and underclothing.

For the week ending April 20th, 1895, the entire earnings of the family amounted to £2 3s. 9d.; the household expenses were as follows:

Saturday Tripe cuttings for Sunday's dinner
(six persons) . . . . .3½d.
Saturday Potatoes and parsley for Sunday's
dinner (six persons) . . . . .2½d.

Monday Dinner (2 bloaters) ....2*d.*
Tuesday No dinner
Wednesday (pledged pair of blankets for 4/-)
Wednesday Stew for dinner ....9*d.*
Wednesday Paid coal man 2/- owing to him
(as he refused otherwise to send in any more coal,
and family had no fire) ....2*s.*
Thursday Dinner (potatoes and dripping) ....4*d.*
Friday No dinner
Saturday Dinner (haddock and butter) ....4*d.*
Bread for week ....2*s.* 3*d.*
Tea, Sugar, and Milk for week ....1*s.* 5½*d.*
Oil ....3*d.*
Sundries ....9*d.*
Total expenditure for week ....8*s.* 9½*d.*

The absence of any item of expenditure for beer or other alcoholic drinks is noteworthy. Moreover, with the exception of one item of 2/11 for boots for one of the children, there is no mention made of clothes, the cost of which, for a family of six persons, would necessarily be great.

Arthur Sherwell, *Life in West London*, 1897

FLATS

In few points does London, or, indeed, English life in general, differ from that of the Continent more remarkably than in the almost absolute ignoring by the former of all possibility of having more than one house under the same roof. Within the last few years, however, symptoms have appeared of a growing disposition on the part of Londoners to avail themselves of the Continental experience which the increased travelling facilities of the day have placed within the reach of all, and to adopt the foreign fashion of living in flats. The progress of the new idea has been slow, as is the progress of all new ideas in this most conservative of countries. But progress has been made, and signs are not wanting that it will before long be more rapid. At present almost the only separate etages to be found in London are those in the much-talked-of Queen Anne's Mansions, a good number of sets in Victoria-street, a few in Cromwell-road, just between the railway-bridges, and a single set in George-street, Edgware-road. Of all these, however, the last named, with a few sets in Victoria-street, are the only examples of the real self-contained "flat," the inhabitant of which, whilst relieved from all the responsibility and most of the troubles of an isolated house, yet enjoys to the full all the advantages of a separate establishment. The houses in Cromwell-road, nominally divided off into flats, are really mere shapeless buildings, the exigencies of whose site have necessitated a plan of construction incompatible with the dealing with each building in its entirety, and which have therefore perforce been let off in tenements, to which has been given the name of "flats." In the case of the Queen Anne's Mansions the building has been constructed with an especial view to the separation into tenements but in this case the self-containing principle has been deliberately set aside, and one kitchen has been built for the use of the entire establishment. One great obstacle to the building of houses laid out in regular flats on the Continental principle has been in the Building Act; under the provisions of which the expense of construction of houses for such a purpose on any really convenient scale is enormously increased in proportion to that of the ordinary ten, twelve, or fifteen-roomed dwelling house with its 9-inch walls, its five or six narrow storeys piled one above the other, and its domestic treadmill of six or seven dozen weary stairs, the mere climbing of which necessitates the keeping of at least one or two extra servants.

Charles Dickens (Jr.), *Dickens's Dictionary of London*, 1879

FLOGGING, CORPORAL PUNISHMENT BY

Then the executioner produced his cat-o'-nine tails. I think that everybody saw the terrible implement but Regan, and his eyes were closed in dreadful expectation. I was heartily glad that he did not see it. Had it been otherwise, I should not be surprised if, in his ignorance of how much a little whip could make a back smart, he had turned his villainous gaze on it and laughed in the hangman's face. I don't recollect whether Mrs Joe Gargery's "tickler," which was the terror of Pip's life, was minutely described in "Great Expectations;" but if it was nothing more formidable than this article, all I can say is that Pip was very easily scared. Judging from appearances, I would ask for nothing more than the handle of a hearthbrush, and a penn'orth of string of the thickness of a tobacco-pipe, and I would wager to produce that dreadful scourge's exact counterpart. The handle was about two feet in length, and the "tails" about fourteen inches. The hangman spat on his hand, and "swish!" Mr Regan had tasted cat.

He did not writhe or yell, or utter any agonised exclamation; but I was not in the least surprised, for really there was nothing to yell about. His back was marked – that is to say, you could see where the tails had struck the skin, marking it pinkish ; but that was all. Swish again; but the hangman might as well have flogged a brick wall for any cry of pain that was elicited from the sturdy young garotter. Swish, swish, till ten more lashes had been administered, and then Mr Regan was flogged out of his determination to "take it dumb," and he growled out "Oh!" If his punishment had been limited to ten lashes – no uncommon sentence – the culprit might afterwards have bragged to his comrades of his utter contempt of the Newgate cat. After the fourteenth or fifteenth, however, the punishment began to tell, and Regan cried "Whooo!" and "Ah!" but it was behind his clenched teeth, and in not at all a loud tone.

About the eighteenth lash he turned his face to the hangman, and said, in tones of reproach rather than entreaty, "Lay it on fair, will yer?" and then planted his forehead against the board to take the other twelve. When he had received them, from under his left shoulder-blade to the top of his right there was an ugly beer-coloured patch about six inches in width but he was not made to bleed at all, and when his limbs were released he needed no assistance in putting his shirt on. Reckoning from the moment Mr Calcraft spat in his hand until now, exactly a minute and three-quarters had elapsed.

James Greenwood, *In Strange Company,* 1874

FOG

Many lives have been lost through foot-passengers mistaking the steps at the foot of some of the bridges for the opening of the bridge itself, and, ere they were aware of it, rolling head-foremost into the river. Strong iron-railings have been erected during the last few years, and have put an end to such dreadful accidents at the foot of Blackfriars-bridge, many, we have heard, thus lost their lives.

At this time the pavement is greasy, and, though you keep lifting up your legs, you are hardly positive whether or not you are making any progress. You seem to go as much backward as forward, and some old Cockneys do aver that the surest way of reaching Temple-bar from Charing-cross would be to start off with your face turned towards King Charles's statue, to walk away manfully without once turning your head, and that, by the end of three hours, you would be pretty sure of reaching the point aimed at, should you not be run over.

Thomas Miller, *Picturesque Sketches of London Past and Present,* 1852

The winter-fogs of London are, indeed, awful. They surpass all imagining; he who never saw them, can form no idea of what they are. He who knows how powerfully they affect the minds and tempers of men, can understand the prevalence of that national disease—the spleen. In a fog, the air is hardly fit for breathing; it is grey-yellow, of a deep orange, and even black at the same time, it is moist, thick, full of bad smells, and choking. The fog appears, now and then, slowly, like a melo-dramatic ghost, and sometimes it sweeps over the town as the simoom over the desert. At times, it is spread with equal density over the whole of that ocean of houses; on other occasions, it meets with some invisible obstacle, and rolls itself into intensely dense masses, from which the passengers come forth in the manner of the student who came out of the cloud to astonish Dr. Faust. It is hardly necessary to mention, that the fog is worst in those parts of the town which are near the Thames.

> Max Schlesinger, *Saunterings in and about London*, 1853

I went home by way of Holborn, and the fog was denser than ever,—very black, indeed, more like a distillation of mud than anything else; the ghost of mud,—the spiritualized medium of departed mud, through which the dead citizens of London probably tread, in the Hades whither they are translated. So heavy was the gloom, that gas was lighted in all the shop-windows; and the little charcoal-furnaces of the women and boys, roasting chestnuts, threw a ruddy, misty glow around them. And yet I liked it. This fog seems an atmosphere proper to huge, grimy London; as proper to London, as that light neither of the sun nor moon is to the New Jerusalem.

On reaching home, I found the same fog diffused through the drawing-room, though how it could have got in is a mystery. Since nightfall, however, the atmosphere is clear again.

> Nathaniel Hawthorne, *The English Note-Books*, 1857

Mond. Jan. 9. Hideous fog; bad cold. …

Tuesd. Jan. 10. Fog still; cold worse. …

Wed. Jan. 11. Fog denser than ever. Cold so much worse, had to lie up in house. …

Thursd. Jan. 12. A terrible day; the fourth that we have not seen the sky. Happily began to clear in the evening. My cold too bad to let me go forth. …

Frid. Jan. 13. Fog hanging about still, until 3 in afternoon. then clearing. Got up at 10; cold almost gone, but did not go to Grahame. …

Sat. Jan. 14. Black fog at noon, then cleared, and at night thanked heaven for showing its stars once more. …

Thursd. Jan. 19. Sent cheque to mother. Walked to Tott. Ct. Rd. for tobacco etc. … Cold and cloudy. Must be several weeks since there was a single gleam of sunlight.

George Gissing, *Diary*, 1888

Foggy weather is propritious to amatory caprices. Harlots tell me that they usually do good business during that state of atmosphere, especially those who are regular nymphs of the *pavé*, and who don't mind exercises in the open air. Timid men get bold and speak to women when they otherwise would not. That is my own experience also …

'Walter,' *My Secret Life*, n.d.

FOOTBALL

Football was played a good deal by schools, as I had opportunity of observing on Blackheath, where my own seminary performed a kind of Rugby game every Saturday afternoon in the season.

"Association" was not yet. But as a popular sport football was non-existent, and in view of the attention it now receives in the Press it is curious to look for football news in the sporting papers of the [eighteen] fifties and sixties, and, apart from school matches, find it not. But such football as did exist was sport; that of 1924 is, unfortunately, trade – a capitalised gambling counter. The exaggerated importance with which the game is regarded by a large section of the population of Great Britain is nothing less, in my opinion, than a national misfortune. If newspaper notices of English football were few they did not exist at all about Scottish.

Were none but those able to play the game allowed to attend football matches the nation might gain something in physical development: and Sport would smile again.

Cup ties were very modest affairs when "Association" was young. They were often played in public parks, without charge for admission. I have in mind one decided in West Ham Park in the early 1880*s*. It was between Upton Park and Preston North End, the second or third round in the English Association Cup. There was neither gate nor gate money; no stands, no seats, while the spectators numbered 300 at most. To-day such a match would attract 40,000; but would the sport be any cleaner or better?

Alfred Rosling-Bennett, *London and Londoners in the 1850s and 1860s*, 1924

FREAK-SHOWS

But, speaking of shops, we must not omit some mention of one certainly peculiar in its appearance, and totally distinct from the many which surround it. It is a dingy, sinister-looking shop, at the corner of Ship-alley, bearing the ambitious name of the "British and Foreign Medicine Institution;" and its proprietor, a tall, white-haired man, clad in a loose-coloured dressing-gown, such as Nicholas Flamel or Cornelius Agrippa might have worn without loss of reputation, rejoices in the rather ominous title of Dr. Graves. Our business, however, is with the window and its collection of horrors, before which Jack stands aghast, his bronzed face changing to the pallor of ashes. Wax models of terrible diseases, "rarely to be met with," says the card attached. We think so too – very rarely, and only then, we trust, in the nightmare-like imagination of Dr. Graves himself. Bottled babies in plenty; children with two heads – who, if we are to believe in time assertion that "two are better than one," must have been invaluable to their parents. Here is a small serpent, taken from the body of a sailor; and here the skeleton of a small sailor, taken from the body of a serpent – with other horrors, too numerous to mention. Sick at heart, we turn away, and seek amusement and instruction elsewhere.

Watts Phillips, *The Wild Tribes of London*, 1855

Among the many interesting sights of this wonder-fraught season is "the Fairy Queen," who has recently changed her place of exhibition near Leicester-square to the corner of Hall-street, Goswell-road. This interesting and diminutive little girl, when born, weighed only one pound and a half. She is now fourteen months old, weighs five pounds, and measures sixteen inches in height; her feet are but two inches in length and she possesses the utmost regularity of limb and feature.

Illustrated London News, 1851

Sir, – I am authorized to ask your powerful assistance in bringing to the notice of the public the following most exceptional case. There is now a little room off one of our attic wards a man named Joseph Merrick, aged about 27, a native of Leicester, so dreadful a sight that he is unable even to come out by daylight to the garden. He has been called "the elephant man" on account of his terrible deformity. I will not shock your readers with any detailed description of his infirmities, but only one arm is available for work.

Some 18 month ago, Mr. Treves, one of the surgeons of the London Hospital, saw him as he was exhibited in a room off the Whitechapel-road. The poor fellow was then covered by an old curtain, endeavouring to warm himself over a brick which was heated by a lamp. As soon as a sufficient number of pennies had been collected by the manager at the door, poor Merrick threw off his curtain and exhibited himself in all his deformity. He and the manager went halves in the net proceeds of the exhibition, until at last the police stopped the exhibition of his deformities as against public decency.

Unable to earn his livelihood by exhibiting himself any longer in England, he was persuaded to go over to Belgium, where he was taken in hand by an Austrian, who acted as his manager. Merrick managed in this way to save a sum of nearly £50, but the police there too kept him moving on, so that his life was a miserable and hunted one. One day, however, when the Austrian saw that the exhibition was pretty well played out, he decamped with poor Merrick's hardly-saved capital of £50, and left him alone and absolutely destitute in a foreign country. Fortunately, however, he had something to pawn, by which he raised sufficient money to pay his passage back to England, for he felt that the only friend he had in the world was Mr. Treves of the London Hospital. He therefore, though with much difficulty, made his way there, for at every station and landing-place the curious crowd so thronged and dogged his steps that it was not an easy matter for him to get about. When he reached the London Hospital he had only the clothes in which he stood. He has been taken in by our hospital, though there is, unfortunately, no hope of his cure, and the question now arises what is to be done with him in the future.

He had the greatest horror of the workhouse, nor is it possible, indeed, to send him into any place where he could not insure privacy, since his appearance is such that all shrink from him.

The Royal Hospital for Incurables and the British Home for Incurables both decline to take him in, even if sufficient funds were forthcoming to pay for him.

F.C. Carr-Gomm, letter to *The Times*, 1886

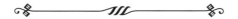

FUNERALS

I can quite well recollect the orthodox funeral of the fifties and sixties when two red-nosed men, similar to those in George Cruikshank's picture, stood outside the door from early morning until the funeral was over, each bearing a mysterious bauble, something like a broom tied up in black silk squares at the head and finished at the middle of the stave with black silk bows. These worthies were called mutes, and were supposed to stand motionless, no matter what the weather; indeed, a rather good story was told about a couple who, on a very cold winter day, sent in to ask for "a glass of somethink 'ot to keep them alive." Unfortunately, the request was made to a man who had neither generosity nor humour, and who in return sent back a message: "Nonsense! Certainly not! if they are cold, tell them to jump about and warm themselves" – the idea of the melancholy, silent, black-garbed mutes jumping hilariously about on the doorstep not having struck him as being either indecorous or absurd! The hearse itself was a nightmare: an enormous black vehicle, crowned with nodding plumes of ostrich feathers, the number and splendour of which determined the financial status of the "corpse," or the esteem in which he was held by his friends; the four splendid black horses, with tremendous manes and tails, were adorned with more plumes of feathers on their heads, and great velvet coverings on their backs, and as all the attendants wore vast cloaks, and wide silk hat-bands round their hats, and the mourners were one and all provided with hat-bands and wide scarfs of silk and black gloves, and were lent cloaks by the undertaker, I leave my readers to imagine the actual amount of money that used to be spent, often enough at a time when the unfortunate survivors could ill afford it.

Mrs. J.E. Panton, *Leaves from a Life*, 1908

Funeral costing £3 5s.-Patent carriage, with one a horse; smooth elm coffin, neatly finished, lined inside, with pillow, &c.; use of pall, mourners' fittings, coachman with hat-band; bearers; attendant with hat-band, &c.

Funeral costing £5 5s.-Hearse, with one horse; – mourning coach, with one horse; stout elm coffin, covered with fine black, plate of inscription, lid ornaments, and three pairs of handles, mattress, pillow, and a pair of side sheets; use of velvet pall; mourners' fittings, coachmen with hat-bands and gloves; bearers; attendant with silk hat-band, &c.

Funeral costing £6 6s.-Hearse, with pair of horses; a mourning coach and pair; strong elm coffin, covered with a black, plate of inscription, lid ornaments, and three pairs of handles, mattress, pillows, &c.; use of velvet pall, mourners' fittings; coachmen with hat-bands and gloves; bearers; attendant with silk hat-band, &c.

Funeral costing £8 15s.-Hearse and pair of horses; mourning coach and pair; velvet covering for carriages and horses; strong elm coffin, covered with fine black, a plate of inscription, lid ornaments, three pairs of cherub handles and grips, and finished with best black nails, mattress, pillow, and side sheets; use of silk velvet pall; two mutes with gowns, silk hat-bands, and gloves; four men as bearers, and two coachmen with cloaks, hat-bands, and gloves; use of mourners' fittings; and attendant with silk hat-band.

Funeral costing £14 14s.-Hearse and pair of horses; a mourning coach and pair, fifteen plumes of black ostrich-feathers, and complete velvet covering for carriages and horses; stout inch elm coffin, with inner lid, covered with black cloth, set with two rows all round of best black nails; lead plate of inscription, lid ornaments, four pairs of handles and grips, all of the best improved jet and bright black; tufted mattress, lined and ruffled, and fine cambric winding-sheet; use of silk velvet pall; two mutes with 2 gowns, silk hat-bands, and gloves, eight men as pages and coachmen, with truncheons and wands, crape hatbands, &c.; use of mourners' fittings; and attendant with a silk hat-band, &c.

Funeral costing £23 10s.-Hearse and four horses, two mourning coaches, with pairs, nineteen plumes of rich ostrich-feathers, and complete velvet covering for carriages and horses . . . . .

Cassell's Household Guide, c.1880

FURNISHING, FASHIONABLE

On my arrival at North Villa, I was shown into what I pre-sumed was the drawing-room.

Everything was oppressively new. The brilliantly-varnished door cracked with a report like a pistol when it was opened; the paper on the walls, with its gaudy pattern of birds, trellis-work, and flowers, in gold, red, and green on a white ground, looked hardly dry yet; the showy window-curtains of white and sky-blue, and the still showier carpet of red and yellow, seemed as if they had come out of the shop yesterday; the round rosewood table was in a painfully high state of polish; the morocco-bound picture books that lay on it, looked as if they had never been moved or opened since they had been bought; not one leaf even of the music on the piano was dogs-eared or worn.

Never was a richly furnished room more thoroughly comfortless than this – the eye ached at looking round it. There was no repose anywhere. The print of the Queen, hanging lonely on the wall, in its heavy gilt frame, with a large crown at the top, glared on you: the paper, the curtains, the carpet glared on you: the books, the wax-flowers in glass-cases, the chairs in flaring chintz-covers, the china plates on the door, the blue and pink glass vases and cups ranged on the chimney-piece, the over-ornamented chiffoniers with Tonbridge toys and long-necked smelling bottles on their upper shelves – all glared on you. There was no look of shadow, shelter, secrecy, or retirement in any one nook or corner of those four gaudy walls. All surrounding objects seemed startlingly near to the eye; much nearer than they really were. The room would have given a nervous man the headache, before he had been in it a quarter of an hour.

Wilkie Collins, *Basil*, 1852

ON the correctness of the taste displayed in furnishing a house, or only a few rooms, depends altogether the air of comfort which either will wear, and a corresponding degree of pleasure or discomfort to those who live in them. Often on entering a strange room one feels a sense of indescribable irritability, aris-ing either from the incongruity of the furniture as regards size, style, and general ornamentation, or from the inharmonious colouring of the draperies, the confusion of pattern on the car-pet, or the dazzling design of the wall-paper, not dazzling from its brilliancy, but from the regular and close recurrence of stripes, circles, and other geometrical forms, which bewilder the sight as if the pattern were in motion. The proper furnish-ing of a house is as much a fine art as painting, and if the rules do not come by an intuitive faculty they may be acquired. The glaring defects in modern house-furnishing are, first, incon-gruity of form and size of furniture with the surroundings and means of the possessor, and next, an elaborate decoration of the rooms out of keeping with the position of the owner. And the third is the elaboration of ornament on the furniture, this not being superadded to utility, but subversive of it – ornament being understood to mean a superfluity above utility – permanently fixed or carved upon the article. Decoration means something portable, as vases, glasses, and pictures. The walls of a room covered with an appropriate wallpaper, a ceiling elaborately worked in moulded forms, as well as its cornices, and carved or beaded doors, are said to be ornamental. The meanings of the two words are very distinct. A person may be decorated with a feather but is not thereby rendered more ornamental. A man's own fine head of hair is an ornament – it is irremovable by ordinary means – but his medals and jewellery are decorations.

Elaboration of ornament and decoration, in a house of great pretension but with small means to support it, is not a mark of good taste, neither is confusion of colour; when blues and greens, reds and violets, are indiscriminately mingled.

Cassell's Household Guide, c.1880

FUR-PULLING

THIS industry is very little known to the general public, but a great many girls and women earn their living by it in Bermondsey and other metropolitan districts. The most unpleasant part of the work consists in pulling the skins of rabbits – namely, in rubbing the loose down off them with a blunt knife, which process prepares them for lining cloaks and jackets. The down is returned to the furrier, who uses it to stuff beds, sofas, and pillows. A fur-puller explained to a Commissioner that this fur is "handsome for rheumatics." Furpullers formerly received 1*s.* 9*d.* per five dozen skins; but now so many women have gone into the business that only 1*s.* 1*d.* is generally paid for that quantity. This fur-pulling cannot be done by machinery at present. At the time of the Crimean war a great many women became furpullers, for large numbers of rabbit-skins were then wanted to line the coats of soldiers. Now the skins are chiefly used for the cloaks and jackets of women and children. The work is very unpleasant. The fur-puller sits in a small barn, or out-house, on a low stool. She has a trough in front of her, into which she drops the down as she pulls it off the rabbit-skins with her knife. Occasionally she stops to rub the knife with whiting, for the skins are greasy. The down gets into her nose and mouth. Her hair and clothes are white with it. She generally suffers from what she calls "breathlessness," for her lungs are filled with the fine down, and she is always more or less choked.

Another branch of the fur-pulling business consists in cutting open the tails of rabbits in order to extract the little bone in the middle. The bones are returned to the manufacturer, who sells them for manure. The fur is paid by the *lb.*, and the worker generally receives 8*d* per *lb.* for it after the bones have been extracted. This fur is used to make cheap blankets, and those fur hats which are sold at such low prices.

Anon., *Toilers in London; or Inquiries
concerning Female Labour in the Metropolis*, 1889

G is for Gymnasia

An 1896 photograph of the Young Men's Christian Association
in Exeter Hall on the Strand. Note the early model of
exercise bicycle.

GALLANTY SHOWS

There is the "gallanty show" again. Who can give a satisfactory reason why Punch's theatre should still hold its own, while its exact counterpart – except that the "gallanty" was an evening and illuminated exhibition, and the audience, instead of the substantial puppets, saw only their shadows cast on a sheet – has almost, if not entirely, disappeared ? Without prejudice, the gallanty was far more entertaining than Punch; and if the two were weighed in the scales of morality, there can be no question as to which would kick the beam. Goodness forbid that the rising generation should go Punchless, but really there is much that is reprehensible in the conduct of Toby's master! He is a shameful old wife-beater, and he never makes a joke that is not emphasised with a murderous blow of his too-ready bludgeon. Whereas the gallanty show dealt in only innocent domestic drama and farce. A Quaker's children might without contamination witness the spirited play of the broken bridge, or the eccentricities of Mr. Jobson, the inebriated shoemaker. But the gallanty has gone. To be sure it always had its disadvantage from a financial point of view – that is to say, the performance being capable of taking place at dark was against the proprietors. It is notorious, and an ever-rankling thorn in the side of Punch-and-Judy men, that in the broad daylight there are even grown people who are so mean as to stand and witness the performance right up to the part where Mr. Ketch comes in, and then sneak off the moment there are symptoms of the hat coming round; and if folk will behave thus shabbily in the open face of day, is it likely they will do otherwise with the cloak of evening to screen them from detection? It is not pleasant to be driven in this way to account for the despairing retirement of a once popular exhibition. It does not indicate an improved moral tone amongst the people.

James Greenwood, *The Mysteries of Modern London*, 1883

GAMBLING HOUSES

The chain was withdrawn and the door was opened. The party was admitted. Chichester led the way and his companions followed, up to a suite of rooms on the first floor. These were brilliantly lighted. On one side of the front room stood a bouffet covered with wines and liquors. In the middle of that same apartment was the rouge et noir table. On each side sat a Croupier, with a rake in his hand, and a green shade over his eyes. Before one of them was placed a tin case; this was the Bank; – and on each side of that cynclosure of all attention, stood piles of markers, or counters.

Two or three men, flashily dressed, and exhibiting a profusion of Birmingham jewellery, sat at the table. These were the Bonnets – individuals in the pay of the proprietor of the establishment, whose duties consist in enticing visitors to play. The Bonnets were compelled to affect joy when they won, and grief or rage when they lost. When none save the Croupiers and Bonnets are present, they laugh, joke, chatter, smoke and drink; but the moment steps are heard upon the staircase, they relapse with exactitude into their business aspect. The Croupiers put on their imperturbable countenances as easily as if they were masks; and the Bonnets appear to be as intent on the game, as if its results were to them perspective life or death. The Croupiers are trustworthy persons well known to the proprietor, or shareholders in the establishment. The Bonnets are young men of education and manners, who have lost the fortunes wherewith they commenced life, in the whirlpool to which, for a weekly stipend, they are employed to entice others.

George Reynolds, *The Mysteries of London*, 1844

GREAT EXHIBITION, FOOD SOLD AT THE

Bread, quarterns 52,094
Bread – cottage loaves 60,698
Bread – French rolls 7,617
Pound cakes 68,428
do. at 3*d* 36,950
Savoury cakes 20,415
Savoury cakes – Pies 33,456 *lbs*
Savoury Patties 23,040 *lbs*
Italian cakes 11,797
Biscuits 37,300 *lbs*
Bath buns 934,691
Plain buns 870,027
Banbury cakes 34,070
Sausage rolls 28,046
Victoria biscuits 73,280
Macaroons 1,500 *lbs*
Rich cakes 2,280 *lbs*
Pastry at 2*d* 36,000
Schoolcakes 4,800
Preserved cherries etc. 4,840 *lbs*
Pine apples 2,000

Pickles 1,046 gallons
Meat 113 tons
Potted meat, tongues, etc.
    36,130 *lbs*
Hams 33 tons
Potatoes 36 tons
Mustard 1,120 *lbs*
Jellies 2,400 quarts
Coffee 14,299 *lbs*
Tea 1,015 *lbs*
Chocolate 4,836 *lbs*
Milk 33,432 quarts
Cream 32,049 quarts
Schweppe's Soda Water,
    Lemonade, & Ginger
    beer 1,092,337 bottles
Masters' Pear Syrup 5,350
    bottles
Rough ice 363 tons
Salt 37 tons

Report of the Commissioners, 1852

GREAT WHEEL, THE

THE WHEEL AT EARL'S COURT—This gigantic wheel, which forms such a prominent object in the landscape anywhere west of London, is extensively patronised by the public during the Exhibitions at Earl's Court, and it matters very little if it is an Indian, or Colonial, or South African Exhibition, the big wheel always has its crowd of patrons who like to experience the exhilarating effects of an ascent into the air, minus the dangers attending a balloon and the probability of making an ascent rather higher than they originally intended, and the improbability of landing on the earth again in a perfect condition. This slowly revolving wheel takes you up to a good height, from which you have a splendid view of bricks and mortar below you; and there is just that touch of danger which always gives piquancy to pleasure, that perhaps it may stop, and refuse to go on, and its patrons may have to be fed on buns and soda water by venturesome sailors until the machinery once more gets into working order, and you slowly descend to your despairing relatives and expectant friends with tumultuous applause and you feel proudly conscious of something attempted and (thank goodness) something done.

George Birch, *The Descriptive Album of London*, c.1896

GREENWICH TUNNEL

New Thames Tunnel.

The London County Council Preparing to Run Another Tunnel Under the River Connecting Greenwich with the Isle of Dogs

Hardly was Blackwall Tunnel out of hand when the London County Council turned its attention to another sub-aqueous scheme. This time the claims of Greenwich and the Isle of Dogs were considered. There is a lot of passenger traffic between the two places, but it is left to the Great Eastern Company's steamers. The hundreds of workmen and workgirls who have to cross morning and night are therefore compelled to pay daily fares. Even workmen's wives on the Millwall side are forced to use the steamers to go marketing in Greenwich.

At first the Council thought to make a tunnel slightly smaller than the one at Blackwall to carry vehicles as well as passengers, but this project was soon dropped. The Millwall Docks on the

Isle of Dogs made it impossible to construct the necessary approaches. Besides, there was little promise of any vehicular traffic, with Blackwall Tunnel so near on the one side, and the promised Rotherhithe tunnel between the island and the Tower-bridge on the other. Communication between the two banks was needed wholly in the interests of the working people of both districts, so it was decided to make a footway tunnel only. Out of four tenders that of Messrs. Cochrane was accepted a few days ago for £109,500. The approach to the tunnel on the Greenwich side will be from the north end of Church-street, in the rear of the famous Ship Tavern. On the Millwall side the approach will be by a footpath 15ft. wide at the western end of Island Gardens. The depth of the tunnel at the centre of the river will be about 72ft. below the ground line.

Municipal Journal and London, 1899

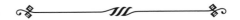

GYMNASIA

Almost every big park has a public gymnasium, the apparatus being specially arranged to meet the differing requirements of children, youths, and adults. Thus no one under 12 is allowed in the "seniors" part, while no one over that age may make use of the juvenile division. In the latter swings and see-saws predominate, whereas the rings, giant-strides, climbing ropes, and poles are always confined to the former section. . . .

The gymnasia proper, many of which have special classes for ladies, are likewise numerous in all parts of London. Possibly, however, the northern half is slightly more favoured in this respect, since in that district are situated, among others, both the Orion Gymnasium and the German Gymnasium. The latter – which claims to be the pioneer of gymnastic societies in this country – is not by any means so Teutonic in composition as its name would imply. In fact, since it was first started some forty years since, out of close on eighteen thousand members about thirteen thousand were English, the actual German element being well under five thousand. In addition there are a few members of other nationalities. Nor can it be said that the foreign element monopolises or even carries off the far greater part of the prizes awarded at the different competitions that the German Gymnasium promotes. These generally include (besides gymnastics proper on the "horse," parallel and horizontal bars, etc.) fencing, boxing, jumping, Indian clubs, and wrestling. Besides this, there is in connection with the gymnasium a cycling club, which is well supported and meets with much success.

It should likewise be borne in mind that the gymnasium forms a part of practically every institute from the Polytechnic downwards, so that its advantages are available to all. The boxing section of most of these organisations is generally largely attended.

Then, too, for those who prefer a more scientific and less violent method of acquiring bodily strength, there are numerous schools of physical culture, for the most part on the Sandow system, and open to both sexes. For women and girls in particular there are many places at which Swedish drill is taught, not to speak of the schools at which this branch of calisthenics forms part of the regular curriculum. So that, even if City life does have a hard physical effect on those subjected to it, it must be admitted that the Londoner is given ample facilities for fighting against its influence with whatever means most appeal to his taste, pocket, or requirements.

George R. Sims, *Living London*, 1902

H is for Horsemonger Gaol

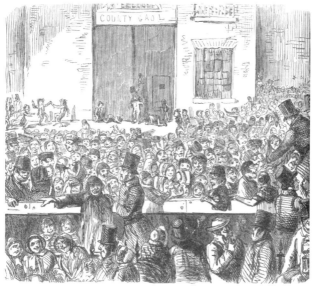

The Great Moral Lesson at Horsemonger Lane Gaol, Nov. 13.

Public executions were performed at both Newgate Prison (now the site of the Old Bailey) and Horsemonger Gaol in the Borough. Riotous crowds and a holiday atmosphere were the norm, as this critical *Punch* cartoon of 1849 indicates.

HAIRDRESSERS

TO the VISITORS of LONDON. Amongst the sights of London, there is none more useful and attractive than the BOWER OF CALYPSO. While surrounded by the sunny sky of the east, listening to the murmuring of the waters, you can have your hair cut; while having your hair dressed by the first-rate artists either English, French, or Italian, you can enjoy the Tale of Telemachus; in the Grotto of Calypso, in sight of the inimitable Mentor and his pupil, you can have your head shampooed in the limpid waters of the Adriatic, always using brushes clean from the stream. So great an influence has the fair island, that premature age, with white heads and whiskers, do not leave the Bower without being restored to their natural colour of brown or black, or when the hand of time has destroyed the luxorious tresses of youth, the invisible fibres of Calypso will restore them to their former beauty.

Observe – HEWLETT'S HAIR CUTTING, HAIR DYEING and WIG MANUFACTORY, 6 Burlington-arcade (five doors from Piccadilly.) Fresh hair brushes to every customer. The head shampooed on the Oxford system.

advertisement from *The Daily News*, 1851

HAIR-SELLERS

The lot under inspection, a little parcel of a couple of hundred-weight, came from Germany. The human hair business has been brisker in that part of Europe than anywhere during the past few years, on account of its yielding a greater abundance of the fashionable colour, which is yellow. Prices have gone up amongst the "growers" in consequence. The average value of a "head" is about three shillings. ... It comes from Italy as well as from Germany, and recently from Roumania. I was informed that an attempt has been made to open a trade with Japan but, though the Japanese damsels are not unwilling, at a price, to be shorn for the adornment of the white barbarian, the crop, although of admirable length, is found to be too much like horsehair for the delicate purposes to which human hair is applied.

Brown hair, black hair, hair of the colour of rich Cheshire cheese, hair of every colour under the sun, was tumbled in heaps on the counters before me, including grey hair – not much of it, as much, perhaps, as might be stuffed into a hat-box; but there it was, the hair of grandmothers. Seeing it to be set aside from the rest, my impression was that it got there through one of those tricks of trade that every branch of commerce is subject to. That lot was stuffed into the middle of a bale, I thought, by some dishonest packer who, while aware how valueless it was, knew it would help to make weight.

"You don't care much about that article I imagine," I remarked to my guide.

"What! that grey hair – not care for it!" he returned, with a pitying smile at my ignorance. "I wish that we could get a great deal more of it, sir; it is one of the most valuable articles that comes into our hands. Elderly ladies will have chignons as well as the young ones; and a chignon must match the hair, whatever may be its colour."

James Greenwood, *In Strange Company*, 1874

HANGING

The tolling of St. Sepulchre's bell about 7.30 a.m. announced the approach of the hour of execution; meanwhile a steady rain was falling, though without diminishing the ever-increasing crowd. As far as the eye could reach was a sea of human faces. Roofs, windows, church-rails, and empty vans – all were pressed into service, and tightly packed with human beings eager to catch a glimpse of seven fellow-creatures on the last stage of life's journey. The rain by this time had made the drop slippery and necessitated precautions on behalf of the living if not of those appointed to die, so sand was thrown over a portion, not of the drop (that would have been superfluous), but on the side, the only portion that was not to give way. It was suggestive of the pitfalls used for trapping wild beasts ...

The procession now appeared, winding its way through the kitchen, and in the centre of the group walked a sickly cadaverous mob securely pinioned, and literally as white as marble. As they reached the platform a halt was necessary as each was placed one by one immediately under the hanging chains. At the end of these chains were hooks which were eventually attached to the hemp round the neck of each wretch. The concluding ceremonies did not take long, considering how feeble the aged hangman was. A white cap was placed over every face, then the ankles were strapped together, and finally the fatal noose was put round every neck, and the end attached to the hooks. One fancies one can see Calcraft now laying the "slack" of the rope that was to give the fall lightly on the doomed men's shoulders so as to preclude the possibility of a hitch, and then stepping on tiptoe down the steps and disappearing below. At this moment a hideous contretemps occurred, and one poor wretch fell fainting, almost into the arms of the officiating priest.

The reprieve was, however, momentary, and, placed on a chair, the inanimate mass of humanity awaited the supreme moment in merciful ignorance. The silence was now awful. One felt one's heart literally in one's mouth, and found oneself involuntarily saying "They could be saved – yet – yet – yet," and then a thud that vibrated through the street announced that the pirates were launched into eternity. One's eyes were glued to the sport, and, fascinated by the awful sight, not a detail escaped one. Calcraft, meanwhile, apparently not satisfied with his handiwork, seized hold of one poor wretch's feet, and pressing on them for some seconds with all his weight, passed from one to another with hideous composure. Meanwhile, the white caps were getting tighter and tighter, until they looked ready to burst, and a faint blue speck that had almost immediately appeared on the carotid artery gradually became more livid, till it assumed the appearance of a huge black bruise. Death, I should say, must have been instantaneous, for hardly a vibration occurred, and the only movement that was visible was that from the gradually stretching ropes as the bodies kept slowly swinging round and round.

'One of the Old Brigade', *London in the Sixties*, 1908

HARMONIC MEETINGS

Like other and better people, the inhabitants of a rookery district must have their amusements. Chief among these – especially with the younger men and women – are the public-house "Harmonic Meetings." Admission to these entertainments is free, the publicans looking for their gain to the extra drinking "for the good of the house," which in these cases it is found in practice music (?) has charms to promote. Mine host supplies the instrumental music, generally a much-worn piano "jangled out of tune," while the audience furnish the vocal "talent." Ladies and gentlemen who fancy they can sing – and to judge from their efforts, such a fancy upon their parts must in most instances involve great powers of imagination – "oblige the company." The company in return drink the "health and song" of each performer, and all goes pleasantly, that is to say, profitably for the landlord, however it may be with his customers. The organ-grinder and the street ballad-singers are welcome visitants in a rookery district. Curiously enough, however, the members of the street-singing fraternity who are resident in a district, or habitual frequenters of its common lodging-houses, find themselves, like prophets, without honour in their own country. The fact is, the modern wandering minstrel is, as a rule, likely to fare better the farther he wanders from where he is best known.

The Riverside Visitor, *The Pinch of Poverty*, 1892

HOOPS

Sir, – I have not for many years read a paragraph in *The Times* which has afforded me greater pleasure than that which heads your "Police" report of this day, conveying Mr. Hardwick's just complaint of, and directions to Inspector Baker, on the hoop nuisance. As a daily passenger along the crowded thorough-fares of London-bridge and Thames-street, where boys and even girls, drive their hoops as deliberately as if upon a clear and open common, I can bear witness to its danger and incon-venience. I have at this moment a large scar on one of my shins, the legacy of a severe wound, which festered, and was very painful for an entire month, inflicted a year ago by the iron hoop of a whey-faced, cadaverous charity-boy from Tower-hill, who on my remonstrating with him on his carelessness, added impudence to the injury, by significantly advancing his extended fingers and thumb to his nose and scampering off. Aware that I had no redress, that the police would not inter-fere, I was compelled to grin and bear it while I hobbled away. The nuisance calls loudly for the interference of the Police Commissioners.

Your daily reader,

September 30. A PEDESTRIAN.

letter to *The Times*, 1842

HORSE-MAKERS

This notable personage locates principally in the neighbour-hood of Whitechapel, though many of his kith and kin are to be met with in or near the neighbourhood of Smithfield, and in the lowest parts of Westminster. In appearance, the horse-maker has nothing Cockneyish or London-like about him; even his dialect, though he be a Cockney born and bred, is in some degree provincial both in idiom and accent. His costume is that of the respectable agricultural yeoman or small farmer; and is always in neat and tidy trim. He affects a rustic gentility and simplicity of behaviour, and disarms suspicion by his cheerful, open, loquacious, and unsophisticated manner: he makes no great parade of himself in the markets, never attend-ing, in fact, when his presence can be dispensed with. By this means his simulated character lasts him the longer, and he is saved from the disagreeable necessity of shifting the scene of his labours. His business is to purchase horses which, from accident, vice, disease, or even old age, are rendered unfit for the service of man, and then, by means best known to himself, to metamorphose the poor beasts into quiet, plausible, service-able-looking steeds, and to sell them, while yet under the influ-ence of his all-potent incantations, to unwary customers. There is hardly a disorder horse-flesh is heir to the symptoms of which he cannot temporarily banish, by means of drug, knife, cautery, or some secret nostrum; while there is no animal so vicious but that he can subdue him for a time to quiet good behaviour. By dint of shears, singeing, currycomb, and brush, under his direction the roughest hide assumes the radiant polish of the turf; by the cunning application of ginger or cayenne to the jaws, the nostrils, the ears, or elsewhere, the dullest worn-out hack is stimulated into sprightliness and demonstrations of blood and breeding; and the poor honest brutes are compelled by his arts to play the hypocrite, and to assume virtues and qualities to which they have perhaps been strangers all their lives.

Charles Manby Smith, *Curiosities of London Life*, 1853

HOUSES

At the first step a German makes in one of the London streets, he must understand that life in England is very different from life in Germany. Not only are the walls of the houses black and smoky, but the houses do not stand on a level with the pavement. A London street is in a manner like a German high-road, which is skirted on either side with a deep ditch. In the streets of London the houses on either side rise out of deep side areas. These dry ditches are generally of the depth of from six to ten feet, and that part of the house, which with us would form the lower story, is here from ten to twelve feet underground. This moat is uncovered, but it is railed in, and the communication between the house door and the street is effected by a bridge neatly formed of masonry.

Every English house has its fence, its iron stockade and its doorway bridge. To observe the additional fortifications which every Englishman invents for the greater security of his house is quite amusing. It is exactly as if Louis Napoleon was expected to effect a landing daily between luncheon and dinner, while every individual Englishman is prepared to defend his household gods to the last drop of porter.

You may see iron railings, massive and high, like unto the columns which crushed the Philistines in their fall; each bar has its spear-head, and each spear-head is conscientiously kept in good and sharp condition. The little bridge which leads to the house-door is frequently shut up; a little door with sharp spikes protruding from it is prepared to hook the hand of a bold invader. And it is said, that magazines of powder are placed under the bridge for the purpose of blowing up a too pertinacious assailant. This latter rumour I give for what it is worth. It is the assertion of a Frenchman, whom the cleanliness of London drove to despair, and who, in the malice of his heart, got satirical.

Max Schlesinger, *Saunterings in and about London*, 1853

Houses—A few general hints upon taking a house may be useful. Having chosen your neighbourhood, and found a house to be let, you will do well to consider if the situation be quiet or noisy; the width of the street; the nature of the paving in front; the outlook at back; whether there are any objectionable busi-nesses or trades carried on in the neighbourhood; any mews, cab-yards, or carriers' premises adjacent, or any public place of resort for folk who like to be merry at midnight; any noisy church or chapel bell to annoy you, or any railway running underneath you; whether near omnibus or tram routes; distance from various railway-stations; and places of public worship and public amusement. Most London houses of any pretensions are let upon lease; and upon the estates of the large landholders, particularly, the restrictive covenants, and the covenants to repair, maintain, and uphold, are very stringent. In taking leases of houses upon such as the Bedford, Portman, or Portland estates, remember that it is often of value to get the lease direct from the freeholder, or to get the whole term remaining in the person between you and the freeholder, as it is the custom on these estates at the expiration of the term to grant to the occu-pying tenant a renewal of lease upon improvement of the premises or payment of fine or increased rental. The next con-siderations are the state of repair and sanitary condition of the house, and on these points you will do well to consult some competent practical architect, otherwise you may unexpectedly find a large outlay necessary for a new roof, new floor, new drainage, or other expensive work. Most London houses have basement storeys below the level of the street, and most basements are damp. Their dampness arises from several causes. The use of porous bricks in the walls, and the absence of a damp-proof course to arrest the absorption of moisture from the earth in contact with the lower portions of the wall, is of frequent occurrence. In some parts of London land-springs may give considerable trouble, and in this case land drains must be laid, care being taken that they are not in direct communication with any soil drain, or with the public sewer. Another source of damp is the absence of air space under the floors, and arrangements for the free admission and passage of air. Air bricks properly distributed, and, perhaps, lowering the level of the ground, will then be necessary. In all cases it is desirable to well drain the subsoil and to have a good layer of concrete 6in. thick under all basement floors. The level of the ground externally being higher than the floor internally is frequently the cause of damp, and in this case the construction of a good open area is often practicable, but, if not, a properly constructed dry area will be the best remedy. One of the greatest dangers to health is the presence of sewage gas in the house.

Charles Dickens (Jr.), *Dickens's Dictionary of London*, 1879

I is for Illumination

After the Paris exhibition of 1878, where electric lighting was used to great effect, it was suggested that a similar system could be used for the Embankment. Despite attracting considerable crowds and interest, the lighting proved costly and unreliable necessitating a return to gas lighting after only six years.

IMMIGRANTS, IRISH

They are Irish, all of them; Irish, every man, woman, and child. Turn whichever way you will, the same "wild, Milesian features, looking false ingenuity, restlessness, misery, and mockery, salute you" on every side. Glance down these narrow courts and filthy alleys that open upon you at every step, and again and again you recognise the race; "there abides he in his squalor and unreason, in his falsity and drunken violence, as the ready-made nucleus of degradation and disorder." Alas! that it should be so; that centuries of neglect – of wrong legislation – should have reduced a people capable of so much to so low an ebb as this; to be a plague-spot upon the garment of her more fortunate sister – a breeder of paupers for a land that has already far too many of her own. Let us take a group, – a fair sample of this unfortunate and improvident class. It is a family picture, and one that it pains the heart of the philanthropist to witness. The man who comes first, in his rough gray coat, and other garments of curious make, lounges slowly along, partly from fatigue, partly from habitual indolence; his hands deep sunk in his pockets, his eyes wide open with astonishment as he contemplates the (to him) wondrous sights around. His wife follows close on his heels; one child held in her arms she endeavours to shelter from the rain beneath her scanty shawl, while another is slung at her back, bending her nearly double with the burden. Three others cling about her garments, and partially running by her side, keep pace with her, as strong in a mother's love and hope, she tramps sturdily along.

This is a family picture, as we said. But a few days ago, these parents, with their wild-looking children, were in Connaught, doing badly enough in all conscience, yet with a "chance" before them. They are now in London, with no chance at all; and but one hope – the workhouse.

Watts Phillips, *The Wild Tribes of London*, 1855

IMMIGRANTS, ITALIAN

There are about 11,500 Italians all told in London, and these can be classed into three groups – (1) merchants, traders, professional men, and householders; (2) working class and Holborn district; (3) Soho and West End. The latter is the largest colony, numbering nearly 6,000, whilst about 4,000 are accounted for in the Saffron-hill district. It is computed that among the latter a thousand grind organs for a living, whilst 2,000 are classed as ice cream, potato and chestnut vendors.

The conditions under which the itinerant vendors of ice-cream live, in whatever part of London a colony is established, are generally more or less modelled, so far as the local circumstances permit of this, upon those which obtain in the Italian quarter itself. Some description of the chief Italian colony in London may therefore be given.

The Padrones and "Chaps."

The colony is largely made up of young men. In 1861 the Holborn registration district contained 598 male Italians and only 31 females. At the time of the last census, however, the want of proportion between males and females was less marked, there being 1,069 males and 382 females. The houses in the streets are rented in some instances by "padrones," and are occupied by the padrone, his family, and the "chaps." The last-named are the young men who, in the ice-cream season, are to be seen presiding over the barrows at street corners in various parts of London. A padrone employs on an average about a dozen "chaps," and his establishment is practically a common lodging-house – unregistered, however, and providing accommodation of an order considerably inferior to that insisted upon in the case of registered houses ...

How the Italians Sleep.

The financial relations existing between the latter and the padrone seem to vary in different cases, In some instances the men are said to pay so much a week – about eighteenpence – for sleeping accommodation, and "something extra" for washing; in other cases the young men are said to enter into an agreement to give their services for a certain period in return for board and lodging and a small allowance of pocket-money. . . . The seasonal fluctuations of the ice-cream trade lead to corresponding variations in the extent of crowding in the Italian colony. The bedrooms almost always contain double beds, and on the supposition that each of these is occupied by two persons, the cubic capacity of the rooms is altogether insufficient in almost all instances for the number of individuals accommodated . . .

Italians Cleaner than English Poor

It is also satisfactory to be assured that the Italians have some regard for cleanliness. Dr. Hamer, as the result of his investigations, says:- The utensils in all instances were being carefully cleansed before use, and we found that the material left over from the preceding day was being thrown down the drain. In the matter of cleanliness, the Italians have, as a rule, a far higher standard than that which obtains among English people of a similar class . . .

Municipal Journal, 1900

IMMIGRANTS, JEWISH

Usually they bring with them no ready-made skill of a marketable character. They are set down in an already over-stocked and demoralized labour market; they are surrounded by the drunkenness, immorality, and gambling of the East End streets; they are, in fact, placed in the midst of the very refuse of our civilization, and yet (to quote from a former chapter), whether they become bootmakers, tailors, cabinet-makers, glaziers, or dealers, the Jewish inhabitants of East London rise in the social scale; "as a mass they shift upwards, leaving to the new-comers from foreign lands and to the small section of habitual gamblers the worst-paid work, the most dilapidated workshops, and the dirtiest lodgings." But this is not all. Originally engaged in the most unskilled branch of the lowest section of each trade, Jewish mechanics (whether we regard them individually or as a class) slowly but surely invade the higher provinces of production, bringing in their train a system of employment and a method of dealing with masters, men, and fellow-workers which arouses the antagonism of English workmen. The East End Jewish problem therefore resolves itself into two central questions :—(1) What are the reasons of the Jews' success? (2) Why is that success resented by that part of the Christian community with whom the Jew comes in daily contact? I venture to end this chapter with a few suggestions touching this double-faced enigma of Jewish life.

First we must realize (in comparing the Polish Jew with the English labourer) that the poorest Jew has inherited through the medium of his religion a trained intellect. For within the Judaic Theocracy there are no sharp lines dividing the people into distinct classes with definite economic characteristics such as exist in most Christian nations: viz, a leisure class of landowners, a capitalist class of brain-workers, and a mass of labouring people who up to late years have been considered a lower order, fit only for manual work.

The children of Israel are a nation of priests. Each male child, rich or poor, is a student of the literature of his race. In his earliest childhood he is taught by picturesque rites and ceremonies the history, the laws, and the poetry of his people; in boyhood he masters long passages in an ancient tongue; and in the more pious and rigid communities of Russian Poland the full-grown man spends his leisure in striving to interpret the subtle reasoning and strange fantasies of that great classic of the Hebrews, the Talmud. I do not wish to imply that the big-otted Jew is a "cultured" being, if we mean by culture a wide experience of the thoughts and feelings of other times and other races. Far from it. The intellectual vision and the emotional sympathies of the great majority of Polish Jews are narrowed down to the past history and present prospects of their own race. But the mechanical faculties of the intellect—memory, the power of sustained reasoning, and the capacity for elaborate calculation—have been persistently cultivated (in orthodox communities) among all classes ... In the Jewish inhabitants of East London we see therefore a race of brain-workers competing with a class of manual labourers. The Polish Jew regards manual work as the first rung of the social ladder, to be superseded or supplanted on the first opportunity by the estimates of the profit-maker, the transactions of the dealer, or the calculations of the money-lender; and he is only tempted from a life of continual acquisition by that vice of the intellect, gambling.

Charles Booth, *Life and Labour of the People in London*, 1903

IMPURITY

1. One of the greatest evils wherever young men congregate is that of obscene conversation. It very often happens that a boy brought up strictly is entirely ignorant till he goes to a boarding-school. A feeling of false shame prevents his confessing that ignorance. He listens greedily to his companions, and in a short time is initiated. There are certain rhymes and stories which, once learned, cleave to the imagination and taint it almost irretrievably. They often remain for a lifetime, and refuse to be forgotten. Thus the seeds are sown of future evil.

2. Loose reading. This is a much smaller evil though it threatens to grow greater. Almost every Londoner knows the streets about the Strand where indecent books and pictures are sold.

These shops are now under pretty rigorous supervision, and the business has to be conducted with great caution. The ordinary spectator will notice in the window pamphlets with long titles, promising entertainment of a certain kind, bad photographs of dancers, and a few books, of which "Maria Monk" seems to be the most common.

3. The influence of theatres, music-halls, etc. We have said so much on this subject that we need only touch on it briefly. Correspondents have written to us defending theatres, and we readily admit there is much reason in what they say, so far as they are concerned. That many go to a good play, and spend an evening pleasantly and without much injury, is undeniable. But the thing has to be considered in its total influence. The first thing to be remarked is that morality among actors and actresses is very low. We need not enter into what excuses or explanations there may be for this; suffice it to say that it is from theatrical managers that we have received the darkest account of the morality of the stage.

4. We mention in addition the great difficulties in the way of marriage. Salaries, never very high, are now distinctly on the down grade, and while the rent of houses in London is diminishing, and some household expenses are diminishing along with it, a revolution must take place before living in London can become really cheap. When there is no escape from the monotony of the office except to the monotony of lodgings it is no cause for wonder that many become entangled in vice.

5. The last incentive we shall mention is drink. The first lapse from morality, which counts for so much, is almost invariably smoothed by drink, and drink accompanies all the rest. We said in one of the earliest of these chapters that if drink could be avoided absolutely by young men they would comparatively speaking, be safe. We repeat it with, if possible,

greater emphasis. Only let there be no mistake about it; it is total abstinence in the fullest sense that we mean.

Anon., *Tempted London: Young Men*, c.1889

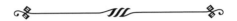

INDECENCY

MARLBOROUGH STREET- On Monday a respectably-dressed gray-haired elderly person, who gave the name of Richard Simpson on the charge-sheet, but who is a wealthy baronet, whose name was not further divulged than that was Sir F–, as the person who was going to give the name corrected himself in time, was charged in company with George Stacey, butler to Sir Frederick Roe, with indecently exposing and behaving themselves in Hyde-park on Saturday night last. ... Police-sergeant Everitt, 17 A, stated, that while on duty in Hyde-park, in company with police-constable Guy, 72 A, about five minutes to 9 o'clock on Saturday evening, they saw the two defendants walk together towards "a woody clump of trees," near the gravel-pits. They hid themselves behind a tree, and watched them (the prisoners). The witness then described the manner in which they acted towards each other. While they were acting so, and he and the constable watching, a man and women crossed the path, and the prisoners moved to the railing by the side of the gravel-pit. They then separated for two or three yards, and after looking about to see whether they were observed, again joined company, and stood five or six minutes with their heads inclined, as if they were looking at the grass. Witness and his brother constable "pounced upon them," and found their trousers were unbuttoned ...

The Times, 1843

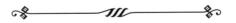

INDUSTRY
GREAT INDUSTRIAL ESTABLISHMENTS.

STRANGERS interested in industrial operations would, if properly introduced, have no difficulty in obtaining permission to inspect some of the great engineering works, such as Maudsley and Field's in Westminster Road, Lambeth, or some of those at Millwall. The manufacture of gas on a large scale, as conducted by some of the great companies, is also an interesting sight. ... The printing establishment of *The Times* newspaper, in Printing-House Square, Blackfriars, is highly deserving of a visit, and may be seen by ticket obtained from the printer. ... Then there are the great BREWERIES, so remarkable for the vast amount of their operations. Taking the twelve largest concerns, the annual consumption of malt ranges from 15,000 quarters to 200,000. The establishments of Messrs. Barclay, Perkins, & Co., Park Street, Southwark, and Messrs. Hanbury, Buxton, & Co., Bricklane, Spitalfields, are larger than the others. By procuring a letter of introduction to either firm, there will be no difficulty in obtaining permission to view the brewery. ...

Another vast manufacture is that of candles, as conducted by Price's Patent Candle Company. ... The company has works both at Belmont, Vauxhall, and at Battersea. At the latter place the works cover 11 acres; the capital invested in apparatus and machinery is £200,000, and 800 persons are employed, although machinery is used as much as possible. For permission to inspect the works apply by letter to the managing director.

The stranger in London will also do well to see Bryant and May's match works at Bow; the railway works at Stratford; the cabinetmakers' shops in and about Shoreditch; the sugar brokers' in Commercial Road, Whitechapel; the Sunday clothes market in Petticoat Lane, Aldgate; the Saturday night market in the New Cut; the pianoforte manufactory of Messrs. Broadwood, in Soho; the billiard-table factory of Messrs.

Thurstons, in Catherine Street, Strand; the hatters' shops in
Lambeth; the tanneries in Bermondsey; the shipwrights in the
Isle of Dogs; the silk-weavers in Spitalfields; the jewellers'
workshops in Clerkenwell; the plaster image works in Saffron
Hill; the potters in Lambeth; the carriage-builders in Long
Acre; the toy and doll makers at Hoxton; the chemical works
on the banks of the Lea; the paper-makers on the Wandle; the
iron-founders and anchor-smiths at Millwall; and the boat-
builders at Chelsea.

Black's Guide to London and Its Environs, 1882

INNS OF COURT

The Inns of Court are themselves sufficiently peculiar to give a
strong distinctive mark to the locality in which they exist; for
here are seen broad open squares like huge court-yards, paved
and treeless, and flanked with grubby mansions – as big and
cheerless-looking as barracks – every one of them being destitute of doors, and having a string of names painted in stripes
upon the door-posts, that reminds one of the lists displayed at
an estate-agent's office and there is generally a chapel-like
edifice called the "hall," that is devoted to feeding rather than
praying, and where the lawyerlings "qualify" for the bar by eating
so many dinners, and become at length – gastronomically –
learned in the law. Then how peculiar are the tidy legal gardens
attached to the principal Inns, with their close-shaven grass-
plots looking as sleek and bright as so much green plush, and
the clean-swept gravel walks thronged with children, and
nursemaids, and law-students. How odd, too, are the desolate-
looking legal alleys or courts adjoining these Inns, with nothing but a pump or a cane-bearing street-keeper to be seen in
the midst of them, and occasionally at one corner, beside a
crypt-like passage, a stray dark and dingy barber's shop, with its

seedy display of powdered horsehair wigs of the same dirty-white hue as London snow. Who, moreover, has not noted the windows of the legal fruiterers and law stationers hereabouts, stuck over with small announcements of clerkships wanted, each penned, in the well-known formidable straight-up-and-down three-and-fourpenny hand, and beginning – with a "This-Indenture"-like flourish of German text – "The Writer Hereof" &c. Who, too, while threading his way through the monastic-like byways of such places, has not been startled to find himself suddenly light upon a small enclosure, comprising a tree or two, and a little circular pool, hardly bigger than a lawyer's inkstand, with a so-called fountain in the centre, squirting up the water in one long thick thread, as if it were the nozzle of a fire-engine.

But such are the features only of the more important Inns of Court, as Lincoln's and Gray's, and the Temple; but, in addition to these, there exists a large series of legal blind alleys, or yards, which are entitled "Inns of Chancery," and among which may be classed the lugubrious localities of Lyon's Inn and Barnard's ditto, and Clement's, and Clifford's, and Sergeants', and Staple, and the like. In some of these, one solitary, lanky-looking lamp-post is the only ornament in the centre of the backyard-like square, and the grass is seen struggling up between the interstices of the pavement, as if each paving-stone were trimmed with green chenille. In another you find the statue of a kneeling negro, holding a platter-like sun-dial over his head ... In another you observe crowds of lawyers' clerks, with their hands full of red-tape-tied papers, assembled outside the doors of new clubhouse-like buildings. Moreover, to nearly every one of these legal nooks and corners the entrance is through some arch way or iron gate that has a high bar left standing in the middle, so as to obstruct the passage of any porter's load into the chancery sanctuary; and there is generally a little porter's lodge, not unlike a French conciergerie, adjoining the gate, about which loiter livened street-keepers to awe off little boys, who would otherwise be sure to dedicate the tranquil spots to the more innocent pursuit of marbles or leap-frog.

Henry Mayhew and John Binny,
The Criminal Prisons of London, 1862

K is for King's Cross

An 1845 lithograph from the *Illustrated London News* showing
the demolition of the monument to George IV, erected in 1836,
which gave the area of King's Cross its name. It proved an
obstruction to traffic and was removed.

JOURNALISTS

The police have very speedily made a sanitary cordon round about the blazing premises, and let none pass save those who have special business near the place. The firemen are "welcome guests" within the magic cordon, as also the fussy, self-important sergeants and inspectors of police, who often do more harm than good with their orders and counter-orders. There are some other gentlemen, too, who slip in and out unquestioned and unchallenged. They don't pump at the fire-engines, and they don't volunteer to man the fire-escape. But they seem to have an undisputed though unrecognised right to be here, there, and everywhere, and are received on a footing of humorous equality by the police, the fire-escape men, the firemen, and the very firemen's dogs. They are not official-looking persons by any means. They wear no uniforms, they carry no signs of authority, such as truncheons, armlets, or the like. They are rather given, on the contrary, to a plain and unpretending, not to say "seedy," style of attire. Napless hats, surtouts tightly buttoned up to the throat and white at the seams, pantaloons of undecided length, unblackened bluchers, and umbrellas, seem to be the favourite wear among these gentlemen. They are, not to mince the matter, what are termed "occasional reporters" to the daily newspapers, and, in less courteous parlance, are denominated "penny-a-liners." It is the vocation of these gentlemen (worthy souls for the most part – working very hard for very little money) to prowl continually about London town, in search of fires, failings in and down of houses, runnings away of vicious horses, breakings down of cabs, carriages, and omnibuses; and, in fact, accidents and casualties of every description. But especially fires. Fatal accidents are not unnaturally preferred by the occasional reporters, because they lead to coroners' inquests, which have of course also to be reported; and, in the case of a fire, a slight loss of life is not objected to. It entails "additional particulars," and perhaps an inquiry before the coroner, with an examination of witnesses relative to the cause of the fire; nay, who knows but it may end in a trial for arson?

George Augustus Sala, *Twice Round the Clock*, 1859

I proceeded to a suite of rooms occupied by the subeditor and the principal reporters. In the outermost of these rooms is arranged the electric-telegraph apparatus – three round discs, with finger-stops sticking out from them like concertina-keys, and a needle pointing to alphabetic letters on the surface of the dial. One of these dials corresponds with the House of Commons, another with Mr. Reuter's telegraph-office, the third with the private residence of the proprietor of my journal, who is thus made acquainted with any important news which may transpire before he arrives at, or after he leaves, the office. ... On the sub-editor's table lie the weapons of his order: a gigantic pair of scissors, with which he is rapidly extracting the pith from the pile of "flimsy" copy supplied by the aid of the manifold-writer and tissue-paper, by those inferior reporters known as penny-a-liners; and a pot of gum, with which he fits the disjointed bits together here also are proofs innumerable in long slips; red, blue, and yellow envelopes, with the name of my journal printed on them in large letters – envelopes which have contained the lucubrations of the foreign and provincial correspondents; an inkstand large enough to bathe in; a red-chalk pencil like the bowsprit of a ship; and two or three villanous-looking pens. At another table a gentleman, gorgeous in white waistcoat and cut-away coat, is writing an account of a fancy-fair, at which he has been present; printers, messengers, boys, keep rushing in asking questions and delivering messages; but they disturb neither of the occupants of the room. The fancy-fair gentleman never raises his eyes from his paper, while, amid all the cross-questioning to which he is subjected, the sub-editor's scissors still snip calmly on.

Next to the composing-room, where I find about seventy men at work "setting" small scraps of copy before them. The restless scissors of the head of the room divide the liner's description of horrible events at a position of breathless interest, and distribute the glorious peroration of a speech among three or four compositors, who bring up their various contribution of type to the long "galley" in which the article is put together. These men work on an average from four P.M. till two A.M., or half-past two (in addition to these there are the regular "day-hands," or men employed in the daytime, who work from nine till five). They are mostly from twenty-five to thirty-five years of age; though there is one old man among them who is approaching threescore-and-ten, and who is reported almost as good as any of his juniors, They earn from three to four guineas a-week each. The room is large, and though innumerable gaslights are burning, the ventilation is very good.

Edmund Yates, *The Business of Pleasure*, 1879

KING'S CROSS

This is King's Cross. It is the centre of a foul network of London vice and ruffianism. Four Railway Stations are here – stations of the gay and dissolute, who glide serpent-like upon the platforms, and parade their sensual and daring visages before respectable members of society. The profligate finds here a haven for his vicious desires, and he can be seen from an early hour in the evening till early dawn, or until the recuperative powers of nature no longer lend their aid for a prolongation of their animal enjoyment. "Gentlemen" who reside in various parts of North London find this arena a very secluded spot to carry on their drunken debauch. Here, as in many other parts of London, disorderly houses of the most disreputable kind exist ad libitum, under the very eyes of the police, and wherein, night after night, a calling of the most iniquitous kind is carried on with the sanction of all the departments of officialism. Shops, with side doors which stand ajar, and small windows adorned with nondescript refreshments, and wherein you would imagine you could procure tea, coffee, or cocoa to renew your almost exhausted energies, form deceptive gateways into houses consecrated to immoral purposes. Private houses, in streets occupied by well-to-do tradesmen and City business people, are made centres of corruption into which the unwary are taken, robbed of all that's dear, then trampled and beaten to earth by the hoofs of passion, appetite and mad indulgence. The owners of these dens are known to so quickly accumulate their ill-gotten wealth, that many of them reside in aristocratic dwellings, in high-class districts, where they rear a young family in entire ignorance of their parent's vocation. They there guard jealously over the honour of their own daughters with one eye, while with the other they watch with deadened feelings the skilful sensualist as he carries out his nefarious plans, and blights the flower of innocent girlhood.

Look at the state of this Euston Road. Count them up:- three hundred street walkers, from grey haired decrepitude, to the slender girl of twelve or thirteen – some of them once the cherished, almost idolised, inmates of happy homes; once beautiful, innocent and good, – all now the blighted, wretched inmates of the brothels which abound at the rear of their present public promenade. The police are alive to the state of this thoroughfare, but they affirm that they are powerless in remedying it.

Henry Vigar-Harris, *London at Midnight*, 1885

KNOCKERS-UP

"Look here, then," said he, "are you ever out early – very early, I mean - in the morning, and chance to go through streets where working men live? Very well, you are; and didn't you ever notice chalked on the pavement, or on the door or wall of the houses all manner of figures, '½ past 3,' '¼ to 4,' '5 o'clock,' and such like? There you are, then. That's what you may call the key to the knocking-up business. There are many men, factory hands and those who ply at market, who have no reglar time for getting up. They don't know themselves what time it will be needful till they get home the night before. Well, they depend on the knocker-up to have 'em out at the time. He makes an engagement to do it, don't you see, for sixpence or ninepence a week, and of course he has to be on his beat very early, as he don't know what time the first one wants to be roused. It will be three o'clock, maybe, and then he must be out by two so as to have time to run through all his streets, and make sure; or he'll take a turn overnight, last thing, and before he turns in his-self. It's a ticklish job, I've heard him say, with some of the heavy sleepers. They take such a lot of hammering to wake 'em that the neighbours don't like it; and he's been pelted from windows and had water chucked down on him, and all manner of things. Then the police are awfully hard on knockers-up. It's a job they've got a fancy for, and can do it easy in general, being on duty there; but there's no knowing when they may have a station-house job on, and they can't be in two places at the same time, and that's why the people would rather have a private knocker-up if they can get one."

"Does it pay ?"

"Well, it's according to the number, I should say. About nine shillings a week the man I'm speaking of makes while he's at it. But then, don't you see, it's in all weathers, and it means a good many miles if the streets are far apart and the times are various."

'One of the Crowd' [James Greenwood],
Toilers in London, 1883

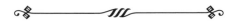

144

LIGHTING, ELECTRIC

Electric Light.—The electric light first practically introduced into London by Mr. Hollingshead at the Gaiety Theatre, has been made, during the last few months, the subject at a great number of experiments both public and private. Of the former the most important has been that on the Thames Embankment where the great width of, and the entire absence of all extraneous light from shop windows or public houses on either hand, enabled the rival systems of gas and electricity to try their strength against each other on equal terms. On the conclusion of the period allotted to the first experiment the Board of Works decided upon continuing it on a somewhat larger scale, and an additional length, of the Embankment parapet has accordingly been supplied with electric burners. The principal experiment elsewhere was on the Holborn Viaduct, also a very excellent situation, with the same advantages as those possessed by the Thames Embankment. It would, perhaps, be well to essay the experiment under other conditions, and try the effect of the electric light along-side of the ordinary shop window; but up to the date of our going to press this had not been done. The chief private experiments have been, externally at the Gaiety Theatre, and at the Regent-street establishment of the London Stereoscopic Company—the latter with one of the old-fashioned machines in use by the company for photographic purposes for the last twenty years—and internally at Messrs. Shoolbreds and the Albert Hall, where the Good Friday performance of the Messiah was given under its light. At the two former of these places it understood to be established en permanence.

Charles Dickens (Jr.), *Dickens's Dictionary of London*, 1879

LIGHTING, GAS

The first street in London lighted with gas was Pall Mall in 1807, and the last street lighted with oil was Grosvenor-square in 1842.

Peter Cunningham, *Hand-Book of London*, 1850

Most regular and reliable is a third medium for the lighting-up of London—the gas. The sun and moon may be behind their time, but the gas is always at its post. And in winter, it happens sometimes that it does service all day long. Its only drawback is, that it cannot be had gratis, like the light from the sun, moon, and stars; but the same inconveniences attend the gas on the Continent, and after all, it is cheaper in England than anywhere else. The Germans are mere tyros in the consumption of gas. The stairs of every decent London house, have generally quite as much light as a German shops, and the London shops are more strongly lighted up than the German theatre. Butchers, and such-like tradesmen, especially in the smaller streets, burn the gas from one-inch tubes, that John Bull, in purchasing his piece of mutton or beef, may see each vein, each sinew, and each lump of fat. The smaller streets and the markets, are literally inundated with gaslight especially on Saturday evenings. No city on the Continent offers such a sight. In the apothecary's shops, the light is placed at the back of gigantic glass bottles, filled with coloured liquid, so that from a distance you see it in the most magnificent colour. The arrangement is convenient for those who are in search of such shop, and it gives the long and broad streets of London a strange and picturesque appearance.

Max Schlesinger, *Saunterings in and about London*, 1853

LODGINGS, DECENT

LODGINGS – The visitor who wishes to make a lengthened stay in the Metropolis, will find it most economical to take lodgings. These he may get at all prices, from the suite of elegantly furnished rooms in the West End, at 4 to 15 guineas a week, to the bed-room and use of a breakfast parlour, at 10 shillings a week. In the West End the best kinds of lodgings are to be found in the streets leading from Piccadilly - such as Sackville-st., Dover-st., Half-Moon-st., Clarges-st., and Duke-st, and in streets leading out of Oxford-st., and Regent-st., St. James's-st., Jermyn-st. The apartments of the best class are those in private houses, let by persons of respectability, generally for the season only. A list of such apartments is to be found, however, at the nearest house-agent's, who gives cards to view, and states terms. An advertisement in *The Times* for such rooms, stating that "no lodging-house-keeper need apply," will often open to the stranger the doors of very respectable families, where he will be more likely to get all the quiet and comfort of a home, than in a professed lodging-house.

FURNISHED HOUSES for families can always be obtained at the West End, on application to a house-agent, at prices varying from 5 to 25 guineas a week, according to size, situation, &c.

CHEAPER LODGINGS. – Strangers requiring moderate lodgings in a central situation, should seek for apartments in some of the secondary streets leading from the Strand, such as Cecil- st., Craven-st., Norfolk-st., Southampton-st., Bedford-st., or the Adelphi. Also in the neighbourhood of Pimlico, and round Victoria Station, in Vauxhall-bridge-rd., Warwick-st., Ebury-st., Chester-st., or near the Marble Arch and Edgware-road, in Cambridge-st., Connaught-st., &c., &c., good rooms may be obtained at a moderate rate. In the season, the prices range from 1 to 4 guineas for a sitting and bed-room. The middle-class visitor who is bent on sight-seeing should obtain a bedroom in a healthy locality, and the use of a breakfast-room. Such lodgings may be had for half-a-guinea a week. He can either provide his breakfast himself or get his landlady to provide it for him. The various chop-houses and dining-rooms, of which there are nearly 600 in the Metropolis, will supply him with his dinner; whilst the 900 coffee-houses will afford him a cheap tea in any quarter of the town.

Murray's Handbook to London As It Is, 1879

LODGINGS, LOW

The proprietor has heard of his establishment being mentioned even in print, in a police report, as a "thieves' kitchen" a title which he holds to be altogether libellous; there is a kitchen there, as in all common lodging-houses, for the use of the customers, but he don't own that his customers are thieves, and don't know them to be thieves; "some of 'em," he is "quite certain, aint," and others, he has no doubt, are, but he asks no questions, and he don't want thieves; if a thief goes there, he perhaps knows him, and them that he thinks are only just going wrong he talks to, and tries to persuade them to keep themselves right.

Does he ever give credit?

Well, yes; sometimes he does to his regular lodgers, or if he knows that a young fellow is hard-up he don't mind letting him come for a night or two, if he's well disposed and tries to get work; and as for thieves, he don't want 'em to come, and they know that he won't harbour 'em; nor, on the other hand, won't ask questions, and then he can't know nothing. As to the police, they got no information from him; he never has any to give 'em, and he's determined not to have anything to do with the police, and not to have his men made a show of, like wild beasts . . .

Did he enter the name of his lodgers in that book?

Yes, such names as the regulars chose to give, or such as he knew 'em by they mostly put against the numbers of the rooms they occupied, so that there should be no mistake.

Some of the names chosen are either evidence of a peculiar taste on the part of those who chose them, or are highly illustrative, for I notice that the list includes "Dick Turpin," while some modest lodger, who is, I suppose, his companion, is satisfied to be recognised as "Dick Turpin's mate." Similarly, "Cock Sparrow" is followed by "Sparrow's mate," while "Oxford," "Jeweller," "Bos," "Countryman," "Rubbing-up Jack," "Rubbing-down Bill," "Coachman," and a few others, rely entirely upon their own attractions.

During the time that we are conversing the lodgers are coming in. Their chamber candlesticks have already been prepared in the shape of half inches of rushlight stuck upon small shards of broken crockery, of which ingenious adaptations there are perhaps forty on the table. It is comparatively early, and yet the larger number of the men and lads, as they come in, pay their three-pence, and go off to bed at once, with a tired look which seems to disregard everything but sleep . . . a man who has been driving a hearse, a stableman who leaves part of a harness in care of the proprietor, a plasterer, a couple of bricklayers, two or three whose occupation is not to be discovered from their appearance – one of them a shabby buttoned-up man with a hang-dog look, and another, an elderly man who looks as though he sold books or pamphlets in the streets or at the bars of public-houses – one or two unmistakable young London thieves, and two boys who came in upon the introduction of a third, and stand laughing and kicking at each other in the passage until they come just within the door to pay their money; when the proprietor "reckons 'em up," (as he says,) at a look, and at once informs them that he won't have any tricks, and that if they make a disturbance he shall "be with 'em, and throw 'em down stairs in half a minute."

Thomas Archer, *The Pauper, The Thief and The Convict*, 1865

It has struck two by St. George's chimes. The gas jet that makes a transparency of the dingy red or yellow blind that drapes the parlour window, and on which is inscribed "Good single beds at threepence half-penny," may be turned low for economy's sake. The upper windows, where the dormitories are, may show no sign of light or life, but push open any one of the battered old street doors (they're all on the latch), and there will be found the lodging-house "deputy," dozing, perhaps, beside his brazier of glowing coke, but ready to rouse at the swinging of the door, and to receive threepence half-penny and give in exchange the tin ticket that entitles the holder to join the seven times seven sleepers in the well-packed apartment where the good beds are.

But who is the man, the dozen men, that, after the clock has struck two, push open the the street-door and walk in without ceremony? The "deputy" asks no questions, and therefore he hears no lies, as probably he would were he to show himself inquisitive. It is no part of his duty to pry into the private affairs of the customers of the establishment. It is not as it used to be at these places. Time was, and that not so many years since, when the threepenny lodging-house-keeper was almost invariably a retired thief content to pass the evening of his life as a peaceful purchaser of stolen property, and who, if ever there was any unpleasantness in the shape of policeman hammering at his door at an unseasonable hour, would regard it as his duty to slip upstairs, and, for the benefit of any one whom it might particularly concern, throw out a hint that the back door was unbolted.

Now, however, there is no lodging-house so "common" but that the law has a kindly regard for it. It must be conducted under a police licence, and inspectors are appointed to see that every lodger gets his fair share of breathing space, and that the sheets are changed something oftener than once a month. But in no part of the Act of Parliament is it insisted on that every person shall on application for a lodging produce to the deputy a certificate of character.

You must take care of yourself if you are doubtful of the company you may find yourself in. The proprietor takes care of himself. He is a man not given to make himself or others uncomfortable by an affectation of delicacy. He brands his sheets "Stop Thief," with indelible marking ink and in inch-long letters. The backs of the shoe-brushes, the knives and forks, the very gridiron handle, is marked, "Stolen from Dodger's Lodging House." Why not? To a person incapable of an act of dishonesty what is there in mere words? The sheets are as snug to lie in; the bristles of the shoe- brushes are not at all depressed by the shameful brand on their backs; the vile insinuation on the gridiron will not taint the toothsome rasher grilled on its bars. It is assumed that the man who comes to Dodger to lodge is not straight from the country. Even if he be he will get fair treatment as far as possible.

'One of the Crowd' [James Greenwood],
Toilers in London, 1883

LUNATICS & ASYLUMS

ST. LUKE'S HOSPITAL for Lunatics was first established 1751 . . . The Hospital was incorporated 1838; the end infirmaries added in 1841; a chapel in 1842, and open fire-places set in the galleries; when also coercion was abolished, padded rooms were provided for violent patients, and an airing-ground set apart for them; wooden doors were substituted for iron gates, and unnecessary guards and bars removed from the windows. In 1843 were added reading-rooms and a library for the patients, with bagatelle and backgammon-boards, &c. By Act 9 and 10 Vict., c. 100, the Commissioners of Lunacy were added to the Hospital direction. In 1848, Sir Charles Knightley presented an organ to the chapel, and daily service was first performed. The Hospital was next lit with gas; the drainage, ventilation, and supply of water improved, by subscription at the centenary festival, June 25, 1851.

On St. Luke's Day (October 18), a large number of the Hospital patients are entertained with dancing and singing in the great hall in the centre of the Hospital, when the officers, nurses, and attendants join the festival. Balls are also given fortnightly.

The mode of treatment at St. Luke's has undergone so complete a metamorphosis within the last few years, by the institution of kindness for severity, and indulgence for restrictions, that the maladies of the brain have been rendered as subservient to medical science as the afflictions of the body. Modern experience shows that the old terrors of the prison, brutal execrations and violence, and those even worse scenes which were exhibited for a small money payment to the curious, in the madhouses of the metropolis and elsewhere, were errors. The percentage of recoveries was, from 1821 to 1830, 47 1/3 per cent.; 1831 to 1840, 56¼ ditto; 1841 to 1850, 60 3/5 ditto; showing the results of the improved treatment. But the largest percentage of recoveries, with one exception, was 69 1/3, in 1851.

John Timbs, *Curiosities of London*, 1867

The visitors thus describe one of the women's galleries: "One of the side-rooms contained about ten patients, each chained by one arm or leg to the wall, the chain allowing them merely to stand up by the bench or form fixed to the wall, or sit down again. The nakedness of each patient was covered by a blanket gown only. The blanket gown is a blanket formed something like a dressing gown, with nothing to fasten it in parts. The feet even were naked." Many women were locked up in cells, naked and chained, on straw, with only one blanket for a covering; and the windows being unglazed, the light in winter was shut out for the sake of warmth. In the men's rooms, their nakedness and their mode of confinement, continues the report from which we have already quoted, gave this room the appearance of a dog-kennel. At this period the committee for months together made no inspection of the inmates. The house surgeon was in an insane state himself, and still oftener drunk; and the keepers were often in the latter state; yet at this very time the governors spent £600 in opposing a bill for regulating mad-houses, and I dare say they cried out lustily, No centralization! - no interference with vested interests! as enlightened Englishmen and parochial dignitaries are wont to do in our days.

Could we not do without lunatic asylums, if society gave up its drinking customs? Not exactly; but their number might be very much decreased. Two-thirds of our lunatics become so through drink. "They are very bad at first, sir," said one of my inform- ants to me, "but after a little while they get quieter, and perhaps they are cured in two or three months." And yet I find all these lunatics are supplied with beer. "They has two half-pints a day, sir, and when they work they gets two half-pints more, and very good beer it is, sir," continued my informant, "as strong as any man need drink." Now is not this preposterous? Men who drink till they become lunatics should be taught to do without it; but they are allowed their beer even in the asylum, and when they go out they begin drinking again, and of course relapse. Thus we keep feeding our lunatic asylums, at the very time we profess to cure lunatics. I admit these places are in many respects well managed – that the buildings are commodious – that the attention is good – that the governors are humane, and the medical officers vigilant; but which is the truer humanity, to take care of the man when in a lunatic asylum, or to keep him out of it altogether?

J. Ewing Ritchie, *The Night Side of London*, 1858

M is for Mugging

This 1856 cartoon is one of several humorous suggestions from *Punch* upon how to defend oneself against muggers. Street crime in London was very much a concern of the middle-classes in the 1850s and 1860s.

MAGDALEN HOSPITAL, THE

The Magdalen Hospital, St. George's Fields, was founded about the year 1758, in a great measure through the exertions of the Reverend and ill-fated Dr. Dodd. It was intended to receive and reclaim unfortunate females from the paths of prostitution; and has been eminently successful in restoring many thousands of lost women to their families and society. The buildings are spacious, and include an octagonal chapel, in which a select portion of the females of the institution are permitted to sing during Divine service, though secluded from the public eye by a screen.

The London Female Penitentiary, established at Pentonville in 1807, and the Female Refuge for the Destitute, in Hackney Road, of more recent origin, may be considered as adjuncts in the meritorious design of this Hospital.

> *Mogg's New Picture of London and Visitor's Guide to its Sights*, 1844

MAGDALEN HOSPITAL, ST. GEORGE'S FIELDS, for the reformation and relief of penitent prostitutes. Instituted 1758, chiefly by the exertions of Mr. Dingley, Sir John Fielding, Mr. Saunders Welch, and Jonas Hanway. The first house of the society was in Prescot-street, Goodman's-fields. A subscription of 20 guineas or more at one time, or of 5 guineas per annum for five successive years, is a qualification of a governor for life. A subscription of 5 guineas entitles the subscriber to the privileges of a governor for one year.

> Peter Cunningham, *Hand-Book of London*, 1850

MARRIAGE, PROPOSALS OF

Answer to a Proposal.

London, September 4th.

DEAR SIR,

I was very much surprised by your letter, and I will add, much pleased at being the object of your preference. I am fully sensible that it is the greatest compliment you could pay me.

I have had frequent opportunities of learning your worth, and must candidly admit that I both like and esteem you.

But an engagement is a very serious affair, and I am sure that I may safely appeal to your generosity for time to give the matter due consideration, especially as I do not feel at liberty to give a decisive answer without previously consulting my relatives. Trusting that you will see the propriety of my request,

I remain,

Yours very sincerely,

JANE ANDREWS.

Accepting.

The Oaks, March 9.

MY DEAR MR. SMITH,

I feel much flattered by your proposal, and if my father makes no objection to you; I shall esteem myself happy in having secured the affection of so good a man.

Pray excuse the shortness of this letter; it is the most awkward one I ever had to write – but I have good cause to know that you will pardon the shortcomings of

Yours sincerely,

–

Answer to a proposal.

Belvoir Terrace April 1, 18–.

DEAR CHARLES,

Your letter was a surprise, although our long and affectionate friendship, and the many proofs you have given of tender care for me, ought to have prepared me for it. But it was a very happy surprise too, Charlie. I do not doubt you have a shrewd guess that I care a wee bit for my old friend; indeed I should be very ungrateful if I did not.

You must speak to my father and mother on the subject. That they may consent to our union is the sincere wish of

Your very sincerely attached,

–

Accepting

London, April 5th, 18–.

DEAR MR.–

I scarcely know how to reply to your letter or to express what I feel at finding that you have given me your affection. I am not worthy of you in any way, but if you really think that I could make you happy. I will gladly try my best to do so.

Of course my consent to your proposal must now depend on that of my father, to whom pray apply at once. I have prepared him for your letter.

Believe me,

Very truly yours,

–

Refusing a proposal.

London, August 5th.

DEAR MR. –,

My father has placed your letter to him in my hands, and desired me to answer the flattering proposal which it contains. It is with profound regret that I obey him; for I cannot—unhappily—respond to the feelings you are good enough to entertain for me.

As a friend I shall ever like and esteem you, but I cannot feel for you the love which alone can make married life happy.

Allow me, however, to thank you very heartily for the great compliment that you have paid me, and to entreat your forgiveness if anything in my manner has unconsciously given rise to the hopes I am obliged to disappoint.

You will doubtless meet with some far worthier object by-and-by on whom to bestow your affections. That such may be the case is the sincere prayer of

Your obliged friend,

L. M.

From a Lady to her Betrothed, who has not written to her.

Elm Grove, November 13th.

DEAR JOHN,

It is more than a month since you wrote to me. Are you ill? or what causes your silence? I have thought lately also that your letters were constrained and cold, as well as few and far between. Has your affection for me changed? If so, speak frankly to me, dear John. I would not for the world hold you to your promise to me, if you desired to be released from it.

Write to me immediately, and answer me truly.

I am, ever,

Yours affectionately,

The Ladies' and Gentleman's Model Letter
Writer, c.1870

MATCHES

There are six or seven match manufactories in the East End, and they give employment to some thousands of women and girls. Until within a few years ago this industry was associated with a system of slavery of the very worst description; but I am happy to say that since the great strike at Bryant and May's in 1888, matters have considerably improved.

This firm, or, rather, company, is the largest of the kind in London, and, in the busy seasons, employs about twelve hundred hands. In 1877 the business paid a dividend at the rate of twenty-five per cent., and at that time the hours of work were from six a.m. to six p.m. in the summer, and from eight a.m. to six p.m. in the winter, an hour being allowed for dinner and half an hour for breakfast. The earnings of the great majority of the girls were from four shillings to eight shillings a week. Strict discipline was maintained, and penalties were inflicted for the slightest breach of the regulations. If, for instance, a girl arrived at the factory five minutes behind time, she was frequently shut out for half a day; and for any little act of untidiness, such as omitting to clear away the litter from under the bench, a fine was imposed.

The business is now much more humanely managed, and the labour of the workers has been considerably lightened by the introduction of improved machinery.

Next to Bryant and May's comes Bell's, where some five hundred girls and women are engaged; and the Salvation Army have a match manufactory which gives employment to about sixty persons. On visiting these establishments, you will find that the women are very contented and cheerful. They work with great rapidity—which is but natural, for they are paid by results. Men are employed in mixing the materials into which the matches are dipped; the girls prepare the wood and make the boxes.

Speaking generally, the factory hands are a healthy class. One woman who was interviewed had worked continuously in the same establishment for twenty years, and she was as robust as could be wished. Nevertheless, it is a mistake to suppose that phosphorus poisoning is a thing of the past. There is still a terrible amount of the disease, which is termed "phossy jaw." The first sign of the disorder is toothache, accompanied by swollen cheeks. As soon as these symptoms appear the sufferer has several teeth removed, in order, if possible, to save the entire jaw.

Montagu Williams, *Round London: Down East and Up West*, 1894

MECHANICS' INSTITUTIONS

The LONDON MECHANICS' INSTITUTION, 29 South-ampton Buildings, Chancery Lane, is the oldest, and, in fact, may be considered the originator of all the Mechanics' or Popular Institutes for education, literature, and science, in England. The late excellent philanthropist, Dr. Birkbeck, founded it in 1823, deriving much assistance from the support of Lord Brougham and many other public spirited men. Its library contains 4000 volumes. There are reading-rooms, class-rooms, a capacious "theatre" or lecture-room, in which for thirty-five years the lectures have been given weekly, and the usual appurtenances of a literary institute.

Of a similar class are: The London Institution, Finsbury Circus, Moorfields, established in 1806, – the present building erected in 1814, – the library containing 60,000 volumes; the Crosby Hall Institute, Bishopgate Street; the Southwark Institution. Southwark Bridge Road; the Pimlico and Belgravia Institute, near St. George's Road, Pimlico; the Russell Institution, 55 Great Coram Street, Russell Square, has a large and excellent library, and caters for a superior class of subscribers (in the library is a fine picture of the first sight of the sea by Xenophon and his army, in the retreat of the ten thousand, painted by Haydon, and presented by the Duke of Bedford, the patron of the institution, in 1836); the Marylebone Institution, 17 Edward Street, Portman Square; and the Working Men's College, Great Ormond Street, established by the Rev.F. D. Maurice, and providing first class instruction for artisans, mechanics, and others, in arithmetic, pure and mixed mathematics, mechanics, English composition, drawing, bookkeeping, English history, &c., at a cost of from 2*s*. 6*d*. to 5*s*. per term of eight weeks.

Cruchley's London in 1865: A Handbook for
Strangers, 1865

MEDICINE

The domestic arrangements of those days were very different to what they are now, and as such, I think, deserve a few words here. My mother was a great believer in medicine, especially in domestic medicine, and we suffered in due course. Every year in the early spring she made a jorum of treacle and brimstone, which she kept on the washing-stand shelf in Papa's dressing-room, a wooden spoon in it coming through a hole in the paper cover, and for about a fortnight she enacted the part of Mrs. Squeers on her unfortunate offspring. But at last, the devil having entered us, we incited Willie to eat the lot at one sitting, and the result was so disastrous that she gave up the brimstone and treacle régime from that day. Then there was an awful dose the nurses called "sinner and pruines" (senna and prunes), which was brought hot and odoriferous at dawn to the unhappy invalid. Rhubarb and magnesia had been tried, but as we invariably rose, smashed the cup, and sprinkled the bed and bearer, it was given up; and our worst dose was hot castor oil and milk, shaken together in a bottle and poured from the bottle down our throats. A strong peppermint lozenge some-what mitigated our woes, while those who had not been dosed incited the invalid to dance, so that the hideous liquid might be heard to wobble about inside the victim, which shows what imagination will do! Then we had powders, but these the doctor brought; Mama did not make these. It fell to her and Miss Wright to conceal them in different vehicles, hoping to take us in, and cause us to take them in in their turn. But we always found out in time to avoid the gritty deposit, and at one time the two busts which stood half-way up the stairs on red pedestals were full of figs which we concealed there, and were never discovered, as far as we knew; or if our dear friend, the housemaid, found them she at all events never told of us, but simply burned them. In October Mama brought out her small and precious silver saucepan, and over a fire lighted specially in her bedroom – fires were never allowed upstairs except in cases of real and severe illness – she would concoct camphor balls for chapped hands, which we were allowed to roll up in silver paper to preserve them for use, and a salve for the lips made from wax and a sweetly scented rose-essence, which we fetched from the chemist's shop in Oxford Street

Mrs. J.E. Panton, *Leaves from a Life*, 1908

MESMERISTS

ELECTRO BIOLOGY – The MARYLEBONE LITERARY and SCIENTIFIC INSTITUTION, 17 Edward-street, Portman-square – Every TUESDAY, WEDNESDAY, THURSDAY, and SATURDAY EVENINGS – At the above Institution, Dr. DARLING and Mr. STONE will give a SERIES OF LECTURES, accompanying each with a series of EXTRAORDINARY EXPERIMENTS upon persons coming forward from the audience, who in a perfectly wakeful state will be deprived of the power of SPEECH, SIGHT, and HEARING, their voluntary motions controlled, and all their sensations. They will forget their own names, and declare that water tastes like vinegar, milk, brandy, or whatever the operator designates. – Commence at 8, doors open at half-past 7; and, to prevent interruption, will be closed at half-past 8 o'clock. – Admission: reserved seats, 2*s*; back-ditto, 1*s*.

advertisement from the *Daily News*, 1851

MIDLAND GRAND HOTEL, THE

Alighting under a magnificent porch, the guest will find himself in a large hall. Immediately to the right are the offices of the manager, for "information," and of the bedroom clerk; and on the left is one for hall porters, and for letters and parcels. Passing along the corridor, there is a small sitting or waiting room on the left; then a gentlemen's lavatory; and above, up a mezzenin, or half-flight of stairs, a ladies' lavatory. Further on is the passenger lift, and in a recess to our left the luggage lift, both of which ascend to the fifth story, and are worked by hydraulic power. Immediately to our right we enter the general coffee room, which sweeps along the whole curved wing of the building, 100 feet long by 30, and 24 feet high, and ventilated with shafts. Close by are the waiters' pantry and the still-room, whence dinners and tea and coffee are served.

Turning through a door at our left, we find ourselves at the foot and in front of the grand staircase. It rises to the third floor, is lighted by three two-light windows which continue up to the roof, a height of 80 feet, and are divided by four transom windows; the whole being crowned by a groined ceiling, with stone ribs and carved bosses at the intersections, filled in with Portland concrete a foot thick, the face being finished with Parian cement, which some day will be coloured and decorated. The groined ribs spring from stone corbels, and are supported by polished green Irish marble columns.

Ascending the first floor of this staircase, on turning to the right we again pass the lifts and lavatories, and reach the general drawing and reading room, a spacious and beautifully decorated and furnished apartment. The five front windows look into Euston Road, over a terrace, which will be adorned with flowers and plants, and covered with an awning in summer. Three side windows look westward down Euston Road, and three others eastward along the whole frontage of the building. From hence we enter the music room, another splendidly furnished apartment; and immediately adjoining there will be "the private coffee room," for the use of which it is intended to make a somewhat higher charge, in order to keep it more select. We are now near the west end of the corridor, which runs from one end of the building to the other, a total distance of some 600 feet, and conducting to the noble suites of bedrooms and sitting-rooms with which present visitors to the hotel are familiar.

We pass along the deep-piled silent Axminster carpet. On our right are suites of rooms, with a balcony in front, looking out upon the wide space in front of the hotel and on to the Euston Road. The spacious and lofty apartments, the handsome furniture, the Brussels carpets, the massive silken or woollen curtains, and the pinoleum blinds; the wardrobes, chests of drawers, clocks, writing tables, sofas, arm-chairs, with which they are supplied, leave nothing to be desired by the wealthiest and the most refined.

> Frederick S. Williams, *The Midland Railway: Its Rise and Progress*, 1878

MODEL HOUSING

THE TRUSTEES OF THE PEABODY DONATION FUND started with sums given and bequeathed by Mr. Peabody, amounting in all to half a million of money. The added money received for rent and interest has brought this capital to the magnificent sum of (in round numbers) £700,000. The principle of this fund is to devote the profits gradually to the purchase of land and the erection of buildings. At the end of 1875 nearly £150,000 was in hand and available for these purposes. Up to the present time the trustees have provided for the artisan and labouring poor of London 5,170 rooms, exclusive of bath-rooms, laundries, and wash-houses. These rooms comprise 2,348 separate dwellings, occupied by nearly 10,000 persons. It was for some time feared that the class of accommodation provided was somewhat too good, and consequently too expensive for the actual artisan and labouring classes. But the table showing the employ of the tenants, which is appended to the report for 1878 is reassuring on this head. Bricklayers, cabmen, charwomen, letter-carriers, messengers, needlewomen, police-constables, porters, &c., comprise large numbers of persons who can afford to pay but very moderate rentals. The average weekly earnings of the head of each family were £1 3*s.* 8*d.* The average rent of each dwelling was 4*s.* 4*d.* per week, and if it be considered that these rents are somewhat too high, it must be remembered that many of the dwellings comprise as many as three rooms, and that the free use of water, laundries, sculleries, and bath-rooms, is included. The cheapest lodgings are naturally in Shadwell, where the rents are, for one room, 2*s*. to 2*s*. 3*d*.; two rooms, 3*s*. to 3*s*. 6*d*.; and three rooms, 4*s*. to 4*s*. 6*d*. In Southwark-street the charges for the same accommodation are respectively 3*s*., 4*s*. 3*d*. to 4*s*. 9*d*., and 5*s*. 3*d*. to 5*s*. 9*d*. The same average prevails in Pimlico, where there are also sets of four rooms at 7*s*. 6*d*. The death-rate of the Peabody Buildings is about 180 per 1,000 below the average of all London.

Charles Dickens (Jr.), *Dickens's Dictionary of London*, 1879

MORTALITY, INFANT

II. Table showing the Rate of Infant Mortality (i.e., children under one year of age) in (a) Soho, and (b) the wealthy districts of the West.

Sanitary Area // Deaths under one year of age per 1000 births, 1894

Strand (including St. Anne, Soho) 179
Hampstead 113
St. George's, Hanover Square 115
Chelsea 131
Paddington 137
Kensington* 173
[*The figures for Kensington are remarkable and are probably to be explained by special circumstances. It must not, however, be forgotten that 25% of the total population of Kensington live under crowded conditions]

III. Table showing the Rate of Infant Mortality (i.e., children under one year of age) in (a) Soho, and (b) the most crowded districts in other parts of London

Sanitary Area // Deaths under one year of age per 1000 births, 1894

Strand (including St. Anne, Soho). 179
St. George-the-Martyr, Southwark 186
St. George's-in-the-East 185
Holborn 180
Limehouse 174
Rotherhithe 161
Whitechapel 154
Bethnal Green 151
St. Saviour's, Southwark 145
Clerkenwell 145
St. Giles-in-the-Fields 132
St. Luke, City Road 123

Arthur Sherwell, *Life in West London*, 1897

MOURNING

THE blinds of the windows of the house should be drawn down directly the death occurs, and they should remain down until after the funeral has left the house, when they are at once to be pulled up. As a rule, the females of the family do not pay any visits until after the funeral. Neither would it be considered in good taste for any friends or acquaintances to visit at the house during that time, unless they were relatives of the family, when of course it would be only proper for them to do so. With regard to the time that ought to elapse after death before the funeral is performed, it may be said that in many cases – especially in the summer – the corpse is retained too long, and thus becomes injurious to the health of those living in the house.

This is most especially the case when the deceased died of typhus or some other fever, and complaints of a similar infectious character. Under these circumstances, the practice is attended with danger to the neighbourhood, and should be most strictly avoided. Perhaps, as a rule, it may be said that funerals in winter should take place within one week after death, and in summer in a still shorter time.

It sometimes happens among the poorer classes that the female relatives attend the funeral; but this custom is by no means to be recommended, since in these cases it but too frequently happens that, being unable to restrain their emotions, they interrupt and destroy the solemnity of the ceremony with their sobs, and even by fainting. As soon as the funeral is over it is usual for the mourners to separate, each one taking his departure home.

While on the subject, we would caution our readers against, out of a mistaken and thoughtless kindness, offering, and even forcing wines, spirits, and other liquors upon the undertaker's man. If they were given instead a cup of tea or coffee and a sandwich, it would, in the generality of cases, be both more acceptable to them, and also keep them in the condition necessary for the proper performance of their duties.

Cassell's Household Guide, c.1880

MOVING HOUSE

WE write upon the eve of quarter-day, and as it happens to be the Midsummer quarter that is impending, we are reminded by demonstrations at this season, always very numerous, and which meet us as we walk the streets, that a pretty large section of the London population are about changing their abodes, or are even now in the very act of so doing. First, there is the sudden apparition of "This house to let – enquire within," or somewhere else, stuck into parlour and drawing-room windows, or mounted on a board in the front garden. Then there is the spectacle of respectable fathers of families, or agitated young wives, flitting backwards and forwards like unquiet phantoms, and turning their heads constantly on this side and that, in search of a new domicile. Again, there are those long ominous-looking vans, upon whose fronts are inscribed the words "Goods removed," either standing open-mouthed at the greengrocer's doors, with their shafts reared perpendicularly like rampant skeleton arms, or their cavernous throats filled with the household goods of a migrating family, creaking slowly along the highway on the route to a new domestic retreat. These outward signs, which we cannot escape if we would, forcibly recall to our recollection the events of that last flitting, when, leaving the southern banks of the Thames we took our flight northwards, to the suburban precincts of merry Islington.

First came the preparations for the event, which preparations consisted of no end of packing and bundling, sorting, arranging, and rejecting, all accompanied with so many appeals to old memories and sympathies, so many mementoes of vanished pleasures, and, no less touching, of vanished pains too – so many dumb and dusty witnesses of the fateful and remorseless passage of that "time which is our life," that it required no little stock of moral courage to look them all in the face with an unmoved countenance. Think of unearthing thirteen gratuitous blue-papered hat-boxes, consigned one by one at forgotten dates to the gloom of an upstairs cupboard, but unscrupulously unkennelled at once by Betty to scare our astonished senses! Worse than that – think of her marshalling a battalion of physic-bottles a hundred strong, each with a label like a clerical band at its neck, and each one recalling the undelightful sensations – "ventral, subventral, internal and central," of which, in the course of that long illness, it had been the bitter occasion.

Think of the awful dilemma into which we were cast, as a host of forgotten and unmentionable articles were dragged forth from their hidden recesses, and the question was asked, "Will master take this to the new house?" and the impossibility of a sagacious decision upon numberless calls so suddenly made. Think of the dismay, the spasmodic squall, the resulting ill-humour and consequent ill-management, of Betty herself, who, having rushed heedlessly to work with the bed-key to take down her own four-poster, had smashed in the roof of her purple-splashed bonnet-box, and jammed her best puce silk bonnet into a colossal facsimile of a Norfolk biffin! Think of dining for the last time upon the deal dresser in the kitchen, without chairs, only the brewer's unclaimed barrels to sit upon – with borrowed knives and forks to carve and eat with, and nothing but a battered pewter pot to drink out of!

Charles Manby Smith, *The Little World Of London*, 1857

MUDLARKS

Mudlarks are boys who roam about the sides of the river at low tide, to pick up coals, bits of iron, rope, bones, and copper nails that fall while a ship is being repaired. They are at work sometimes early in the morning, and sometimes late in the afternoon, according to tide. They usually work from six to seven hours per day. My informant, a quick intelligent little fellow, who has been at the business three years, tells me the reason they take to mudlarking, is that their clothes are too bad to look for anything better, and that they are nearly all fatherless, and their mothers are too poor to keep them; so they take to it because they have nothing else to do. This boy works with about twenty to thirty mudlarks every day, and they may be seen, he tell me, at daybreak, very often, with their trousers tucked up, groping about, and picking out the pieces of coal from the mud. They go into the river up to their knees, and in searching the mud they very often run pieces of glass and long nails into their feet. When this is the case, they go home and dress the wounds, and return directly, for, should the tide come up without their finding anything, they must starve that day. At first it is a difficult matter to stand in the mud, and he has known many young beginners fall in. The coals the mudlark finds he sells to the poor people in the neighbourhood at a penny the "pot," the weight of which is 14 *lb*. The iron, bones, rope, and copper nails he sells to the rag shops. They sell the iron 5 *lb*. for a penny, the bones 3 *lb*. for one penny, rope a half-penny per pound wet, and three farthings dry. The copper nails fetch four-pence per pounds but they are very difficult to find, for the mudlark is not allowed to go near a vessel that is being coppered (for fear of their stealing the copper), and it is only when a ship has left the docks that the nails are to be had. They often pick up tools – such as saws, hammers, etc. – in the mud; these they either give to the seamen for biscuits and beef, or sell to the shops for a few halfpence. They earn from 2½*d*. to 8*d*. per day, but 8*d*. they consider a very good day's work, and they seldom make it; their average earnings are three-pence a day. After they leave the river they go home and scrape their trousers, and make themselves as tidy as possible they then go into the streets and make a little by holding gentlemen's horses, or opening cab-doors. In the evening they mostly go to the ragged schools. My informant and his sister keep their mother – the boy by mudlarking, the girl by selling fish. The poor little fellow owes 5*s*. rent; he has a suit of clothes and a pair of boots in pawn for 4*s*.; if he could get them out he would be enabled to find something better to do.

Henry Mayhew, *'Labour and the Poor'*
(in the *Morning Chronicle*), 1849

MUFFINS AND CRUMPETS

The street-sellers of muffins and crumpets rank among the old street-tradesmen. It is difficult to estimate their numbers, but they were computed for me at 500, during the winter months. They are for the most part boys, young men, or old men, and some of them infirm. There are a few girls in the trade, but very few women.

The ringing of the muffin-man's bell – attached to which the pleasant associations are not a few – was prohibited by a recent Act of Parliament, but the prohibition has been as inoperative as that which forbad the use of a drum to the costermonger, for the muffin bell still tinkles along the streets, and is rung vigorously in the suburbs. The sellers of muffins and crumpets are a mixed class, but I am told that more of them are the children of bakers, or worn-out bakers, than can be said of any other calling. The best sale is in the suburbs. "As far as I know, sir," said a muffin-seller, "it's the best Hackney way, and Stoke Newington, and Dalston, and Balls Pond, and Islington; where the gents that's in banks – the steady coves of them – goes home to their teas, and the missuses has muffins to welcome them; that's my opinion."

I did not hear of any street-seller who made the muffins or crumpets he vended. Indeed, he could not make the small quantity required, so as to be remunerative. The muffins are bought of the bakers, and at prices to leave a profit of 4*d*. in 1*s*. Some bakers give thirteen to the dozen to the street-sellers whom they know. The muffin-man carries his delicacies in a basket, wherein they are well swathed in flannel, to retain the heat: "People likes them warm, sir," an old man told me, "to satisfy them they're fresh, and they almost always are fresh; but it can't matter so much about their being warm, as they have to be toasted again. I only wish good butter was a sight cheaper, and that would make the muffins go. Butter's half the battle." The basket and flannels cost the muffin-man 2*s*. 6*d*. or 3*s*. 6*d*. His bell stands him in from 4*d*. to 2*s*., "according as the metal is."

The regular price of goodsized muffins from the street-sellers is a halfpenny each; the crumpets are four a penny. Some are sold cheaper, but these are generally smaller, or made of inferior flour.

Henry Mayhew, *London Labour and the London Poor*, 1851

MUGGING

Returning about midnight homeward, by Regent's Park, two young men, one about 5ft. 7in., the other 5ft. 5in. or 6in., rather fashionably dressed, going in the same direction, accosted me as I passed between them, when, after a few remarks on the weather, &c., in an instant I found myself prostrate, and, recovering, as from a shock, with my pockets rifled, I struggled and threw one or both over, but found my mouth bandaged round with some machine composed of strands of whipcord or whalebone, and my head constricted as in a vice. Immediately I was again felled, by a blow from behind, as from a life-preserver, and, on again rising I heard distinctly the footsteps of the Thugs running away at perhaps 60 or 70 yards distance. Having power just barely sufficient to call "Murder!" it occurred to me that chloroform was used on their infernal mask; and, in about three minutes, three policemen came to my aid, one of whom said he had met the runaways near the toll-gate, who then affected to be drunk, or "fresh," as he termed it, and that "one challenged the other to run towards the turnpike for a sovereign." "This," said the constable, "put me off my guard, as I thought they were 'gents' after dinner."

letter to *The Times*, 1850

MUSIC HALL

Music Halls—The music-hall, as it is at present understood, was started many years ago at the Canterbury Hall over the water. The entertainments proving popular, the example was speedily followed in every quarter of the town. The performance in no way differs, except in magnitude, from those which are to be seen in every town of any importance throughout the country. Ballet, gymnastics, and so-called comic singing, form the staple of the bill of fare, but nothing comes foreign to the music-hall proprietor. Performing animals, winners of walking. matches, successful scullers, shipwrecked sailors, swimmers of the Channel, conjurers, ventriloquists, tight-rope dancers, campanologists, clog-dancers, sword-swallowers, velocipedists, champion skaters, imitators, marionettes, decanter equilibrists, champion shots, "living models of marble gems," "statue marvels," "fire princes," "mysterious youths," "spiral bicycle ascensionists," flying children, empresses of the air, kings of the wire, "vital sparks," "Mexican boneless wonders," "white-eyed musical Kaffirs," strong-jawed ladies, cannon-ball performers, illuminated fountains, and that remarkable musical eccentricity the orchestre militaire, all have had their turn on the music-hall stage. Strangers to the business may be warned that the word "turn," as understood in the profession, means the performance for which the artist is engaged, and frequently comprises four or more songs, however much or little of pleasure the first effort may have given the audience. Furthermore, as many of the popular performers take several "turns" nightly, it is undesirable to visit many of these establishments on the same evening, as it is quite possible to go to four or five halls in different parts of the town, and to find widely diverse stages occupied by the same sets of performers. Among the principal halls may be mentioned the Bedford, in Camden Town; the Canterbury, Westminster-bridge-road; the Foresters, Cambridge-rd, E.; Gatti's, Westminster-bridge-road; the London Pavilion, at the top of the Haymarket; Evans's, Covent-garden; the Metropolitan, Edgware-road; the Oxford, Oxford-street;

the Cambridge, 136, Commercial-street; Lusby's Palace, Mile End-road; the Royal, High Holborn; the South London, London-road, SE.; and Wilton's in Wellclose-square, in the far east. Of these the Canterbury, the Metropolitan, and the South London have a specialty for ballet on a large scale. The Canterbury has an arrangement for ventilation peculiar to itself. A large portion of the roof is so arranged as to admit of its easy and rapid removal and replacement. The entertainments at the other halls vary only in degree. The operatic selections which were at one time the distinguishing feature of the Oxford have of late years been discontinued. A curiosity in the way of music-halls may be found by the explorer at the "Bell," in St. George-street, Ratcliff-highway, where, contrary to precedent, the negro element preponderates among the audience instead of on the stage. The hours of performance at most music-halls are from about 8 till 11.30, and the prices of admission vary from 6*d.* to 3*s.* Private boxes, at varying prices, may be had at nearly all the music-halls.

Charles Dickens (Jr.), *Dickens's Dictionary of London*, 1879

MUSIC IN THE HOME

The social morceaux, which belong to "little music", are peculiar. All those songs which you see in Regent Street music-shops, often adorned with very pretty sentimental lithographs, and rejoicing in such titles as "Mary Anne", "Love Always" (with a counter-song dedicated to the composer, called, "Do not Love at all"), "The Troubadour was a gallant Youth", "Hasten back from the Crusades", all these are the celebrities of "little music". They belong to no opera: they have been sung at almost no concert, save by the single vocalist whose name appears on the title-page, and who gave them a fillip by one single performance. They descend to no barrel-organ – they are whistled by no butcher's boy; they are never parodied in burlesques; the name of the composer does not strike you as remarkably familiar – he may, perchance, be a letter of the Greek alphabet. He who passed his life at public places would think that these works were buried in the deepest obscurity. Not at all. Seek them in the drawing-room, and you shall find them honourably enveloped in smart cases, and you shall even hear them declared "sweet." They are usually sung by young ladies in a voice so soft as to be almost inaudible three yards from the piano; and, on the whole, we may say that they are more popular with the performer than the listener.

Albert Smith, *Sketches of London Life and Character*, 1849

N is for Nightmen

Nightmen emptied privies and cesspools under cover of darkness. The "night-soil" went to local "night-yards" where it was mixed with other waste matter, left to dry, and turned into manure. The smell of the yards was reportedly "quite awful, and enough to kill anybody". After public health legislation was introduced in 1848, metropolitan "night-yards" were banned and "night-soil" had to be transported directly to the countryside.

NIGHT CLUBS

The entrance to Kate Hamilton's may best be located as the spot on which Appenrodt's German sausage-shop now stands, although the premises extended right through to Leicester Square.

"Don't go yet, dear," appealed a sweet siren as Bobby, looking at his watch, swore that when duty called one must obey, but eventually succumbed to a voice like a foghorn shouting, "John, a bottle of champagne," and the beautiful Kate bowed approvingly from her throne. Kate Hamilton at this period must have weighed at least twenty stone, and had as hideous a physiognomy as any weather-beaten Deal pilot. Seated on a raised platform, with a bodice cut very low, this freak of nature sipped champagne steadily from midnight until daylight, and shook like a blancmange every time she laughed.

Approached by a long tunnel from the street – where two janitors kept watch – a pressure of the bell gave instant admittance to a likely visitor, whilst an alarm gave immediate notice of the approach of the police.

Finding oneself within the "salon" during one of these periodical raids was not without interest. Carpets were turned up in the twinkling of an eye, boards were raised, and glasses and bottles – empty or full – were thrust promiscuously in; every one assumed a sweet and virtuous air and talked in subdued tones, whilst a bevy of police, headed by an inspector, marched solemnly in, and having completed the farce, marched solemnly out.

What subsidy attached to this duty, and when and how paid, it is needless to inquire. Suffice to show that the hypocrisy that was to attain such eminence in these latter enlightened days was even then in its infancy, and worked as adroitly as any twentieth-century policeman could desire.

"Now we're all right," exclaimed the foghorn, as the "salon" resumed its normal vivacity. "Bobby, my dear, come and sit next me," and so, like a tomtit and a round of beef, the pasty-faced youth took the post of honour alongside the vibrating mass of humanity. The distinction conferred upon our hero was a much-coveted one amongst youngster, and gave a "hall-marking" which henceforth proclaimed him a "man about town." To dispense champagne ad libitum was one of its chief privileges – for the honour was not unaccompanied with responsibilities – and Florrie or Connie (or whoever the friend for the moment of the favoured one might be) not only held a carte blanche to order champagne, but to dispense it amongst all her acquaintances, by way of propitiation amongst the higher grades, and as an implied claim for reciprocity on those whose star might be in the ascendant later on.

'One of the Old Brigade', *London in the Sixties*, 1908

We are now at Barnes's, a famous night house, or, rather, an infamous night house, in the Haymarket. When the dancing places and music-hells of the metropolis close, this door remains open to catch all stray night birds who can find no other resting place. The place is an ordinary drinking saloon, with a confectionery and pastry counter, and the attendants are five or six over-dressed young ladies, all of whom have their hair dyed of a light color, and are very free and chatty in their manner. These girls are well supplied with jewelry and lockets. Their salary is not large enough to furnish them with the trinkets, as they only get one pound five shillings a week; yet they manage to dress expensively, and Champagne is so common to their palates that they have become indifferent to it and it absolutely palls upon them. Yet there is a percentage on every bottle that is consumed here, and consequently they do their best to sell Moet & Chandon at ten shillings a bottle to the customers – and will even drink with them.

This is a great place for rump-steaks and native oysters – late at night, and a good business is done here in those articles of food. The oysters are small, black, and have a bitter, copperish taste. A New Yorker, used to Sounds and East Rivers, would leave them in disgust; but Englishmen, whose throats are parched with the liquors they get at the Argyle and in the Haymarket, prefer them to the most luscious Saddle Rocks. There is a large screen in the center of the room, the bar glitters with costly mirrors, and behind the screen are a number of small boxes partitioned off, and having red plush seats. In these are several noisy women, inflamed with liquor, eating and drinking and halhooing at their male companions. One girl, in a black silk dress, with her hair hanging down in disorder, is crying drunk at one of the tables, and has just spilled a bottle of wine over her handsome dress. She is cursing the waiter, who is also drunk, with much earnestness of purpose, and as soon as she sees the detective she halloos at him in a harsh voice:

"I say, Bobby, you don't want me, do you? I 'avent done nothink, although I wos wonst in Newgate for taking a swell's watch, which he guv to me for my wedding present, as was just four year ago, come Micklemas Goose. I wish I could throw meself in the Thames ...

Daniel Joseph Kirwan, *Palace and Hovel:*
Phases of London Life, 1878

NUISANCES

Nuisances.—A few of the *desagremens* to which metropolitan flesh is heir have been legally settled to be "nuisances".

(a) THE FOLLOWING WILL be summarily suppressed on appeal to the nearest police-constable:

Abusive language; Advertisements, carriage of (except in form approved); Areas left open without sufficient fence.

Baiting animals; Betting in streets; Bonfires in Streets; Books, obscene, selling in streets.

Carpet-beating; Carriage, obstruction by; Cattle, careless driving of; Coals, unloading, between prohibited hours; Cock-fighting; Crossings in streets, obstructing.

Defacing buildings; Deposit of goods in streets; Dogs loose or mad; Doors, knocking at; Drunk and disorderly persons; Dust, removal of, between 10 a.m. and 7 p.m.

Exercising horses to annoyance of persons; Exposing goods for sale in parks.

Firearms, discharging; Fireworks, throwing in streets; Footways, obstructions on; Footways unswept; Furious driving; Furniture, fraudulent removal of between 8 p.m. and 6 a.m.

Games, playing in streets.

Indecent exposure.

Lamps, extinguishing.

Mat-shaking after 8 a.m; Musicians in streets.

Obscene singing; Offensive matters, removal of, between 6 a.m. and 12 night.

Posting bills without consent; projections from houses to cause annoyance.

Reins, persons driving without; Ringing door bells without excuse; Rubbish lying in thoroughfare.

Slides, making in streets; Stone-throwing.

Unlicensed public carriage.

(b) THE FOLLOWING WILL require an application to the police-courts:

Cesspools, foul.

Dead body, infectious, retained in room where persons live; Disease, person suffering from infectious, riding in public carriage, or exposing himself, or being without proper accommodation; Disorderly houses; Drains, foul.

Factory, unclean or overcrowded. Furnace in manufactory not consuming its own smoke; Food unfit for consumption, exposing.

Gaming houses.

House filthy or injurious to health.

Infected bedding or clothes, sale of.

Letting infected house or room; Lotteries.

Manufactures (making sulphuric acid, steeping skins, &c.); Manure, non-removal of; Milk, exposing, unfit for consumption.

Obstructions in highways, bridges, or rivers; Overcrowding of house.

Powder magazine, or keeping too large a quantity.

Theatres, unlicensed; Trades, offensive (keeping pigs, soap-house, slaughter-house, or manufactures in trade causing effluvia, &c.).

Want of reparation of highway; Warehousing inflammable materials; Water-fouling or polluting.

Charles Dickens (Jr.), *Dickens's Dictionary of London*, 1879

OMNIBUSES

We are going to take a ride in a penny omnibus. Here we are at Holborn-hill: the omnibus, a white one, has just turned round, and we are the first to jump in and ensconce ourselves in a further corner. Now we can ride to Tottenham Court-road for a penny, or to Edgware-road, if we choose, for two-pence. We are hardly seated, when an elderly dame literally bundles in, having a large brown-paper parcel, almost as big as a pannier, and a crushed and semi-collapsed bandbox, which she quietly arranges on the cushioned seat, as though she had engaged that whole side to herself. She is followed in an instant by an elderly and portly figure in patched boots, and well-worn dingy great coat, who takes the right-hand door corner, where he sits with clasped horny hands, nursing a corpulent umbrella, upon the handle of which he rests his unshaven chin, as with rueful face he peers over the low door. Bang! goes something on the roof; the explosion startles him from his contemplations, and causes him to poke out his head, which is instantly drawn in again, as the conductor opens the door, and keeps it open while a living tide rushes in – one, two, three, four, five, six, seven, eight, nine! "No more room here, conductor: full here!" "Full inside!" roars the conductor, in reply. But we don't move on yet; there is a vision of muddy high-lows, corduroy garments, and coat- tails, clambering up consecutively in the rear under the guidance of the conductor, and making a deafening uproar on the roof in the ceremony of arranging themselves upon what has been not inappropriately styled the "knife-board." "All right" bursts involuntarily from the lips of the conductor, as the last pair of bluchers disappears above our heads. Now the "bus" gets under way, and we begin to look around us, and find that we form one of a very mixed company indeed. Opposite us sits the old lady with the bandbox and monster bundle. By her side is a very thin journeyman baker in his oven undress, and next to him a young man carrying a blue bag, and wearing a diamond ring on his little finger, a pair of false brilliants by way of shirt-studs, and a violet-coloured neck-tie. To his left is the wife of a mechanic, carrying a capless, bald-headed fat baby in her arms – baby sputtering, staring, and kicking in an ecstasy of delight, and stretching out its little puddings of fingers to reach the diamond-ringed hand that grasps the blue bag. Next to the mother of the baby is a blue-jacket, a regular tar, who, it would seem, has entered the omnibus for the sake of enjoying a "turn-in," and is endeavouring to compose himself to sleep.

Charles Manby Smith, *Curiosities of London Life*, 1853

When the London General Omnibus Company – the capital for which was largely subscribed in Paris – began its operations, its promoters held an Exhibition somewhere near Charing Cross, of models of improved omnibuses; and among these I recall several with staircases on the outside, like those attached to the Russian "isbas," and by means of which the "knife-board" could be reached. This eventually led to the adoption of what is known as the "garden-seat" system, and to me it is positively delightful to watch, looking out of window, the transformation of the formerly barren, or at the most, men-folk frequented roofs of the buses, into so many brilliant parterres of tastefully dressed ladies, who gaily ascend the staircases, and seat themselves on the commodious benches, at right angles with the longitudinal sides of the bus.

I have fallen hopelessly in love with hundreds of brilliant bonnets, and handsome hats, to say nothing of skirts and sunshades of every colour of the rainbow; and I only regret that the altitude of my apartments precluded me from scanning the countenances of the doubtless lovely occupants of the garden-seats. Perhaps, for the sake of domestic peace and quiet, it is better that I should have admired the costumes, and not become acquainted with the fascinating lineaments of the wearers thereof.

George Augustus Sala, *London Up to Date*, 1895

OPIUM DENS

"Close up, gentlemen, don't lose sight of me," says our dragoman, as we sidle in single file through a fog-choked little covered passage. Presently we reach Victoria Court, and stop outside

Eliza's door. (Eliza is the original of the woman opium-smoker in "Edwin Drood.) Our dragoman calls up the pitch-dark staircase, "You at home, Eliza?" Being answered in the affirmative, he leads the way up the narrow, how, corkscrew-like little staircase – or rather, we have to stumble up it the best way we can. In a dirty little room there is a dirty little bedstead, outside the dirty clothes on which a black-moustached, swarthy Lascar, who passes for Eliza's husband, lies rolled up in a rug. He pretends to be asleep, but now and then gives a grunt of inquiry, and Eliza answers him in his own tongue. She is a sallow-faced, carelessly-dressed woman, reclining on the other end of the bed, with her opium-pipe, lamp, &c, ready to her hand.

Some wet clothes are hung up to dry before the little fire. She is asked whether she is getting ready to go to church or chapel next day. "Ah, no," she answers in a canting whine, "that's what I can't do, but it's where I should like to go if I was prepared." When asked how she came to take to opium-smoking, she says that she can speak Hindi and Hindustani, and used to be with those that spoke them, and one would say to her, "Have a whiff," and another would say to her, "Have a whiff," and she knew no better, and so she got into the habit, and now she cannot leave it off.

In intervals between her talk she scoops out prepared opium from a little gallipot, sticks it on the needle that crosses the broad shallow bowl of her ruler-like pipe, turns the bowl to the orifice in the glass cover of her lamp, humours the pill with the spatula end of another needle to get it to kindle, and then takes a long pull, – sometimes sending back the smoke through her nostrils and her ears.

"It's very healthy, gentlemen," she says, when we remark upon its not unpleasant odour.

Richard Rowe, *Life in the London Streets*, 1881

P is for Pollution

The scientist Michael Faraday wrote a letter to *The Times* in 1855, describing the river's polluted condition, and how he used a piece of white card to test the water's opacity. The river would eventually be cleansed by Joseph Bazalgette's new system of sewers, built during the following decade.

PARKS

THERE is no park in London which, in point of fashion, at all approaches to Hyde Park. There is Victoria Park away in the eastern part of London, amid beggars and poor people, mechanics and small tradesmen – its acres have God's sky over them like those in Hyde, but never a man of *town* sets his foot there, for it is too vulgar, too plebeian ground! Its grass is just as green and soft as that in wealthier quarters – and the poor bless God for it – but splendid carriages are never to be seen in it, nor people of wealth and respectable standing in society, reckoning after the English manner.

St. Jame's Park is beautiful, but it is not fitted for carriages like Hyde, and Fashion never deigns to walk in town during the season.

Green Park spreads out in front of Piccadilly, and is pleasant, but it has no Serpentine river to add to its beauty. It is a famous place for the children to romp in, and scream, and dance, and play wild sports. Poor men's children are fond of coming there to catch a sight of the blue skies, and to play in the free breezes which sweep across it. The stomachs of the élite are altogether too delicate to bear the sight of these ragged and dirty-faced children – if they were as delicate in the treatment of their consciences, it would be better for themselves and the world lying in misery about them.

Regent's Park is of greater extent than any other in the Metropolis It has its Botanical and Zoological Gardens, its Hippopotamus, and in fact all manner of wild beasts, so that the million go there, not for fresh air, or to exhibit themselves, but to see its curious sights, just as they flock to the National Gallery, or the Museum.

The only park where people may be said to go to see, and be seen, is Hyde Park, and as it is the only fashionable one in London ...

David W. Bartlett, *London by Day and Night*, 1852

PARTY ENTERTAINERS

ENTERTAINMENTS OF EVERY DESCRIPTION, SUITABLE FOR

At Homes, Balls, Banquets, Bazaars, Concerts, Conversaziones, Evening, Garden or Juvenile Parties; Institutes; Receptions, School Treats, &c., &c. . . . . .

45 Comic Variety Entertainment, including White Magic, Juggling, Balancing, and Comic Sketch by two Grotesques in Costume . . . . .1 hour

46 Ditto, with addition of Ventriloquism, Comic Blondin Donkey, Sketch, three or four performers . . . . . .1½ hours

47 Variety Entertainment, including Modern Magic and Ventriloquism, Juggling, Balancing, and Educated Dog; two Musical Grotesques, four performers, including Pianoforte Accompanist . . . . .2 hours

48 Juggling, Balancing, &c. .½hour

49 Comic Conjuror, Juggler, and Balancer, in Costume or Evening Dress . . . . ¾hour

50 Comic Conjuror, Juggler, and Balancer, in Costume or Evening Dress 1hour

51 Ditto, Two performers, introducing Funny Musical Sketch . . . . .1 hour

52 Ditto, with Comic Nigger, three performers 1½hours

53 Hand Shadowist (Comical Shadow Pantomime) combined with Juggling and Mimicry, with Piano-forte Accompanist 1hour

54 Father Christmas, in propria persona, by Harry Phillips, with Conjuring and Characteristic Songs, and carrying an immense Plum Pudding, from which to distribute Presents. Pianoforte Accompanist. Two performers . . . . .¾hour

55 Comic Nigger with Banjo .... ½hour

56 Comic Nigger with Banjo, two performances, half-an-hour each. First part, White as Musical Clown, Second half as Negro Comedian.

57 Ditto ditto by two clever performers, very refined ....
....1 hour

58 Two Musical Clowns, playing eccentric instruments .....
....1 hour

59 Harry Phillips' Original Komical Kidgets, or Living Marionettes, from the Crystal Palace, Royal Aquarium, &c. The largest and most elaborate fit-up of its kind. Preceded by Juggling, Conjuring, &c. Four performers, including Pianist, suitable for Drawing-room or Hall
....................................1½hours

60 Troupe of Negro Minstrels, any number from three upwards

61 The Original Royal Campanologists (Hand-bell Ringers and Glee Singers, Vocal Quartette), five performers, including Pianoforte Accompanist . . . 2hours

62 Hand-bell Soloist (silver bells) . . . ½hour

63 Telepathist (Thought reading, extraordinary) without contact, very clever, by Mr. Carl B. King

64 Troupe of Eight Performing Dogs, Boxing Kangaroo and Goat, performed before Royalty, exceedingly clever
..................................about ¾hour

65 Ditto ditto with two performing ponies

66 Small troupe of performing dogs

Civil Service Supply Association Price List, 1900

PARTY GAMES

The dark evenings of winter and early spring call into request games for round parties, and we shall devote the present paper to some of these. To commence with a very simple one, we will describe a game of German origin, known as

The Ball of Wool- The party are seated round a table, from which the cloth must be drawn. A little wool is rolled up into the form of a ball, and placed in the middle of the table. The company then commence to blow upon it, each one trying to drive it away from his own direction, and the object of all being to blow it off; so that the person by whose right side it falls may pay a forfeit. The longer the ball is kept on the table by the opposing puffs of the surrounding party, the more amusing the game becomes, as the distended cheeks and zealous exertions of the players afford mirth to lookers-on as well as to themselves. ...

The Messenger- The party are seated in line, or round the sides of the room, and some one previously appointed enters with the message, "My master sends me to you, madam," or "sir," as the case may be, directed to any individual he may select at his option. " What for?" is the natural inquiry. "To do as I do;" and with this the messenger commences to perform some antic, which the lady or gentleman must imitate – say he wags his head from side to side, or taps with one foot incessantly on the floor. The person whose duty it is to obey commands his neighbour to the right or to the left to "Do as I do," also and so on until the whole company are in motion, when the messenger leaves the room, re-entering it with fresh injunctions. While the messenger is in the room he must see his master's will obeyed, and no one must stop from the movement without suffering a forfeit. The messenger should be some one ingenious in making the antics ludicrous, and yet kept within moderate bounds, and the game will not fail to produce shouts of laughter.

Cassell's Household Guide, c.1880

The following are examples of the forfeits which may be allotted . . .

Say Half-a-dozen Flattering Things to a Lady, without using the Letter l. This may be done by such phrases as "You are pretty," "You are entertaining, &c.," but such words as graceful, beautiful, and charitable are, of course, inadmissible.

To try the Cold Water Cure, the gentleman is first blindfolded, and then a tumbler filled with cold water, and a teaspoon, are produced. Not to be too hard upon him, he is allowed to take a seat. Each member of the company is then privileged to give him a spoonful; but if he can guess at any time the name of the person who is "curing" him, he is at once released from a further infliction of the remedy.

To play the Learned Pig. To do this, the gentleman must first put himself as nearly as possible in the attitude of one. He must go on all fours, and he is then to answer questions that may be put to him either by the company or by somebody who may volunteer as his master, to show his attainments. The questions asked are something like the following: "Show us the most agreeable person in the company," or, "the most charming," "the greatest flirt," &c. After each question, the victim is to proceed to any one whom he may select and signify his choice by a grunt. The learning as well as the docility of a pig has its limits, and the game must, therefore, not be prolonged too far.

Cassell's Household Guide, c.1880

PATTERERS
The street-sellers of stationery, literature, and the fine arts, however, differ from all before treated of in the general, though far from universal, education of the sect. They constitute

principally the class of street-orators, known in these days as "patterers," and formerly termed "mountebanks," – people who, in the words of Strutt, strive to "help off their wares by pompous speeches, in which little regard is paid either to truth or propriety." To patter, is a slang term, meaning to speak. To indulge in this kind of oral puffery, of course, requires a certain exercise of the intellect, and it is the consciousness of their mental superiority which makes the patterers look down upon the costermongers as an inferior body, with whom they object either to be classed or to associate.

Patterer Slang

Word.	*Meaning.*
Crabshells	Shoes
Kite	Paper
Nests	Varieties
Sticky	Wax
Toff	Gentleman
Burerk	Lady
Camister	Minister
Crocus	Doctor
Bluff	An excuse
Balamy	Insane
Mill Tag	A shirt
Smeesh	A shift
Hay-bag	A woman
Doxy	A wife
Flam	A lie
Teviss	A shilling
Bull	A crown
Flag	An apron

Henry Mayhew, *London Labour and the London Poor*, 1851

PAVING

In the *New York Sun* of August 18th, some interesting facts are given regarding pavements in London, by its correspondent in that city. He says that until 1839 the road ways of the London streets were paved almost exclusively with granite blocks. Macadam was indeed somewhat used then, and is even now employed to some extent, but it was not durable enough and too soon wore into holes. Its defect was, that it did not sufficiently resist heavy traffic. Granite blocks are durable, but the noise made by vehicles passing over them is almost deafening. In 1839, the first wood pavement was laid in the Old Bailey, which runs past Newgate Prison, and this was soon followed by many others. As then made, however, these pavements were not at all satisfactory, and when they wore out they were mostly replaced by granite. Wood pavement for heavy traffic was, in those early experiments, a sign of failure. Stone again had the field undisputed.

In May 1869, Threadneedle street was paved with compressed asphalt by the Val de Travers Company. Several other varieties of asphalt pavement have been tried, but the Val de Travers is the only one that has come into extensive use. It is as smooth as marble slabs and not noisy, and the only objection to it comes from horse owners, members of the Society for the Prevention of Cruelty to Animals, and the horses themselves. Unfortunately, the horses cannot vote, or the asphalt would all be removed at once. The general public, who like to travel on a smooth roadway and object to noise, are very well suited with it.

At present the greater part of the streets are still paved with granite blocks. The early stone pavements were of large square blocks of uniform size, laid in rows across the street. The stone now used is oblong and between three and four inches thick. It is an improvement on the old stone pavement. The fashionable quarter of the West End, where traffic is not so trying, uses mostly macadamized roadways, and desires nothing better. In Central London, where traffic is heavy, there have been most frequent changes, and here improved wood and asphalt prevail to a considerable extent. The streets radiating from the Bank of England are nearly all asphalted.

To macadam the only objection is that it does not resist heavy traffic well enough. But where traffic is light it is likely to be the favorite road. Stone is so noisy that the more fashionable quarters reject its use altogether, and no locality uses it except under protest. Almost any change is welcome. But its cheapness and durability appeal strongly to the pockets of the tax-payers, and this is a very cogent argument.

Manufacturer and Builder, 1878

PAWNBROKERS

The pawnbroker's shop is situated near Drury-Lane, at the corner of a court, which affords a side entrance for the accommodation of such customers as may be desirous of avoiding the observation of the passers-by, or the chance of recognition in the public street. It is a low, dirty-looking, dusty shop, the door of which stands always doubtfully, a little way open: half inviting, half repelling the hesitating visitor, who, if he be as yet uninitiated, examines one of the old garnet brooches in the window for a minute or two with affected eagerness, as if he contemplated making a purchase; and then looking cautiously round to ascertain that no one watches him, hastily slinks in: the door closing of itself after him, to just its former width. The shop front and the window-frames bear evident marks of having been once painted; but, what the colour was originally, or at what date it was probably laid on, are at this remote period questions which may be asked, but cannot be answered. Tradition states that the transparency in the front door, which displays at night three red balls on a blue ground, once bore also, inscribed in graceful waves, the words 'Money advanced on plate, jewels, wearing apparel, and every description of property,' but a few illegible hieroglyphics are all that now remain to attest the fact. The plate and jewels would seem to have disappeared, together with the announcement, for the articles of stock, which are displayed in some profusion in the window, do not include any very valuable luxuries of either kind. A few old china cups; some modern vases, adorned with paltry paintings of three Spanish cavaliers playing three Spanish guitars; or a party of boors carousing: each boor with one leg painfully elevated in the air, by way of expressing his perfect freedom and gaiety; several sets of chessmen, two or three flutes, a few fiddles, a round-eyed portrait staring in astonishment from a very dark ground; some gaudily-bound prayer-books and testaments, two rows of silver watches quite as clumsy and almost as large as Ferguson's first; numerous old-fashioned table and tea spoons, displayed, fan-like, in half-dozens; strings of coral with great broad gilt snaps; cards of rings and brooches, fastened and labelled separately, like the insects in the British Museum; cheap silver penholders and snuff-boxes, with a masonic star, complete the jewellery department; while five or six beds in smeary clouded ticks, strings of blankets and sheets, silk and cotton handkerchiefs, and wearing apparel of every description, form the more useful, though even less ornamental, part, of the articles exposed for sale. An extensive collection of planes, chisels, saws, and other carpenters' tools, which have been pledged, and never redeemed, form the foreground of the picture; while the large frames full of ticketed bundles, which are dimly seen through the dirty casement up-stairs – the squalid neighbourhood – the adjoining houses, straggling, shrunken, and rotten, with one or two filthy, unwholesome-looking heads thrust out of every window, and old red pans and stunted plants exposed on the tottering parapets, to the manifest hazard of the heads of the passers-by – the noisy men loitering under the archway at the corner of the court, or about the gin-shop next door – and their wives patiently standing on the curb-stone, with large baskets of cheap vegetables slung round them for sale, are its immediate auxiliaries.

If the outside of the pawnbroker's shop be calculated to attract the attention, or excite the interest, of the speculative pedestrian, its interior cannot fail to produce the same effect in an increased degree. The front door, which we have before noticed, opens into the common shop, which is the resort of all those customers whose habitual acquaintance with such scenes renders them indifferent to the observation of their companions in poverty. The side door opens into a small passage from which some half-dozen doors (which may be secured on the inside by bolts) open into a corresponding number of little dens, or closets, which face the counter. Here, the more timid or respectable portion of the crowd shroud themselves from the notice of the remainder, and patiently wait until the gentleman behind the counter, with the curly black hair, diamond ring, and double silver watch-guard, shall feel disposed to favour them with his notice – a consummation which depends considerably on the temper of the aforesaid gentleman for the time being.

Charles Dickens, *Sketches by Boz*, 1836

PEDESTRIANISM

Some years since, the feat of walking one thousand miles in one thousand hours was considered next to an impossibility; but here we have to record the wonder doubled. This has been accomplished on the Surrey Cricket-ground, Kennington Oval, by Richard Manks, whose feats of walking present instances of the capability and endurance of the human frame altogether unparalleled. Manks commenced this feat on Friday, the 26th of last September; but, being suddenly attacked with diarrhoea, he was compelled to give up on the Monday following, after having walked 129 miles. His surgeon ordered Manks to rest for a time to recruit his health and strength. This the pedestrian reluctantly yielded to, and for a fortnight he remained under medical treatment. On Friday the 10th October, he re-commenced his great task, starting for the first mile at four o'clock in the afternoon . . . the 1000th mile was gone over in 7 min. 49 sec., in the presence of upwards of 3000 spectators, besides a great crowd outside the Oval.

To perform every 100 miles, 50 hours were required, including rest, meats, change of clothing, ablution, &c. The average rate of walking for the first 300 miles was about 14 minutes per mile, leaving about 16 minutes only for rest &c. The next 300 miles took 16 minutes on an average for a mile, leaving less than 14 minutes for sleep, &c. The third 300 miles averaged 16 min. 30 sec. per mile, allowing about 13 minutes respite between each mile; and up to the finish about the same time per mile was taken. . . .

Manks's appetite remained good, and his general health excellent: ten minutes sufficed to refresh him at any one time. He partook of animal and other nourishing food eight or ten times during the twenty-four hours; including game and poultry, roast beef and steaks, mutton, and chops &c.; strong beef tea he drank in considerable quantities. Old ale was his favourite beverage; and he took tea with brandy in it during the night.

Manks has been heard to declare that never again will he attempt such a frightful feat. At half-past two o'clock on Friday morning he refused to rise, cried like a child, and said to the timekeeper, "I shall walk no more," asking, "Do you want to kill me?" But he at length was induced to persevere unto the finish.

Illustrated London News, 1851

PEDESTRIANS

The necessity of expeditious and cheap locomotion in the streets of London has called forth a variety of methods of travelling. The cheapest, simplest, oldest, and most natural of them is walking. In the narrow and crowded streets of the City, where conveyances make but little progress, this method is certainly the safest, and, withal, the most expeditious. Strangers in London are not fond of walking, they are bewildered by the crowd, and frightened at the crossings; they complain of the brutal conduct of the English, who elbow their way along the pavement without considering that people who hurry on, on some important business or other, cannot possibly stop to discuss each kick or push they give or receive. A Londoner jostles you in the street, without ever dreaming of asking your pardon; he will run against you, and make you revolve on your own axis, without so much as looking round to see how you feel after the shock; he will put his foot upon a lady's foot or dress, exactly as if such foot or dress were integral parts of the pavement, which ought to be trodden upon; but if he runs you down, if he breaks your ribs, or knocks out your front teeth, he will show some slight compunction, and as he hurries off, the Londoner has actually been known to turn back and beg your pardon.

Of course all this is very unpleasant to the stranger, and the more delicate among the English themselves do not like it. None but men of business care to walk through the City at business hours; but if, either from choice or necessity, you find your way into those crowded quarters, you had better walk with your eyes wide open. Don't stop on the pavement, move on as fast you can, and do as the others do, that is to say, struggle on as best you may, and push forward without any false modesty. The passengers in London streets are hardened; they give and receive kicks and pushes with equal equanimity.

Much less excusable is the kicking and pushing of the English public at their theatres, museums, railway stations, and other places of public resort. Nothing but an introduction to every individual man and woman in the three kingdoms will save you from being, on such occasions, pushed back by them. You have not been introduced to them; you are a stranger to them, and there is no reason why they should consult your convenience.

Max Schlesinger, *Saunterings in and about London*, 1853

PENNY DREADFULS

Before me I have twelve penny packets of the poison, gathered at random out of a choice of at least twice as many offered me at the little shop – one of a thousand – devoted to its propagation. It was not on account of their unpromising titles that the remaining pen'orths of poison were not secured. There was "The Boy Bandit," "The Black Monk's Curse," "Blueskin," "Claude Duval, the Dashing Highwayman," "The Vampire's Bride," "The Boy Jockey," "The Wild Boys of London," and many more, of the names of which I have not a distinct recollection. The dozen I received in return for my shilling are entitled, "The Boy King of the Highwaymen," "The Skeleton Crew," "Roving Jack, the Pirate Hunter," "Tyburn Dick," "Spring Heel'd Jack," "Admiral Tom, the King of the Boy Buccaneers," "Starlight Nell, "Hounslow Heath, or the Moonlight Riders," "Red Wolf, the Pirate," "The Knight of the Road," "The Adventures of an Actress," and "The Pretty Girls of London."

Nasty-feeling, nasty-looking packets are every one of them, and, considering the virulent nature of their contents, their most admirable feature is their extremely limited size. Satisfactory as this may be from one point of view, however, it is woefully significant of the irresistibly seductive nature of the bane with which each shabby little square of paper is spread. ... They are enabled to hold out strong inducements to the needy shopkeepers of poor neighbourhoods. The ordinary discount to the trade on ordinary publications is 25 per cent., but the worthy publishers of "Alone in the Pirates' Lair" and "The Skeleton Crew" can afford to allow double that, and more. Wholesale you may buy the precious pen'orths at the rate of fivepence a dozen, and there is no risk to the dealer, since all unsold copies from last week are changed for a similar number of the day's date. This is the lure that tempts the tobacconist and the sweetstuff vender and the keeper of the small chandlery, and induces these worthy tradesmen to give to this pernicious, though profitable, class of goods all the publicity of which their shop window is capable.

James Greenwood, *The Wilds of London*, 1874

'I tell you what,' said the woman, I have thought of an excellent plan to make Fanny useful.'

'Well, Polly, and what's that?' demanded the man.

'Why,' resumed his wife, 'I've been thinking that Harry will soon be of use to you in your line. He'll be so handy to shove through a window, or to sneak down a area and hide himself all day in a cellar to open the door at night – or a thousand things.'

'In course he will,' said Bill, with an approving nod.

'Well, but there's Fanny. What good can she do for us for years to come? She won't beg – I know she won't. Now I've a great mind to do someot that will make her beg – and beg too in spite of herself.'

'What do you mean?'

'Why, doing that to her which will put her at our mercy, and render her an object of such interest that the people must give her money.'

'But how?' said Bill, impatiently.

'By putting her eyes out,' returned the woman. Her husband was a robber – yes, a murderer: but he started when this proposal met his ear. 'There's nothin' like a blind child to excite compassion,' added the woman. 'I know it for a fact,' she continued. 'There's old Kate Betts, who got all her money by travelling about the country with two blind girls: and she made 'em blind herself too – and that has put the idea into my head.'

'And how did she do it?' asked the man.

'She covered the eyes with cockle-shells, the eye-lids being open: and in each shell there was a black beetle. A bandage tied tight round the head, kept the shells in their place: and the shells kept the eyelids open. In a few days the eyes got blind, and the pupils had a dull white appearance.'

'And you're serious, are you?' demanded the man,

'Ah! why not?' pursued the female; 'one must make one's children useful. So, if you don't mind, I'll send Harry out alone tomorrow morning and keep Fanny at home. The moment the boy's out of the way, I'll try my hand at Kate Betts's plan.'

George Reynolds, *The Mysteries of London*, 1844

PENNY GAFFS

We went next into a "penny gaff." Two floors of a house had been knocked into one to form the concert-room. Rough wooden seats, rising at the end of the room nearest the door like a flower-stand, with a villanously dark, dirty, narrow, and malodorous passage behind the same, were devoted to those disposed to pay only a penny for their entertainment. Two-pence was charged for a seat in the more aristocratic gallery, or perhaps I ought to call it "balcony-stalls." The accommodation and the audience seemed precisely of the same stamp in both; the latter consisting chiefly of boys of from ten to sixteen, some of whom favoured my companion with a furtive scowl from beneath their heavy, low-pitched brows. At the farther end of the room was a tiny, tawdry stage, like that of a cheap child's theatre slightly magnified, and on it a tall woman, who looked quite a giantess in that narrow space, was singing something. Probably it was too sentimental, or not highly flavoured enough, for the taste of her hearers, for they sat as glumly silent, and as puzzled-looking as jurymen listening to "points of law" of which they can make neither head nor tail. A drearier specimen of "enjoyment" never witnessed. As we went out, we were met by the male "star" of the establishment with a sheaf of benefit-tickets in his hand; which he pressed us to purchase on the ground that he was going to sing on his benefit night "The Eel-pie Shop" – I think he added "as performed before His Royal Highness."

Richard Rowe, *Life in the London Streets,* 1881

A notice was here posted, over the canvass door leading into the theatre, to the effect that "Ladies and Gentlemen to the front places must pay Twopence."

The visitors, with a few exceptions, were all boys and girls, whose ages seemed to vary from eight to twenty years. Some of the girls – though their figures showed them to be mere children – were dressed in showy cotton-velvet polkas, and wore dowdy feathers in their crushed bonnets. They stood laughing and joking with the lads, in an unconcerned, impudent manner, that was almost appalling. Some of them, when tired of waiting, chose their partners, and commenced dancing grotesquely, to the admiration of the lookers-on, who expressed their approbation in obscene terms, that, far from disgusting the poor little women, were received as compliments, and acknowledged with smiles and coarse repartees. The boys clustered together, smoking their pipes, and laughing at each other's anecdotes, or else jingling halfpence in time with the tune, while they whistled an accompaniment to it. Presently one of the performers, with a gilt crown on his well greased locks, descended from the staircase, his fleshings covered by a dingy dressing-gown, and mixed with the mob, shaking hands with old acquaintances. The "comic singer," too, made his appearance among the throng – the huge bow to his cravat, which nearly covered his waistcoat, and the red end to his nose, exciting neither merriment nor surprise.

To discover the kind of entertainment, a lad near me and my companion was asked "if there was any flash dancing." With a knowing wink the boy answered, "Lots! show their legs and all, prime!"

Henry Mayhew, *London Labour and the London Poor*, 1851

PHOTOGRAPHERS

DAGUERREOTYPE OR PHOTOGRAPHIC PORTAITS

PORTRAITS by Mr. CLAUDET'S INSTANTANEOUS PROCESS under the Patronage of her Majesty, are taken daily at the ADELAIDE GALLERY, LOWTHER ARCADE, STRAND. The Sitting generally occupies less than One Second, by which faithful and pleasing Likenesses are obtained, with backgrounds, the patented invention of Mr. Claudet, representing Landscapes, the Interior of a Library, &c. &c.

Price of a Single Portrait, usual size, One Guinea. Portraits and Groups are also taken on Plates of an enlarged size, and for Lockets or Broaches as small as may be required.

advertisement from *The Builder*, 1842

LIKENESSES.
Have no more bad Portraits!
CAUTION!!!

advertisement, 1857

The parks, commons, gardens, in fact all pleasure-grounds, are
overrun with eager caterers to the public. They offer for sale
objects of the most modest description; but on such occasions the

worst oranges, suspicious sweets, faded flowers, and the dingiest of ornaments, find comparatively speaking a ready sale. Clapham Common is of course one of the most accessible rendezvous for these itinerant vendors but certain industries are more particularly successful on this spot. The place is especially attractive to itinerant photographers. During the season they flock to the Common; though the demand for the class of portrait they produce is of so constant a character, that one photographer at least has found it worth his while to remain in the neighbourhood even during the winter. This faithful frequenter of Clapham Common will be recognized in the accompanying illustration, and he is there represented engaged with the class of subject which generally proves most profitable. Nurses with babies and perambulators are easily lured within the charmed focus of the camera. They are particularly fond of taking home to their mistresses a photograph of the child entrusted to their care; and the portrait rarely fails to excite the interest of the parents. Nor does the matter rest here. The parents are often so satisfied that the nurse is commissioned to obtain one or more likenesses on her next visit to the common. Thus practically she becomes an advertising medium, and the photographer generally relies on receiving more orders when he has once secured the custom of a nurse-girl. It need scarcely be remarked that at Clapham Common there are not only a large number of nurses and children, but these are generally of a class which can well afford the shilling charged for taking their likeness.

Success depends, however, more on the manners than on the skill of the photographer. Many practised hands, who have highly distinguished themselves in the studio, when the work is brought to them, are altogether unable to earn a living when they take their stand in the open air. They have not the necessary impudence to accost all who pass by, they have no tact or diplomacy, they are unable to modify the style of their language to suit the individual they may happen to meet, and they consequently rarely induce any one to submit to the painful ordeal of having a portrait taken. On the other hand, men who are far less skilled in the art often obtain extensive custom by the sheer force of persuasion. Example, also, is contagious, and if in a throng of people, one person ventures to step forward, others soon follow his example, and this renders the large gathering on holidays doubly advantageous. Thus, I know of one photographer, who obtained on Clapham Common no less than thirty-six shillings in the course of one hour.

J.Thomson and Adolphe Smith, *Street Life in London*, 1877

PICKING OAKUM, PUNISHMENT OF

A large square lobby, in appearance like a wheelwright's shed, in which coils of rope occupy some high shelves, and where men, standing at wooden blocks, are cutting old cable into chunks with small hatchets, leads to the series of rooms in which the prisoners are engaged in that most common employment for vagrants or incorrigible paupers and convicted felons – picking oakum.

The hard pieces of junk are placed in a scale and weighed before being consigned to the basket in which they are conveyed to the oakum rooms, the quantity which each prisoner has to pick daily, varying according to his sentence, that is to say, whether it be to hard labour or only to common imprisonment; the former condemning him to pick from three to six pounds a day, in proportion to the hardness and tarriness of the junk, the latter to pick only two pounds a day. Notwithstanding that the carpenters', coopers', smiths', and other shops are busy, that the prison work in the way of plastering, painting, shoemaking, and tailoring, is done by convicts, and that the very tin porringers in which the food is dispensed are made by the prison tinsmiths, oakum picking is the busiest employment in the place, since the demand for oakum is insatiable. It is a trade soon learnt, and requires but little space for its execution. There are three oakum rooms, one for those imprisoned for misdemeanour and two in the felons' prison, and in all of these the men sit about two feet apart, on low forms, each picker with a heap of junk cut in pieces of a few inches long beside him, and with a small iron hook strapped just above his knee. As each length of rope is taken from the heap it is untwisted into separate strands, which are rolled backward and forward on the knee, or rubbed briskly under the iron hook, after which the fibre is easily picked into a fluffy ball, which goes to the heap of oakum on the right hand of the operator.

As the prisoners sit in these large rooms, twisting, rolling, rubbing, until their soft, thievish fingers grow red and sore, and afterwards hard by their contact with those stiff chunks of tarry hemp, the expression is so varied that a careful observer might trace a whole theory of physiognomy by a half-hour's stay. Many of the prisoners return the gaze of the visitor with an impudent look of careless or mocking bravado, others scowl darkly as they bend over their work, and some go stolidly on without changing a muscle of their faces . . .

Thomas Archer, *The Pauper, The Thief and The Convict*, 1865

PICKPOCKETS
THE ORANGE BOY

Sir, – As *The Times* is always open for the insertion of any remarks likely to caution the unwary or to put the unsuspecting on their guard against the numerous thefts and robberies committed daily in the streets of London, I am induced to ask you to insert a case which happened on Saturday last, and which I trust may serve as a warning to those of your lady readers who still carry purses in their pockets.

A young lady (and, as the police reports add,) of very prepossessing appearance, a relation of the narrator's, was walking between 12 and 1 o'clock with another young lady, a friend of hers, in Albany-street, where she resides, when she was accosted by a boy about 11 years of age, who asked her in the most beseeching tones "to buy a few oranges of a poor orphan who hadn't a bit of bread to eat." She told him to go away, but he kept alongside, imploring assistance, and making some cutting remarks about "the ingratitude of the world in general and of young ladies in particular." As his manner became very troublesome the lady threatened to give him in charge of a policeman, and looked down every area to find one; but there was not one even there, and the boy kept up his sweet discourse and slight pushes alternately (the latter with the basket on which he carried his oranges), until the lady reached her own door-step. It then occurred to her that in the boy's ardour to sell his oranges he might have taken her purse; her friend thought so too. A trembling hand was inserted into the pocket; the purse was gone, and so was the lady's happiness. She flew after the thief, who, knowing young ladies were not made for running, coolly deposited his basket on a door-step a little way off and ran away whistling. This brave young lady ran also, shouting "Stop thief! stop thief!" (but then young ladies are not made for shouting, God forbid!) and she looked in the fond hope that a policeman might be found. But no such luck, the culprit got safely off with the purse and its contents; and no kind passer by tried to help the young lady, who was thus shamefully duped and robbed. Ladies, young and old, never carry your purses in your pockets; beware of canting beggars, and beggars of all sorts, that infest the streets; and, above all, keep a watchful eye about you and give the widest possible berth to THE ORANGE BOY.

letter to *The Times*, 1850

PLEASURE GARDENS

THE FETE FOR THE MILLION!

ROYAL GARDENS, CREMORNE.

ELLIS'S NIGHT,

Monday, July 29th 1861.

Be it remembered, MR. JAMES ELLIS was the Original Projector of these delightful Gardens, which now stand confessedly the noblest among all the public places of resort in England, on the Continent, or in any part of the habitable world.

THE DAY AND NIGHT

Entertainments on this occasion will have the additional aid of many novelties too numerous to be specified in the programme, but particular attention is called to the following important arrangements. The brilliant, matchless, and unparalleled performances of

THE WONDROUS LEOTARD.

MR. D'ALBERTE,

The English Rope-Walker, and Blondin's Challenger, who will go through his extra ordinary and incredible performances on the

ILLUMINATED ROPE

(By the kind permission of E. Macnamara, Esq., of the Royal Pavilion Gardens, North Woolwich).

MISS HARRIET COVENEY

(By the same kind permission) will appear in her novel Characteristic Entertainment, consisting of New and Original Songs, written expressly for her by W. BROUGH, ESQ.

THE INSTRUMENTAL CONCERT,

Al Fresco, by the Great Cremorne Band, M. RIVIERE, Conductor, will be followed by

A VOCAL CONCERT.

The New Grand Ballet Pantomime, in Six Tableaux, entitled

FORTUNATUS.

Performance of MR. HENRY COOKE's celebrated Circus Troupe of

EDUCATED DOGS AND MONKEYS.

The Celebrated Company of SWISS FEMALE SINGERS.

Grand Equestrian Performances in the Great

CIRQUE ORIENTAL!

SIGNOR BUONO CORE,

The Italian Salamander, or Fire King.

GRAND DISPLAY OF FIREWORKS!

ONE SHILLING.

advertisement, 1861

The gardens are crowded; dense masses are congregated around a sort of open temple, which at Vauxhall stands in lieu of a music-room. The first part of the performance is just over; and a lady, whose voice is rather the worse for wear, and who defies the cool of the evening with bare shoulders and arms, is in the act of being encored. She is delighted, and so are the audience. Many years ago this spot witnessed the performances of Grisi, Rubini, Lablache, and other first-class musical celebrities.

The crowd promenade these gardens in all directions. In the background is a gloomy avenue of trees, where loving couples walk, and where the night-air is tinged with the hue of romance. Even the bubbling of a fountain may be heard in the distance. We go in search of the sound; but, alas, we witness nothing save the triumph of the insane activity of the illuminator. A tiny rivulet forces its way through the grass; it is not deep enough to drown a herring, yet it is wide enough and babbling enough to impart an idyllic character to the scene. But how has this interesting little water-course fared under the hands of the illuminator? The wretch has studded its banks with rows of long arrow-headed gas-lights. Not satisfied with lighting up the trees, and walls, and dining-saloons, he must needs meddle with this lilliputian piece of water also. ...

Following the rivulet, we reach the bank of a gas-lit pond, with a gigantic Neptune and eight white sea-horses. To the left of the god opens another gloomy avenue, which leads us straightway to Fate, to the hermit, and the temple of Pythia, who, in the guise of a gipsy, reclining on straw under a straw-roofed shed, with a stable lanthorn at her side, is in the habit of reading the most brilliant Future on the palm of your hand, for the ridiculously low price of sixpence only. This is specially English; no house without its fortifications—no open-air amusements without gipsies. The prophetess of Vauxhall is by no means a person of repulsive appearance. You admire in her a comely brown daughter of Israel, with black hair and dark eyes; it is very agreeable to listen to her expounding your fate.

Max Schlesinger, *Saunterings in and about London*, 1853

POLICE

The course to be adopted when a person wishes to become a member of the metropolitan police force, is sufficiently easy and simple. He has only to present a petition to the commissioners, accompanied with a certificate as to good character from two respectable householders in the parish in which he resides. Inquiry is then made relative to the parties signing the certificate; and it being found that they are respectable men, whose testimony as to the applicant's character may be relied on, his name is put on the list of eligible candidates for the situation whenever a vacancy shall occur. I need scarcely say that, before appointment, the party is examined by a surgeon, to see that he suffers under no physical defect which would prevent the efficient discharge of his duties. It is also requisite that he should be under thirty-five years of age, and that he be five feet eight inches in height. The average time which an applicant has to wait, after his name has been inserted in the list of persons eligible to the office, is about eight weeks. Should, however, a party deem it an object to get appointed with the utmost practicable expedition, he may succeed in the short space of ten or twelve days, by getting some personal friend of either of the commissioners to use his influence on the applicant's behalf. The usual form of a petition and certificates from rate-payers, and so forth, are dispensed with in such cases.

James Grant, *Sketches in London*, 1838

The old watchmen, immediate precursors of the new police, had been called Charlies, and the modern force was already familiarly known by names still current, Robert, Bobby, Peeler and Copper. The first three appellations were derived from Sir Robert Peel, who had conducted the Police Bill of 1830 through Parliament; the fourth from the slang verb "to cop," i.e. to catch. In addition, he was sometimes called a Bluebottle, by way of graceful allusion to the colour scheme of his uniform; but this, I fancy, has not survived. Yet another name was "Slop," probably purely slang.

The originator of the idea of the new police was not, however, Sir Robert Peel at all, but Vincent George Dowling, editor of the sporting newspaper *Bell's Life in London*, who had suggested and advocated it years before. Strange freak that caused a rebirth of law and order to proceed from a spokesman of a reputedly lawless community! V.G.D. certainly modified life in London by this reform. Had not that erring jade, popular opinion, wrongfully acclaimed Peel as the author, the new enemies of turbulence would probably have been baptized Georges or Dowlers.

The new policeman wore a tall "pot hat," built strongly of varnished leather and warranted to withstand all sorts of assaults and batteries; a brass-buttoned, bob-tailed, stiff-collared coat, and large-legged trousers, all dark blue, although I seem to have some recollection of white unmentionables for summer wear. A black-varnished belt with truncheon, lamp, and rattle completed the awe-inspiring getup, which in winter was concealed under a long overcoat. The rattle, an inheritance from the old Charlies replaced, in recent times, by a whistle, was a noise-creating device consisting of a tongue pressed by a spring against a wooden ratchet-wheel which when swung round by means of a handle gave out an ear-splitting but distinctive and penetrating sound. It told constables near and far that a comrade needed help. In the Police Court Records of the 1850*s* and 1860*s* the expression "the policeman sprung his rattle," or "proceeded to spring his rattle" constantly occurred.

Alfred Rosling-Bennett, *London and
Londoners in the 1850s and 1860s*, 1924

SPECIAL DUTIES.—The following questions have also been submitted to the Metropolitan Police Department, and have received the annexed replies:

Whether when application is made at a station for a married constable to take charge of an empty—furnished—house, any and what responsibility is undertaken by the department, and what are the general terms and conditions on which such applications are entertained?

Police sergeants or constables are permitted by the commissioner to take charge of unoccupied furnished houses on the recommendation of the superintendent of the division, provided they have undivided care; that no servants remain; and that there are no valuables or plate therein. No responsibility whatever is undertaken by the police department. There are no other set terms or conditions. If the man's wife is employed to keep the house clean, it becomes a matter of arrangement between the parties. Sergeants and constables are allowed by the divisional superintendents to occupy unfurnished houses, or houses that have not been inhabited, provided they are reported, on inspection, as not likely to be prejudicial to the health of the officer.

Whether the police on ordinary night duty are allowed to be made available for calling private individuals in time for early trains, &c.?

The police are not only allowed, but are taught that they are bound to render this or any other service in their power to the inhabitants; and any neglect is considered a breach of duty, and dealt with accordingly.

Whether any arrangement is practicable—short of hiring a special constable—by which a house can safely be left empty for a few hours?

Certainly not. The custom unfortunately is a very prevalent one, notwithstanding numerous official cautions, and a large number of offences are traceable to it, as it affords every facility for thieves and housebreakers.

Charles Dickens (Jr.), *Dickens's Dictionary of London*, 1879

POLICE STATIONS

Up a paved alley into a little paved court, in which a number of helmeted, great-coated policemen are drawn up in line; and then up some old-fashioned doorsteps into the outer police-office. Its walls are tapestried with police-notices, one of them illustrated with a photograph of a "wanted" house-breaker. It contains a dock, with a height-gauge behind, and a desk at which a sergeant in uniform is writing. Opposite him is an inspector in uniform, with a ledger-like book before him, framed in a pigeon-hole in a railway booking-office-like partition. We have made a little mistake as to time, and go into an inner office to wait. Its occupants give up their stools to seat us, and, to beguile the time, bring out an assortment of handcuffs, fit them on us, and laughingly snap-to the steel bracelets; a venerable and popular clergyman, the late Dr. Guthrie, who is of the party, looks particularly droll in the "darbies."

True to his time to a minute, our dragoman arrives, but before we start we look into the station's cells. Only one is occupied. When a "bull's-eye" flashes into it, a pallid, dirty, boy of ten, curled up on a bench, tries to cover his face with the rug which is his only bed-furniture. He is "in for" stealing a pound and a half of sugar out of a van. Poor little pale-faced fellow ...

Richard Rowe, *Life in the London Streets*, 1881

The Police Station where I served has given way to a more commodious and modern building of that name. (Rebuilt 1902.) I will, however, give a brief description of the old place as far as I am able to relate. Anyone walking by the footpath through Hyde Park from the Marble Arch to the Magazine, and when about halfway, would pass on their left-hand side a quaint one-storied old brick building, with its long verandah and grass lawn, surrounded with iron rails; this was the Police Station ... so different to the uniform building we see in the streets with the familiar blue glass lamp over the door; not one out of every dozen that passed this place – non-Londoners especially - ever dreamt that it was a Police Station; but a Police Station it had been for the last forty years at least. ... About thirty of us single men resided in the old station, and, antiquated as it may have appeared outside, it was clean and comfortable inside. On entering the doorway, right and left were the Inspector's (or Enquiry) Office, Charge-room and cells respectively; passing a little further on the right, is the mess kitchen or dining-room; continuing through brings you into the library, a nice spacious room, with its full-size billiard table and well-stocked book cupboards; through another door on the left brings you into the cooking kitchen; following on leads along a passage down a few steps into the yard below, where we find the stables for the horses of the Mounted Police. This was the station I made my acquaintance with in April, 1874.

> Edward Owen, *Hyde Park, Select Narratives,*
> *Annual Event, etc, during twenty years'*
> *Police Service in Hyde Park*, 1906

POLLUTION

Various manufactories of an obnoxious kind, besides places for the collection of night soil and other offensive matters, although 30 years since they might have been considered at a sufficient distance from inhabited houses, are now, from the great extent of buildings, much too near for health and propriety, being situated as it were in the very midst of our habitations.

In my own neighbourhood, that of the East India-road, a place exists called Bow-common, which is a nuisance to all the east end of London, but more particularly to the parishes of Stepney, Bow, Bromley, Poplar, and Limehouse, in which live about 80,000 inhabitants. On this spot are manufactories of the most noxious and injurious kind, carried on by chymical compounders, as they call themselves; and amongst whom are some who manufacture ammonia from night soil, a process which deserves special notice. The soil goes under the operation of boiling, and the liquid which exudes from it is allowed to run into the common sewer, whence it emits, through the gratings in North-street and High-street, Poplar, as also in Limehouse-causeway, the most horrid stench polluting the atmosphere until it enters the river at Limekiln-dock.

What the authorities, public and local, are about, to allow such nuisances to exist, I am at a loss to guess. The said Bow-common belongs, as I am informed, to the lord of the manor; and as for building or other common purposes that would increase its value, a good title cannot, it appears, be given. The land under these circumstances is let for purposes the most offensive. In fact, advertisements have at different periods appeared, drawing attention to the eligibility of the spot for manufactures of such commodities as would be deemed nuisances in other neighbourhoods and representing that they might here be carried on with impunity.

Owing to the laxity of those who should interfere in these matters, manufacturing chymists, bone collectors and burners, patent night soil manure manufactures, night and dust men, as well as other obnoxious trades, are now establishing themselves in Mile-end and Limehouse, alongside the Regent's-canal and River Lea-cut, to the serious inconvenience of the inhabitants as to their health and to the detriment of vegetation.

Within the last two or three years a very sensible difference has been apparent in our gardens; the smells are even greater during the night than in the day, and many inhabitants in the surrounding and immediate neighbourhood of Bow-common are awakened from their sleep by a suffocating feeling arising from the stench thence when the wind sets from that quarter, and which sometimes even reaches the densely populated parish of Whitechapel.

No wonder the people complain of the impurity of the Thames water.

letter to *The Times*, 1847

Smoke is a more tangible opponent to fight against than some people think. "It will all end in smoke," is a common expression to describe something which is, after all, nothing. This is a great mistake. Smoke is not nothing: it is a something which the public find it very difficult to get rid of, - an obvious, avoidable evil, – one of our disgraces. ... The soot of the metropolitan chimneys is injurious in various ways. It injures to a certain extent the health of every one. It tinges with its duskiness the palace and the hovel: it coats and spoils the works of our painters and sculptors: it disfigures the works of architects; and it causes a large unnecessary expenditure in washing. Have we no chivalry in this practical age? Cannot the knights of the present time manage to relieve the ladies of Britain from an evil greater than were the dragons and enchantments of the times past?

There are some startling statistics on record touching the effect of London smoke: we have made some calculations of touching import to all who pay washing-bills, and which show that the damage done to clothes and furniture by our smoke is immense,- enough to astonish any one who has not thought seriously on the subject, and also enough, considering how particularly this evil presses on the female portion of the community, from the highest to the lowest, to stir up amongst us the latent spirit of chivalry already alluded to. Down with the Smoke! That is, let us never allow it to go up.

George Godwin, *London Shadows*, 1854

POLYTECHNIC INSTITUTION, THE

POLYTECHNIC INSTITUTION, (ROYAL) 309, REGENT STREET, and 5, CAVENDISH SQUARE. Incorporated 1838, for the advancement of the Arts and Practical Science, especially in connexion with Agriculture, Mining, Machinery, Manufactures, and other branches of industry. Admission to the morning and evening exhibitions, one shilling each; schools, half price. Annual subscription, one guinea. Annual subscribers of two guineas have the privilege of personally introducing a friend, or two children under twelve years of age. The collection is very miscellaneous, and will repay a visit. The articles exhibited are chiefly deposited by the inventors, or others having a pecuniary interest in them. Observe. – The Diving-bell in the Great Hall, composed of cast-iron, open at the bottom, with Beats around, and of the weight of three tons; the interior, for the divers, is lighted by openings in the crown, of thick plate glass, firmly secured by brass frames, screwed to the bell; it is suspended by a massive chain to a large swing crane, with a powerful crab, the windlass of which is grooved spirally, and the chain passes four times over it into a well beneath, to which chain is suspended the compensation weights. It is so accurately arranged, that the weight of the bell is, at all depths, counterpoised by the weights acting upon the spiral shaft. The bell is supplied with air from two powerful air-pumps, of eight-inch cylinder, conveyed by the leather hose to any depth, and is put into action several times daily. Visitors may safely descend a considerable depth into the tank, which, with the canals, holds nearly ten thousand gallons of water, and can, if required, be emptied in less than one minute. This is an interesting and instructive exhibition, worthy of a visit from every stranger in London.

Peter Cunningham, *Hand-Book of London*, 1850

Ah me! the Polytechnic, with its diving-bell, the descent in which was so pleasantly productive of imminent head-splitting; its diver, who rapped his helmet playfully with the coppers which had been thrown at him; its half-globes, brass pillars, and water-troughs so charged with electricity as nearly to dislocate the arms of those that touched them; with its microscope, wherein the infinitesimal creatures in a drop of Thames water appeared like antediluvian animals engaged in combat …

Edmund Yates, *His Recollections and Experiences*, 1885

PORNOGRAPHY

BOW-STREET – Yesterday an idler in Hungerford-market, named Forder, was charged with exposing indecent prints for sale in that locality.

It was proved by an officer in the employ of the Society for the Suppression of Vice that the prisoner was offering his filthy productions to persons of both sexes in the market, and sold one of them to witness for 1*d*., upon which he gave him into custody.

It having been proved that the prisoner was in the habit of dealing in such commodities, Mr. JARDINE committed him to hard labour for six weeks.

The Times, 1846

GUILDHALL – Yesterday Dominique Barsatti, an Italian itinerant vender of plaster casts, was brought up before Mr. Alderman HUNTER, charged with exhibiting some indecent plaster medallions.

Mr. Clarkson, the barrister, stated that he appeared to prosecute on behalf of a society which had been sometimes the object of remarks which he was sure would find no echo in that court, the Society for the Suppression of Vice. The charge was that the prisoner had been offering casts for sale that would disgust the natives of any country, and at prices calculated to suit the pockets of the uneducated and low. The magistrate would see that those who purchased them could not but be corrupted by them. The society, having heard that the prisoner was in the habit of standing in Smithfield, after dark on Saturday evenings, for the purpose of selling his abominable goods, took the necessary steps to apprehend him. He charged the prisoner with wilfully exposing to public view an indecent exhibition.

James Daniels, a newsvender, stated that he was employed by Mr. Pritchard, the secretary to the Society for the Suppression of Vice, to make a purchase of some of these medallions, Mr. Neale, the clerk to Mr. Pritchard, and a policeman accompanied him. He found the prisoner standing in Smithfield, about 8 in the evening, with a basket of medallions before him. These were all representations of Venus and other classical subjects, copies from antique models. The prisoner also had a box with him. Witness asked him if he had any fancy medallions, and he produced a large one. Witness asked him if he had any others. The prisoner produced three others. The Italian had taken him aside to look at them, but Mr. Neale and the policeman came up and looked over his shoulder. Upon seeing the nature of them, Mr. Neale gave charge of the prisoner and his whole stock. He produced the medallions the prisoner exhibited.

These fancy medallions had no pretensions to be of a classical nature, but were copies after some of the vilest French pictures for illustrating infamous books.

The Times, 1845

POST

'Sir –

I believe the inhabitants of London are under the impression that Letters posted for delivery within the metropolitan district commonly reach their destination within, at the outside, three hours of the time of postage. I myself, however, have constantly suffered with irregularities in the delivery of letters, and I have now got two instances of neglect which I should really like to have cleared up.

I posted a letter in the Gray's Inn post office on Saturday at half-past 1 o'clock, addressed to a person living close to Westminster Abbey, which was not delivered till 9 o'clock the same evening; and I posted another letter in the same post office, addressed to the same place, which was not delivered till past 4 o'clock in the afternoon. Now, Sir, why is this? If there is any good reason why letters should not be delivered in less than eight hours after their postage, let the state of the case be understood: but the belief that one can communicate with another person in two or three hours whereas in reality the time required is eight or nine, may be productive of the most disastrous consequences.

I am, Sir, your most obedient servant,

7 May,
K.

letter to *The Times*, 1881

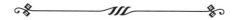

POTATO-THROWER, THE

Witness the performer who, for many years now, has been exhibiting in the streets of London, the tools of his craft being a bag of large-sized raw potatoes. The man is beyond middle age, and his head is bald, or nearly so; and all over his cranium, from the forehead to the base of his skull, are bumps unknown to the phrenologist. There are blue bumps, and bumps of a faded greenish hue, and bumps red and inflamed, and his bald sconce looks as though it had been out in a rain of spent bullets. It is not so, however; it has only been exposed to a downpour of raw potatoes. He is well known, and as soon as he puts his bag down, and divests himself of his coat, is quickly surrounded by a ring of spectators.

"Here I am again!" he says, with a grin, as he takes off his can and exposes his mottled skull; "here is the old man once more, and he's not dead yet. You'll see a treat to-day, for my taters are bigger than ever they were before, and, what's more, they're 'Yorkshire reds,' the hardest tater that grows. I shall do it once too often, there's no mistake about that; but I've served the public faithful for five years and more, and I ain't going to funk over it now. Here you are: here's a tater that weighs half a pound if it weighs an ounce. Chuck threepence in the ring, and up it goes."

And threepence is "chucked" into the ring, and up it does go – high above the houses; and the man with the mottled head folds his arms like Ajax defying the lightning, and gazes skywards, prepared for the descending missile; and presently it strikes him with a sounding thud, and is smashed into a dozen pieces with the concussion, and bespatters his visage with the pulp.

"Now chuck fourpence in," says the exhibitor, wiping his eyes, "and we'll see what we can do with a tater just as large again."

James Greenwood, *The Mysteries of Modern London*, 1883

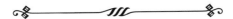

PRAMS

Sir, – I beg leave to draw the attention of the public (I was about to say police) to one of the now existing nuisances. It is that of perambulators. You cannot walk along without meeting several of those novel vehicles; and, as their name implies, they "walk through" the foot-passenger; for you must either go fairly off the pavement or suffer the more pleasant sensation of having your corns (if you are accompanied by those agreeables) run over.

If it were a truck of apples, instead of children, the police would interfere. Why not in this? Apologizing,

I remain yours respectfully,

ONE OF THE INCONVENIENCED PUBLIC

letter to *The Times*, 1855

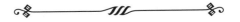

PRISONS & PRISONERS

The Cells are each 13 feet long, by 7 feet broad, and are all of them of one uniform height of 9 feet. The piece or partitions between them are 18 inches thick, and are worked with close joints, so as to preclude as much as possible the transmission of sound. The ceiling is arched, and the light is admitted by a window (a fixture), filled with strong glass, of similar form, in the back wall, and crossed by a wrought-iron bar, in the direction of its length, so so to divide it into two portions, of about 5 inches each. The engraving shows the interior of a cell; on the left is a stone water-closet pan, with a cast-iron top, acting on a hinge let into the wall. Next is a metal basin, supplied with water, to prevent the waste of which, the quantity is limited to one cubic foot, or about 6 gallons; the service-pipe from the water-trough being beat in the form of a trap, to prevent any transmission of sound. Opposite these conveniences is a strong three-legged stool, and a small table, with a shaded gas burner above it. Across the cell is slung from iron staples in the wall the pris- oner's hammock, with mattress and blankets, which are folded up and placed upon a shelf to the left of the door in the day time. Here also is a hand-spring communicating with a bell, which when pulled causes a small iron tablet, inscribed with the number of the cell in the engraving, to project from the wall, so that the officer on duty in the gallery may be apprised of the precise cell where he is required. Each cell is warmed by air, through perforated iron plates in the floor, supplied through flues, communicating with immense stoves in the basement of the wing. The foul air is carried off, and a circula- tion of atmosphere maintained by means of perforated iron plates above the door of the cell, which communicate with an immense shaft ...

The Illustrated London News, 1843

As regards the discipline enforced at Brixton prison, it may be said to consist of a preliminary stage of separation as a period of probation, and afterwards of advancement into successive stages of discipline, each having superior privileges to those which preceded it; so that whilst the preliminary stage consists of a state of comparative isolation from the world, the female prisoners in the latter stages of the treatment are subject to less and less stringent regulations, and thus pass gradually through states first of what are termed "silent association," under which they are allowed to work in common without speaking, and afterwards advance to a state of association and intercommunication during the day, though still sleeping apart at night.

The following are the reasons assigned for this mode of treatment:-

"Until very lately female convicts," the authorities tell us, "were taught to regard expatriation as the inevitable consequence of their sentence; and when detained in Millbank – usually for some months, waiting embarkation – they were reconciled to the discipline, however strict, by the knowledge that it would soon cease, and that it was only a necessary step towards all but absolute freedom in a colony. Now, however, the circumstances being materially altered, and discharge from prison in this country becoming the rule, it is essential that a corresponding change in the treatment of female prisoners should take place, with the view to preparing them to re-enter the world. Hence the necessity for establishing a system commencing with penal coercion, followed by appreciable advantages for continued good behaviour.

> Henry Mayhew and John Binny, *The Criminal Prisons of London*, 1862

Sir, – Instances are now becoming more frequent of paupers preferring a prison to a workhouse, and resorting to the method of window breaking, as described in your police report of yester-day. Now, the law in its present state is merely an incentive to a repetition of the act; and, therefore, as it affords me no redress, I intend to take it into my own hands. I employ two porters on my premises, and have provided them with stout cudgels. If any pauper should deliberately break a large square of glass they will rush out, and thrash them most unmercifully. Where is the advantage in giving them into custody? By that means you confer a favour on the offender; and the very hour he is at liberty he will return and continue to repeat the offence until again incarcerated. It is no argument to tell us to use less expensive glass, as the pauper would soon find other means of accomplishing his object. What is required is this – and I ask the assistance of your all powerful pen in its favour – that a law should be passed condemning the perpetrator to a sound whipping and immediate discharge.

I am, Sir, your obedient servant, A CITY TRADESMAN.

letter in *The Times*, January 5, 1850

A few minutes after ten o'clock on Sunday morning some little excitement was caused in Clerkenwell by the appearance on the western wall of the House of Detention of a man dressed in prison garb. After a few minutes' hesitation he was seen to drop on to the pavement, a height of thirty-five feet, amidst the screams of several women. The next moment the prisoner was again on his legs, and, having first torn the badge off his arm, he ran down Waterloo-passage, disappearing amongst the adjacent courts before the crowd that had witnessed the affair had recovered from the amazement which his extraordinary leap from the prison wall had occasioned.

The man in question is named J. Waters, aged thirty-eight, and was under remand on a charge of housebreaking. He is described by the police as 5ft 2in. in height, of dark complexion, and having blue eyes. He was dressed in a blue pilot-jacket, fustian trousers, and wore a wide-awake cap. That he effected his escape during the progress to the ordinary chapel service seems certain, having climbed a waterpipe to the extremity of the wall within a few yards of Pear-tree-court. At the point indicated an addition of 6 ft. of brickwork has been added since the fatal explosion at the prison; and he was seen standing as if exhausted, for several minutes before he jumped. According to the testimony of a neighbour, a man happened to be passing just as the prisoner reached the ground, and the latter is alleged to have said, "For God's sake, let me go!" the reply being, "All right! take off your badge." It is farther alleged that there being a difficulty in removing the badge, a vendor of watercresses exchanged coats with the prisoner in order to avoid detection. It is thought that the prisoner cannot have gone far from the locality, as when he fell into Rosoman-street he rubbed his legs and moved towards Waterloo-passage, as if in great pain; and, finding there was no thoroughfare there, his movements in the direction of Pear-tree-court, where he was last seen, were inactive. It is said that two other prisoners made a similar attempt to escape, but this was frustrated. The prison authorities instituted an inquiry relative to the matter, and we understand that, negligence being attributed to two of the warders, they were discharged.

The Penny Illustrated Paper, 28 August, 1875

PROFESSIONS

TRADES IN LONDON. The last population returns (1841) exhibit the following tradespeople, &c., residing in London

168,701 domestic servants.

29,780 dressmakers and milliners.

28,574 boot and shoemakers.

21,517 tailors and breechesmakers.

20,417 commercial clerks.

18,321 carpenters and joiners.

16,220 laundrykeepers, washers, and manglers.

13,103 private messengers and errand boys.

11,507 painters, plumbers, and glaziers.

9,110 bakers.

7,973 cabinetmakers and upholsterers.

7,151 silk manufacturers, (all branches).

7,002 seamen.

6,741 bricklayers.

6,716 blacksmiths.

6,618 printers.

6,450 butchers.

5,499 booksellers, bookbinders, and publishers.

4,980 grocers and teadealers.

4,861 tavernkeepers, publicans, and victuallers.

4,290 clock and watchmakers.

Peter Cunningham, *Hand-Book of London*, 1850

PROSTITUTION

'I should say, then, the common opinion that a woman is first betrayed, then deserted and driven to street prostitution, is by no means so general as the universal supposition would make it appear. At the same time, it does frequently take place. Amongst the lower order of unfortunates, their own sex – those who have already fallen – are far more frequently the agents of their ruin.

They entice foolish young girls of sixteen or seventeen to remain out at night till past the permitted hour; then, when frightened to return to their homes, allure them to their dens "just for the one night." But the poor victim, once there, is either talked into "the life," or else, if she resolves to return to her home the next day, finds, when the morning comes, that any place – the streets even are preferable; for, alas, she dare not go home! The evening before she was guilty of what was comparatively a trivial fault; now she is a poor polluted lost creature, despised by others, hateful to herself.

'Another, and I think the most fruitful, source of ruin is indolence. Some girls will do anything sooner than work; and these are the least reclaimable of any.

'A third cause is vanity – a love of dress – a thirst for pleasure. I place them together because they are generally united. These, unlike those possessed by indolence, are very often open to reclamation. The poor painted butterfly sickens at its borrowed colours, and longs, for the quiet home enjoyments it once possessed, instead of the ceaseless round, of dissipation which she knows must end in everlasting misery.

'Of course there are many instances arising from innate depravity – a love of drink, loss of character from dishonesty, and suchlike causes, which lead to the sights we nightly witness in our streets. But if our senses are shocked and our ears horrified often by the things we see and hear, our hearts too are wrung by listening to the sad recital of some of these poor wanderers. How many of them, once innocent happy girls, were driven by dire destitution to pursue the hateful career by which they plunge their souls into everlasting misery, to gain often but the mere crust, which only just saves them from downright starvation!

Thomas Archer, *The Terrible Sights of London*, 1870

Victoria Station, Pimlico, like many other of our railway termini, is made the meeting place of immoral London. For two miles on either side women may be seen towards the shades of evening leaving their houses to ply their nefarious trade about the vicinity of the station. Some of them in gaudy attire, with painted visages, others bedecked with silks and satins, and not a few are poor city workwomen. Here are houses rented and solely used for improper purposes. Whole streets and bye courts are held by the demon of immorality, the occupiers of which are merely servants employed by the owners who live in quite another part of London, and come every morning to receive their ill-gotten gains. Entrance is effected to these houses merely by turning the key which is left in the door, and by the glimmer of the candles flickering in the passage the visitor is able to ascertain how many rooms are vacant. Men of rank and position, local tradesmen and vestrymen, the police inform me, have been known to complain that they have been either robbed or assaulted in these dens. The vicinity is surrounded with public houses, in many of which these women are permitted to remain and drink. Another, and still more heinous aspect of this locality, is the fact that several keepers of these disorderly houses import and export young girls of tender age for the vicious use of home and foreign lordlings. Here servant girls are taken, under the pretence that they are entering respectable lodgings, during the period they are out of situations, and robbed of virtue are induced by horrible representation to lead an immoral life on the streets. Reader! I write of facts indisputable and authenticated which are not generally known, but which our police and local authorities behold with the utmost unconcern.

Henry Vigar-Harris, *London at Midnight*, 1885

THE SOCIETY FOR THE RESCUE OF YOUNG WOMEN AND CHILDREN

Sir, – By your able advocacy of the claims of the Refuges last year this society received about 400*l*., and was by this means enabled to receive about forty young women, who, but for this timely aid, might otherwise have remained slaves to vice and crime. Our wants now are just as great, and we therefore implore your permission to make them known through your extensively-read paper.

In the brief space of 11 years this society has admitted to its Homes (12 in number) 3,940 destitute females – sheltering, clothing, feeding and training them to earn their own liveli-hood, and then placing them out in situations. Of these, 1,792 have been placed in domestic service, 664 restored to friends, 41 sent out as emigrant, 541 otherwise assisted, leaving 679 as unsatisfactory, and 224 in the Homes.

Out of the 676 who were under the society's care during the past year, 479 had lost one or both parents. Although rescued from the streets and dens of London, only 193 were natives of London; the others, 483, being from the country. Hence their destitution and friendlessness.

But the ages at which they fell into evil almost exceeds credibil-ity, and claims for them the deepest sympathy. Out of 472 of the fallen class, two were eight years of age, 4 were 9, 9 were 10, 10 were 11, 37 were 12, 28 were 13, 53 were 14, 52 were 15, 80 were 16, 47 were 17, 56 were 18, 36 were 19, 13 were 20, 12 were 21, 10 were 22, 7 were 23, 7 were 24, 4 were 25, 1 was 26, 1 was 27, 2 were 28 and 1 was 30.

It will be perceived that only 33 fell after arriving at the age of 21, while double the number were victimized when under 13 years of age.

The number of children driven to the streets of London is almost beyond belief. Recent returns quoted in *The Times* show that the number of "unfortunate" girls under 16 years of age was eight times as many in England as in Ireland, according to population, and we fear evil increases. This society is rescuing them by hundreds from the streets of London, and earnestly begs for help from the public.

letter to *The Times*, 1864

"PSYCHO"

Egyptian Hall – At Messrs. Maskelyne and Cooke's entertainment there has lately been introduced a small figure, 22 inches high, called Psycho, which goes through some most wonderful performance. Mr. Maskelyne first invites some of the audience upon the stage to examine the interior of the figure; then Psycho is placed on a hollow glass pedestal and the performance begins. Psycho first multiplies two numbers given by the audience together, and, though he does not speak, shows the numbers one after the other to the audience; he then plays a game of whist with three gentlemen from the audience ...

The Graphic, 1875

Psycho is the figure of a small and melancholy Turk, with lacklustre eyes, and hands having a peculiarly unnatural appearance, even for an automaton, about the nails. He is seated cross-legged on a box, and he has small boxes near him. On the whole, he rather resembles a Turkish gentleman who, having determined upon travelling, had begun to pack up, and having suddenly tired of the occupation had sat down on a trunk, and rested his left arm on a couple of small boxes. However, Psycho is an independent gentleman, for he and his trunk are raised above the floor on a glass pedestal, quite transparent, and he most certainly appears to have no connection with anybody either on, or off, the stage. He does a sum in arithmetic; he takes a hand at whist, and plays (I was told this, not being a whist-player myself) a very fair game. Some clever people say there's a dwarf concealed inside. If so, the dwarf himself would be a fortune in a separate entertainment; but, again, if so, Heaven help that unfortunate dwarf!

Punch, 1875

PUBLIC HOUSES

It was all mahogany – at least, what wasn't mahogany, was gilt carving and ground glass, with flourishing patterns on it. The bar was cut up into little compartments like pawnbrokers' boxes; and there was the wholesale entrance, and the jug and bottle department, the retail bar, the snuggery, the private bar, the ladies' bar, the wine and liqueur entrance, and the lunch bar. The handles of the taps were painted porcelain, and green, and yellow glass. There were mysterious glass columns, in which the bitter ale, instead of being drawn up comfortably from the cask in the cellar below, remained always on view above ground to show its clearness, and was drawn out into glasses by a mysterious engine like an air-pump with something wrong in its inside. There were carved benches in the private bar, with crimson plush cushions aerated and elastic. There were spring duffers, working in a tunnel in the wall, which you were to strike with your fist to try your muscular strength. There were machines to test your lifting power, and a weighing-machine, and a lung-testing machine, or 'vital-power determinator.' There were plates full of nasty compounds of chips, saw-dust, and grits, called Scotch bannocks, which were to be eaten with butter, and washed down by the Gregarach Staggering old Claymore or Doch an' Dorroch ale; but which never should have shown its face in my old house, I warrant you. There were sausages, fried in a peculiar manner, with barbecued parsley, and a huge, brazen sausage chest, supported on two elephants, with a furnace beneath, from which sausages and potatoes were served out hot and hot all day long. There were sandwiches cut into strange devices; and cakes and tarts that nobody ever heard of before; and drinks and mixtures concocted that, in my day, would have brought the exciseman about a landlord pretty soon, I can assure you. The soda-water bottles had spiral necks like glass corkscrews and zigzag labels. The ginger-beer was all colours – blue, green, and violet. Every inch of the walls that was not be – plastered with ornaments and gilding, or bedizened with gilt announcements of splendid ales and unrivalled quadruple stouts I never heard of, was covered with ridiculously gaudy-coloured prints, puffing the 'Cead Mille Failthe Whisky,' the 'Phthisis Curing Bottled Beer,' recommended by the entire faculty . . .

George Augustus Sala, *Gaslight and Daylight*, 1859

PUBLIC TOILETS

The Council of the Society of Arts on the 14th of May requested the following noblemen and gentlemen to act as a committee for establishing forthwith a certain number of model water-closets and urinals in public thoroughfares, with the object of proving that these public conveniences, so much wanted, may be made self-supporting:- The Earl of Carlisle, Earl Granville, Mr. Henry Cole, Mr. S.M.Peto, M.P., and Mr. C. Wentworth Dilke.

The committee consider that the following regulations should be adopted in commencing this experiment:

1. That these conveniences be established on a moderate scale, in connexion with shops, in some public thoroughfares, and be called 'Public Waiting-rooms.'

2. That the public waiting-rooms for men and women be established in distinct shops, on opposite sides of the street.

3. That in each shop there be a waiting-room, having two classes of water-closets and urinals, for the use of which a penny and two pence should be charged.

4. That each set of waiting-room be provided with a lavatory for washing hands, clothes' brushes, &c., at a charge of twopence and threepence.

5. That each set of waiting-rooms have a superintendent and two attendants.

6. That the charges for the use of the lavatories, water-closets, and urinals should include all attendance, and be publicly affixed in the shop.

7. That the police should be requested to cause these establishments to be visited from time to time.

The committee recommend that the Council should undertake to lease several ground floors in the Strand, Holborn and Cheapside.

Mr. Minton having offered to present 24 earthenware urinals and a number of encaustic tiles for labels, and Mr. J. Ridgeway having also offered to present some of his new fountain washhand-stands, the committee recommended that their liberal offers be accepted with thanks.

The committee recommend that it be suggested to manufacturers of lavatories, water-closets, and urinals, who desire to bring their inventions before the public, immediately to present samples for the object in question.

The committee recommend that no time should be lost in inviting respectable persons holding shops in public thoroughfares, who may be desirous of connecting the proposed public waiting-rooms with them, to inform the secretary, Mr. G. Grove, of the accommodation which their premises offer for the purpose. The shops which appear to be most suitable for waiting-rooms for ladies are staymakers', bonnet-makers', milliners', &c. Those most suitable for gentlemen's waiting-rooms are hairdressers', tailors', hatters', taverns, &c.

All communications should be addressed to Mr. George Grove, secretary of the Society of Arts, John-street, Adelphi.

The Times, 1851

PUNCH AND JUDY

The barrel organ is the opera of the street-folk: and Punch is their national comedy theatre. I cannot call to mind any scene on our many journeys through London that struck the authors of this pilgrimage more forcibly than the waking up of a dull, woe-begone alley, to the sound of an organ. The women leaning out of the windows, pleasurably stirred, for an instant, in that long disease, their life, and the children trooping and dancing round the swarthy player!

It is equalled only by the stir and bustle, and cessation of employment, which happen when the man who carries the greasy old stage of Mr. Punch, halts at a favourable "pitch;" and begins to drop the green baize behind which he is to play the oftenest performed serio-comic drama in the world. The milk-woman stops on her rounds: the baker deliberately unshoulders his load: the newsboy (never at a loss for a passage of amusement on his journey) forgets that he is bearer of the "special edition" the policeman halts on his beat, while the pipes are tuning, and the wooden actors are being made ready within, and dog Toby is staring sadly round upon the mob. We have all confessed to the indefinable witchery of the heartless rogue of the merry eye and ruby nose, whose career, so far as we are permitted to know it, is an unbroken round of facetious brutalities.

Wife-beating is second nature to him. To be sure Judy does not look all that man can desire in the partner of his bosom. The dog, indeed, makes the best appearance; and is the most reputable member of this notorious family.

Gustave Doré and Blanchard Jerrold,
London : A Pilgrimage, 1872

QUACKS

STREET vendors of pills, potions, and quack nostrums are not quite so numerous as they were in former days. The increasingly large number of free hospitals, where the poor may consult qualified physicians, the aid received at a trifling cost from clubs and friendly societies, and the spread of education, have all tended to sweep this class of street-folks from the thorough-fares of London. Although of late years much has been done by private charities to supplement the system of parochial relief, there is still a vast field open for the extension of medical missions among the lower orders of the community. Far from being in a position to record the extinction of the race of " herbalists" and "doctors for the million" who practise upon the poor, my investigations prove they are still about as numerous as their trade is lucrative.

It would be unjust to say that the itinerant empirics of the metropolis have advanced with the age, as it is part of their "role" to adhere to all that is old in the nomenclature and prac-tice of their craft. An intelligent member of the fraternity informed me that as members of the medical profession, they are bound to use what may be called "crocus" Latin. "Our pro-fession is known, sir, as 'crocussing,' and our dodges and decoc-tions as 'fakes' or rackets. Many other words make up a sort of dead language that protects us and the public from ignorant impostors. It don't do to juggle with drugs, leastwise to them that are ignorant of the business. I was told by a chum of mine, a university man, that 'crocussing' is nigh as old as Adam, and that some of our best rackets were copied from Egypshin' tombs. ... I have been a cough tablet 'crocus' for nine years, only in summer I go for the Sarsaparilla 'fake.' Sometimes this is a regular 'take-down' – swindle. The 'Blood Purifier' is made up of a cheap herb called sassafras, burnt sugar, and water flavoured with a little pine-apple or pear juice. That's what's called sarsaparilla by some 'crocusses.' If it don't lengthen the life of the buyer it lengthens the life of the seller. It's about the same thing in the end. A very shady 'racket' is the India root for destroying all sorts of vermin including rats. It's put among clothes like camphor. Any root will answer if it's scented, but this racket requires sailor's togs; for the 'crocus' must just have come off the ship from foreign parts. It also requires a couple of tame rats to fight shy of the root. The silver paste is a fatal 'fake.' The paste is made of whiting and red ochre. The 'crocus' has a solution of bichloride of mercury which he mixes with the paste, and rubbing it over a farthing silvers it. He sells it for plating brass candlesticks and such like, but it's the mercury that does the business, he don't sell that. The mercury in time gets into his blood and finishes him. I have known two killed this way.

J.Thomson and Adolphe Smith, *Street Life in London*, 1877

Q

R is for Rollerskating

'Rinkomania' gripped mid-1870s London, with both marble
and 'real-ice' rinks being built throughout the capital.
Rinks were popular with young women, and likely places
to meet unsuitable young men – hence the footman
as chaperone in this *Punch* cartoon of 1876.

RAGGED SCHOOLS

RAGGED SCHOOL UNION, – office, 1 Exeter Hall, – was established in 1844, with the view of bringing a "plain" but sound education within the reach of even the very humblest classes, of providing them with gratuitous shelter from the inclemency of the weather, and stimulating them to industrial and prudent habits. These objects are provided for, as far as the resources of the society will allow, by ragged schools situated in the worst neighbourhoods of London, which already extend their human-ising influence to 27,000 children; by penny banks connected with these schools, in which about 28,000 depositors annually place 4,500*l*.; and by eight Shoe-Black brigades (distinguished each by a cheap coloured uniform), comprising some 350 boys, who earned, last year, 4,647*l*., by cleaning 1,115,280 pairs of boots and shoes, and whose eager cry of, "Have your boots blacked, sir?-only one penny!" salutes the passer by in every busy metropolitan thoroughfare. In certain localities Refuges have been established, which afford to destitute lads and girls a night's shelter and a good supper and break fast. The society also inter-ests itself in procuring employment for deserving industry, and in promoting the emigration of suitable persons. In a word, with a limited income (6,000*l*. yearly), this well-managed institution effects a vast amount of good, and its labours are not the less arduous because never puffed into an unwholesome notoriety.

Cruchley's London in 1865 : A Handbook for Strangers, 1865

Oct. 28, 1849 – ... We prepared the school by placing benches in situations for the division of the scholars into four classes, and as they came tumbling and bawling up the stairs, we directed them to seats .... In mere schooling they are not behindhand, but in decency of behaviour or in respect for the teacher, or in discipline of any kind, they are totally unparalleled. No school can possibly be worse than this. It were an easier task to get attention from savages ... They require more training than teaching. To compose the children, I proposed that we should have a little music ... the first verse of the Evening Hymn. We then invited the children to follow us, and we got through the first line or two very well, but a blackguard boy thought proper to set up on his own account, and he led off a song in this strain:-

"Oh, Susanah, don't you cry for me,
I'm off to Alamabama,
With a banjo on my knee!"

I need scarcely add that every boy followed this leader – aye, girls and all – and I could not check them ... In the midst of the Lord's Prayer, several shrill cries of 'cat's meat,' and 'mew, mew,' ... All our copy books have been stolen, and proofs exist that the school is used at night as a sleeping-room. We must get a stronger door to it.

Diary of a Ragged School Teacher,
English Journal of Education, 1850

RAIL TRAVEL

Q. What is a Railway?
A. An ingenious and complex contrivance for extracting as much money as possible from the travelling public and giving it the least possible amount of convenience and comfort in return. ...

Q. What is a Railway Station?
A. It may best and most briefly be described as a place of public torture.

Q. What are the kinds of torture therein inflicted upon the Public?
A. They are so many and subtly varied as almost to defy exhaustive classification. They may, however, for purposes of illustration, be ranged under various heads, as, for example

1. The torture of Difficult Access.
2. The tortures of Labyrinthine Complexity and Maze-like Muddle.
3. The torture of Hurry-scurry.
4. The torture of Noise.
5. The torture of Imperative Stupidity
6. The torture of Clownish Incivility
7. The tortures of Dirt, Deprivation, and Physical Discomfort generally.

Q. How is difficulty of access secured?
A. By many ingenious devices, such as the multiplication of steep slopes and precipitous staircases, the careful laying out of intricate passages and complicated corridors, the artful adjustment of numerous narrow wickets and the sedulously maintained mystery of many and capriciously used platforms. Perhaps, however, the most successfully tormenting of these devices of delay is the great Ticket trick.

Q. What is the special purpose of this device?
A. To make the procuring of the necessary pasteboard-pass as difficult as possible to the would-be passenger.

Q. For what reason.
A. Reason has nothing whatever to do with Railway regulations.

Q. How is it managed?
A. First, by refusing to issue the ticket for a particular train until that train is about to start, and a long, close-packed, and agitated queue of passengers is in waiting; secondly, by making the species of port-hole through which the tickets are issued so small that only one passenger at a time can obtain a ticket, and that slowly and with exceeding difficulty.

Q. What are the results of these singular arrangements?
A. Uncomfortable hurry, great confusion, needless waiting, and frequent missing of trains. A traveller arriving in good time,

must watchfully linger in a dreary and draughty corridor until it pleases the haughty young gentleman within the rabbit-hutch to raise the hatch thereof. A traveller arriving rather late, must take his place at the end of a long "tail" of eager and angry applicants, with much probability of getting his ticket just in time to lose his train. In any case, he has to stoop and shout his instructions through a little square hole into the reluctant ears of an austere being who is the victim of constitutional supercili-ousness and chronic disgust. This Diogenes in a box is gener-ally hard of hearing, slow of understanding, and much readier with rude questions than with civil answers. When he deigns – after the delay due to his dignity – to understand you arright, he "chucks" your ticket at you in a manner suggestive of lofty contempt or deep resentment. If you require change, he "dabs" it down in a scattered heap, leaving you, if you are nervous or considerate, to claw it up hastily; or, if you are dogged or self-ishly indifferent, to count it carefully. In the former case you may possibly be cheated. In the latter case you will certainly be hated – by the impatient crowd waiting behind you for their turn at the port-hole. In this dilemma, the printed notification, that you are requested to count your change before leaving, as no correction can subsequently be made, will probably strike you as sardonic, if not impertinent.

Punch, 1882

RATTING

Round about the walls were tubs and kennels and railed boxes, and, startled by the incoming of so many strangers, instantly there was a clanking of dog chains and such a chorus of dog music as I had not heard since my visit to the Home at Battersea. With mastiffs and yard dogs and terriers and bandy, blear-eyed bulldogs grinning in malice, and madly struggling against their collars to get at the legs of Mr. Skunko's guests,

I was delighted to hear his cheerful assurance, as he went first with the light, that there was no danger "if we didn't get a joshlin' and scrouging within their reach."

The rat pit was on the frame of the skittle-alley, with boards placed round about breast high. Here we were out of reach of the dogs, and at the end was a sort of raised platform for the more favoured of the company. On a great bunk at hand were several iron-wire cages of rats smelling their doom, and squeaking and scratching to get out; and over these Mr. Skunko presided. Round about the pit were the fanciers who meant to test the killing powers of their dogs, and who carried the pets hugged in their arms.

"Let me have half a dozen, Billy," exclaimed a customer; and at once Billy opened the stocking-leg mouth of a rat cage, and fearlessly plunging his hand into the vermin nest plucked out by their long tails, one after another, six rats, flinging them, as it seemed to me, with unnecessary force into the pit. Instantly the customer dropped his dog over the barricade, and the work of slaughter began, the spectators yelling encouragement to the plucky little terrier, and banging the boards of the pit with their hands and feet to startle back any maddening wretch of a rat that sought so to escape from the inexorable jaws of "Vix," which, as I understood, was a handy abbreviation of "Vixen." In three minutes there remained in the pit six still rats, a few waifs of bloody fur, and a dog licking his lips.

Then came another customer and six more rats. Then a gentleman well known in the pigeon-flying interest, with a new dog he was mighty proud of, and ordered a dozen rats for him all at once. But the pride of the pigeon-fancier was doomed to suffer; the dog was even more afraid than were the rats, and ran away from them ...

James Greenwood, *The Wilds of London*, 1874

REPETITIVE STRAIN INJURY

Telegraph clerks will hear with alarm of telegraphic paralysis, a new malady reported by a French physician to the Academie des Sciences. An employé who had been engaged in a telegraph office for nine years, found that he could not form clearly the letters U, represented by two dots and a stroke, I by two dots and S by three dots. On trying to trace the letters, his hand became stiff and cramped. He then endeavoured to use his thumb alone, and this succeeded for two years, when his thumb was similarly attacked, and subsequently tried the first and second fingers, but in two months these were also paralysed. Finally he had recourse to the wrist which also shortly became disabled. If he forced himself to use his hand, both hand and arm shook violently and cerebral excitement ensued. It appears that this disorder is very common amongst telegraph clerks.

The Graphic, 1875

RESTAURANTS

Few places are more changed, and changed for the better, in the period of my memory, than the dining-rooms and restaurants of London. In the days of my early youth there was, I suppose, scarcely a capital city in Europe so badly provided with eating-houses as ours; not numerically, for there were plenty of them, but the quality was all round bad. And this was not for lack of custom, or of customers of an appreciative kind: for, as I shall have occasion to point out, there were comparatively few clubs at that time, and those which were in existence had not nearly so many members, nor were nearly so much frequented, for dining purposes at least, as they now are. There was not, it is true, in any class so much money to spend as there is now: young men who to-day sit down to soup, fish, entrées – then called "made dishes" – a roast, a bird, a sweet, a savoury, and a bottle of claret, would then have been content with a slice off the joint, a bit of cheese, and a pint of beer; but everything was fifty per cent. cheaper in those times, and there was an ample profit on what was supplied.

The improvement, as I shall show, came in suddenly. There were no Spiers & Pond, and, of course, none of the excellent establishments owned by them; no St. James's Hall, Café Royal, Monico's, Gatti's, Bristol or Continental restaurants, scarcely one of the now fashionable dining-houses. Verrey's was in existence, to be sure, but it was regarded as a "Frenchified" place, and was very little patronized by the young men of the day, though it had a good foreign connection. Dubourg's, in the Haymarket, opposite the theatre, was in the same category, though more patronized for suppers. The Café de l'Europe, next door to the Haymarket Theatre, originally started by Henry Hemming, who had been jeune premier at the Adelphi, was, notwithstanding its foreign name, a purely English house, as far as its cooking was concerned. All these places, however, were far beyond the means of me and my friends. If we wanted foreign fare – and, truth to tell, in those days of youth and health, and vast appetite and little money, we were not much given to it – we would go to Rouget's in Castle Street, Leicester Square; or to Giraudier's in the Haymarket; or, best of all, to Berthollini's in St. Martin's Place, I think it was called – a narrow thoroughfare at the back of Pall Mall East. A wonderful man Berthollini: a tall thin Italian in a black wig – there was a current report that many of the dishes were made out of his old wigs and boots; but this was only the perversion by the ribalds of the statement of his supporters, that the flavouring was so excellent that the basis of the dish was immaterial – who superintended everything himself and was ubiquitous; now flying to the kitchen, now uncorking the wine, now pointing with his long skinny fore-finger to specially lovely pieces in the dish.

Edmund Yates, *His Recollections and Experiences*, 1885

I think that the suggestion to dine at the cheap table d'hôte dinner at one of the very large restaurants, to listen to the music, and look at the people dining, came from me. Our minds made up on this point, there was the difficulty of selecting the restaurant, so we agreed to toss up, and the spin of the coin eventually settled upon the Holborn Restaurant.

In the many-coloured marble hall, with its marble staircase springing from either side, a well-favoured gentleman with a close-clipped grey beard was standing, a sheet of paper in his hand, and waved us towards a marble portico, through which we passed to the grand saloon with its three galleries supported by marble pillars. "A table for two," said a maitre d'hôtel, and we were soon seated at a little table near the centre of the room, at which a waiter in dress clothes, with a white metal number at his buttonhole and a pencil behind his ear, was in attendance waiting for orders. The table d'hôte dinner was what we required, and then I noticed that I had to ask for the wine list, and that it was not given me opened at the champagnes, as is usually the custom of waiters.

The menu, which on a large sheet of stiff paper peeps out from a deep border of advertise-ments, is printed both in French and in English. This is the English side of it on the night we dined:-

SOUPS.
   Purée of Hare aux croûtons.
   Spaghetti.

FISH.
   Supreme of Sole Joinville.
   Plain Potatoes.
   Darne de saumon. Rémoulade Sauce.

ENTRÉES.
   Bouchées a l'Impératrice.
   Sauté Potatoes.
   Mutton Cutlets à la Reforme.

REMOVE.

Ribs of Beef and Horseradish. Brussels Sprouts.

ROAST.

Chicken and York Ham.

Chipped Potatoes.

SWEETS.

Caroline Pudding. St. Honoré Cake.

Kirsch Jelly.

ICE.

Neapolitan.

Cheese. Celery

DESSERT.

We agreed to drink claret, and I picked out a wine third or fourth down on the list.

Lieut.-Col. Newnham-Davies, *Dinners and Diners*, 1899

ROLLERSKATING

We hear of a new West-End Rink of the handsomest description. The Dungannon-Cottage Marble Rink at Knightsbridge (like "The Marble" on the other side of the water) offers to Plimptonians a surface the smoothness of which is unrivalled save by a clear sheet of ice. How beautifully Dungannon Cottage has been fitted-up, by an enterprising gentleman for this healthy if hazardous exercise devotés to the roller-skate will quickly find out for themselves. A praiseworthy feature of this new marble rink is that "ladies desiring to chaperon their daughters" are granted a season-ticket for a merely nominal charge. To give spirit and zest to the skating, an excellent band discourses good music.

Penny Illustrated Paper, 1876

Late in the seventies of our century the social craze of what was called 'rinkomania' set in. Any available buildings were laid down with floors more or less lubricated, on which the sons and daughters of the various sections of the great middle class, shod with a peculiar adaptation of wheels, slipped about, and called it skating. These resorts were no doubt admirably conducted. Acquaintances made at them were probably blameless. They often perhaps ended in blissful and desirable marriage. But not without a shock to her sense of maternal propriety did the english matron of old-fashioned ideas see, or hear of, her daughter being twirled round in the arms of some youth just introduced, or perhaps without even the preliminary of that easy form ...

T.H.S Escott, *Social Transformations of the Victorian Age*, 1897

ROWING MATCHES

ONE of the local matters that soon engaged my youthful attention was the regattas, of which I found there were three at Greenwich every year. They all consisted of sculling competitions in out-rigger racing skiffs with covered-in ends, locally called wager-boats – there were no sliding seats then – between six local men of three different categories: landsmen, for a silver cup; apprentice watermen, for a coat-and-badge and freedom of the Waterman's Guild; and licensed watermen for a brand-new boat or wherry. Several weeks intervened between each regatta, so that rowing interest was sustained during the greater part of the summer and autumn. The competitors wore calico blouses gaudily coloured in red, pink, yellow, green, and dark and light blue, so that they could readily be identified at any part of the course.

There were two trial heats, three men each, during the forenoon; about dinner-time the four losers – known as "the worst four" – met and two were permanently ruled out. In the afternoon the four winners – "the best four" – rowed, and in the evening the two survivors came together for the final heat, or "best two." Men being at work, women cooking, and boys at school, the preliminary heats were not very largely attended, but many spectators mustered for the best four, and in the evening for the grand heat – my word! – what a crowd, what a concourse! The river was covered with boats, and every point ashore was a packed mass of humanity, women almost as numerous as men. The Hospital grounds were thrown open; the pier enclosure was crammed at 1*d*. per head; the wharves, and vessels that happened to lie alongside them (including the rigging if the skippers were propitious); the hotel and tavern windows and balconies; the Harbour Master's pretty paddle-wheel yacht, usually moored off the Trafalgar, and especially the pathway in front of the Hospital and its central landing-steps, – all, all, packed to suffocation. Strange to say, I never knew a regatta to be spoiled by bad weather.

Alfred Rosling-Bennett, *London and Londoners in the 1850s and 1860s*, 1924

ROYAL AQUARIUM, THE
ROYAL AQUARIUM – The pleasantest lounge in London. Open 11 till 11. Always something new. Constant amusement. Admission 1*s*.

—

THE AQUARIUM DEPARTMENT. – Finest collection of MARINE ANIMALS in Europe, 150 different species. Thousands of live specimens.

—

ROYAL AQUARIUM. – At intervals, Fleas, Tubbs' Granville's Entertainment, Farini's Zulus, the new Fine Art Gallery, Reading Room and Library:

3.15. – Royal Acquarium Orchestra

3.30. – Nat Emmett's Wonderful Goats

3.45. – Herr Blitz: Plate Spinning Extraordinary

4.10. – Phillipson's splendid Troupe of Bell Ringers

4.25. – Leclaire, the King of Conjurors

4.40. – Gale St John and Mlle Celia Dwight

4.50. – Poluski Brothers, well known musical clowns

5.20. – Mons. Nathan, marvellous chair manipulator

5.30. – Special performance of Farini's Zulus

6:30. – Recital on Grand Organ by Mr James Halle

8.00. – Vocal and Instrumental Concert. Mons C.Dubois

9.00. – Special performance of Farini's Zulus

9.50. – Second unsurpassed variety entertainment

—

THE marvellous SWORD SWALLOWER, THIS DAY.

—

ROYAL AQUARIUM – FARINI'S ZULUS. Special Performance at 5.40 and 9 o'clock. THE ONLY GENUINE ZULUS in ENGLAND, and the only ones that ever left their country. Admission 1*s*.

advertisement from *The Times*, 1879

S is for The 'Silent Highway'

The "Silent Highway" was the River Thames. Whilst small steamboats provided transport for pleasure-seekers and commuters, the river was dominated by warehouses, docks and commercial traffic. The photograph shows river-workers of the late 1870s, pictured by John Thomson in "Street Life in London".

SANDWICH-BOARD MEN

FEW men who earn their living in the streets are better abused and more persistently jeered at than the unfortunate individuals who let themselves out for hire as walking advertisements. The work is so hopelessly simple, that any one who can put one foot before the other can undertake it, and the carrying of boards has therefore become a means of subsistence open to the most stupid and forlorn of individuals. These facts are so self-evident that the smallest street urchin is sensible of the absurd picture presented by a full-grown man carrying an advertisement "back and front" all day long. The boardmen have therefore become a general butt, and it is considered fair play to tease them in every conceivable manner. The old joke, the query as to the whereabouts of the mustard, has now died out, and it is considered better sport to bespatter the "sandwich men" with mud, or to tickle their faces with a straw when the paraphernalia on their backs prevents all attempt at self-defence. While the street boys indulge in these and various other practical jokes, omnibus conductors also relieve their feelings as they pass by kicking at the boards. These can be conveniently reached from the steps behind an omnibus, and give a jovial clattering sound in answer to a kick well administered with a hob-nail boot. The poor board-man, groaning under this insult, staggers forward, ploughing with his sorry boots the mire of the gutter, and is unable to recover his balance before the omnibus has driven far away. Pursuit is impossible, redress unattainable; the boardman must remain true to his boards, and patiently endure the trials inflicted upon him. But few have escaped receiving ugly cuts from the whips of irate coachmen. If they walk on the pavement the policemen indignantly thrust them off into the gutter, where they become entangled in the wheels of carriages, and where cabs and omnibuses are ruthlessly driven against them. If to these discomforts we add that the mud thrown up by the wheels must bespatter them from head to foot, and that they have no other shelter but the boards themselves to save them from the rain, we may safely conclude that their existence is not fraught with many comforts.

J.Thomson and Adolphe Smith, *Street Life in London*, 1877

SCHOOL FOR THE INDIGENT BLIND

Established in 1799, at the Dog and Duck premises, St. George's Fields; and for some time received only fifteen blind persons. The site being required by the City of London for the building of Bethlem Hospital, about two acres of ground were allotted opposite the Obelisk, and there a plain school-house for the blind was built. In 1826, the School was incorporated; and in the two following years three legacies of 500*l*. each, and one of 10,000*l*., were bequeathed to the establishment . . . The pupils are clothed, lodged, and boarded, and receive a religious and industrial education; so that many of them have been returned to their families able to earn from 6*s*. to 8*s*. per week. Applicants are not received under twelve, nor above thirty, years of age; nor if they have a greater degree of sight than will enable them to distinguish light from darkness. The admission is by votes of the subscribers; and persons between the ages of twelve and eighteen have been found to receive the greatest benefit from the instruction.

The pupils may be seen at work between ten and twelve A.M., and two and five P.M., daily, except Saturdays and Sundays. The women and girls are employed in knitting stockings and needlework; in spinning, and making household and body linen, netting silk, and in fine basket-making; besides working baby-hoods, bags, purses, watch-pockets, &c., of tasteful design, both in colour and form. The women are remarkably quick in superintending the pupils. The men and boys make wicker baskets, cradles, and hampers; rope door-mats and worsted rugs; and they make all the shines for the inmates of the School. Reading is mostly taught by Alston's raised or embossed letters, in which have been printed the Old and New Testament, and the Liturgy. Both males and females are remarkably cheerful in their employment: they have great taste and aptness for music, and they are instructed in it, not as a mere amusement, but with a view to engagements as organists and teachers of psalmody; and once a year they perform a concert of sacred music in the chapel or music-room: the public are admitted by tickets, the proceeds from the sale being added to the funds of the institution. An organ and pianoforte are provided for teaching; and above each of the inmates of the males' working-room usually hangs a fiddle. They receive, as pocket-money, part of their earnings, and on leaving the school, a sum of money and a set of tools, for their respective trades, are given to them.

John Timbs, *Curiosities of London*, 1867

"SECRET VICE", THE

What remains to be said on this subject will be said as briefly and guardedly as possible. The interpretation will not be found difficult by those whom it is meant to reach.

Of the two forms of immorality, secret vice is not the least destructive. We have been urged from the most influential quarters not to pass by this painful subject. We have before us a collection of letters and testimonies which, if we dared to print them, would astound every reader. This vice, in the opinion of many who know the secrets of young men, is at the bottom of more misery than any other. It is generally learnt early at school, and when it gets a hold is rarely shaken off. Its results are in many cases complete collapse of body and mind. It is the cause of nearly all premature break-downs among young men, and every lunatic asylum is full of its victims. The feeling of hopelessness and degradation which it speedily engenders is of the most intolerable kind, and often leads to suicide. The opinion of one whose name, were we permitted to give it, would carry great weight is that it is the great cause of suicide. On this painful subject two things need to be said very plainly –

1. That it is necessary for parents and teachers to warn their sons against this ruinous practice and its consequences. We do not think there can be any doubt about this, whatever difference of opinion there may be on other subjects. We are glad to say that young men's Christian associations are becoming alive to this and are taking means to warn and to save young men. We have found the chief workers among young men in London very much alive on this subject, and doing their part .

2. That advertising quacks are as numerous and as dangerous as ever. There is an impression that they have been less active of late years, and that respectable journals now refuse their advertisements. As a matter of fact this is not so. Now, young men should be told that they will never, under any circumstances, get any help from these men, but harm, and harm only. Their medicines are invariably quite useless.

Anon., *Tempted London: Young Men*, c.1889

SERPENTINE, THE

Sir, – Will you permit me to inquire why it is that the new rule which has been recently, and very properly made, and placed on boards along the northern bank of the Serpentine River, prohibiting any bathing on that side, is so soon to become a dead letter?

I was taking my usual walk last Saturday evening in Hyde Park, after the hours of business were over, when, to my great surprise, I saw several persons bathing, as of old, on the northern bank of the Serpentine River; and, on making the circumstance known to the police, I was politely informed that their orders were not to interfere in the matter. Is it because the great and noble of the land have left town that those less fortunate than themselves are to be subjected to the nuisance, which they flattered themselves had been abated, of seeing hundreds of naked men and boys surrounding that beautiful piece of water, and by their yells and discordant noises preventing any respectable persons from enjoying a quiet walk on either bank of the river?

I am, Sir, your obedient servant,
Sept. 11.   A CONSTANT READER
                        letter to *The Times*, September 12, 1843

Sir, – I read in your paper of this morning a querulous letter from a "Constant Reader" respecting the numbers of poor people who are, I am happy to find, now permitted to bathe in the Serpentine River. I wonder that you, who so lately employed your pen in showing the necessity of providing the means of general ablution for the bodies of our poor working people, should now publish the complaints of this person. What are the poor people to do? There are no free baths provided by the State; the great highway of the Thames is interdicted, perhaps not improperly; but with respect to the Serpentine River, there can be no objection to the use of it as a great public bath.

If "constant readers" and others of such sickly fancies do not like to witness the scene of so much enjoyment, let them go somewhere else and take their "quiet walks" for the walkers, quiet or otherwise, may go to many places, whereas the bathers can go but to this one. For my part, I cannot sufficiently express my gratitude to those in authority who have had the merciful kindness to allow the poor working man to refresh and strengthen his body in the comfort and salubrity of a bath in the Serpentine River.

letter to *The Times*, September 14, 1843

Of course most people who come to the Park of an evening are aware of the swarm of small boys who assemble on the bathing ground (or space), some four hundred yards allotted for that purpose on the south shore, who have been waiting hours before the time, especially after a hot day in July; (they come in droves and batches from all quarters of London) anxiously looking for the signal to plunge in – and this signal was the approach of the Royal Humane Society boats from the opposite side of the water, exactly at half-past seven, to be in readiness to render assistance to any of the bathers that may be in danger of drowning – three as a rule, one at each end of the boundary and one in the centre.

I assure you it is no easy job for the police a few minutes before the approach of these boats to keep them from undressing and plunging in, the eagerness of the young rascals being so great. When I say "undressing" I mean stripping off what little they have on – the word is superfluous, for to keep them from undressing long before the time was a matter of impossibility; it appeared a certain amount of gratification to them to undress, and it was only with firmness and intimidation of sending them away altogether that they could be prevailed upon to squat about with even their shirts on. We usually supplied ourselves with a light stick or cane, and shook it at them in a threatening manner, occasionally impressing upon them the fact that they would get a taste of it, if they did not behave themselves, or we should have been overrun; and even when the boats did appear, and the shout went up – "All in!" I have been in a state of suspense while the boats were coming across, as in sheer excitement the smaller ones were so apt to get out of their depth.

> Edward Owen, *Hyde Park, Select Narratives, Annual Event, etc, during twenty years' Police Service in Hyde Park,* 1906

SERVANTS

Servants vary even more than most commodities. The best way to get one is to select from the advertisements in the daily papers. The next best, to advertise your wants, though this will expose you to the attacks of a considerable class who will call simply for the purpose of extorting their "expenses." In either case insist upon a personal character. Written characters are not worth reading. It is not a safe plan to go to a Registry unless you know all about it first, though there are some which are really trustworthy. But a servant who once finds his or her way to a Registry Office is almost always unsettled, and no sooner in a place than looking out for another. The average London wages may be set down as: Butlers, £40 to £100; Footmen, £20 to £40; Pages, £8 to £15; Cooks, £18 to £50; Housemaids, £10 to £25; Parlour-maids. £12 to £30; "General Servants," Anglice Maids of all Work, £6 to £15. A month's notice required before leaving or dismissing; but in the latter case a month's wages (and board wages if demanded) will suffice. For serious misconduct a servant can be discharged without notice. When left in town, additional board wages will be required at the rate of about 10s. per week. If economy is necessary, bear in mind that the payment of commissions from tradesmen to servants is an almost universal London custom, and a fruitful source of deliberate waste. "Kitchen stuff" is another expensive institution, specially designed to facilitate the consumption of articles, on the replacing of which cook may make her little profit. Dripping, perquisite for which all cooks will make at least a fight, not only means a good deal more than its name would imply, but leads to the spoiling of your meat by surreptitious stabbings that the juice may run away more freely. This ingenious arrangement is also much favoured of late years by the butcher, who nowadays in "jointing" always cuts well into the meat. Give good wages, and let it be clearly understood before hiring that no perquisites are allowed. A serious mistake, and one too often made, is to lay down the hard-and-fast rule "no followers allowed." Servants always have had and always will have followers, whether their masters and mistresses like it or no. It is much wiser to recognise this fact, and to authorise the Visits of the "follower" at proper times and seasons, first taking pains to ascertain that his antecedents and character are good. Police-courts will convict for the annexation of "perquisites" which have not been sanctioned. The giving of a false character to a servant is an offence against the law, and can be prosecuted as such.

Charles Dickens (Jr.), *Dickens's Dictionary of London*, 1879

"I don't care how hard I work," remarked the first maid I beckoned aside, "but I want a place where I'm treated as though I was made of the same flesh and blood as my fellow creatures. I left my last place because I wasn't. Three months I was there; eight of 'em in family, with the washing done at home, and nine pounds a year. Up at six every morning, with the master's and three boys' boots to clean and a whole lot of steps to whiten and the breakfast to get ready before eight; and then, drudge, drudge, scrubbing and getting the dinner ready, going errands, washing up, and getting tea and all that; so that it was never earlier than about seven that I could get my apron off and make myself a bit tidy, with perhaps the gals' – the young missuses' – sweet-hearts coming in the evening, or master bringing home a friend to sup-per, so that I thought myself lucky to get to bed by half-past eleven, that tired that I've felt like passing the night on the attic stairs rather than go up 'em. But I shouldn't ha' minded the work if it hadn't been for the stuck-up ways of Miss Ellen and her sister. They opened my eyes as to the sort they was the first day I was there. I don't say as I'm over partickler; but what I say is that if there is anything a person has got a right to it is the name that their godfathers and godmothers gave them in their baptism. It's their birthright, and you won't catch me a – selling mine for nobody's mess of porridge. Well, and so the first day I went there Miss Ellen began a 'Susaning' me all over the place:

"'This is how we like so-and-so done, Susan. This is how we wish t'other, Susan.'

"So at last I says, 'Scuse me, Miss, but the name of Susan don't apply to me. My name is Hadelaide – Hadelaide 'Obson, Miss, if you ain't got no objections.'

"So she turned it off with a sort of titter, and she says–"That's unfortunate, Hadelaide is my sister's name. Can't you do with Susan? or there's half-a-dozen others you can choose from–Jane, Polly, Ann, Betsey.'

"Only that the parcels delivery had left my boxes not ten minutes before, I'd have had my bonnet on in a jiffy and left at a minute's notice. Just as though I was a creature from the 'sylum for 'omeless dogs, whose name they didn't know."

"'I'm much beholden to you, Miss,' I says, 'but there ain't a name you've mentioned but what I should hate myself if I was mean-spirited enough to answer to. I'd rather drop the 'andle altogether, and be called 'Obson.'"

'One of the Crowd' [James Greenwood],
Toilers in London, 1883

SEWAGE

One Sunday evening last summer, just after low water, we passed along the shore. And all who would have an idea of the extent to which the Thames is used, should visit the landing-place at Hungerford-bridge on a fine Sunday evening. The day had been cooler than some days previously; nevertheless, the stench at the different points was frightful, and produced a sickness which lasted till the next morning. Bad as was the state of affairs at the time referred to, the watermen at the landing-places said the air was "lavender" to what it had been. Early in the morning, they continued, when the first steam-packets begin to move about, the smell is enough to strike down strong men. During a few hours of the night, when there is but little traffic, the heavy matter sinks, and the renewed agitation in the morning causes the escape of pungent gases, of a most poisonous description. Even the dipping of the oars, at early hours, produces a sickening sensation. The weight of the impure portion of Thames water is a peculiarity which formerly caused the water to be held in much favour by sailors for long foreign voyages. Large establishments were formed for the purpose of filtering it; but even so lately as 1840 and 1841, many ships took it without this process from the outside of the docks. A person who has sailed from the Thames, but who is now a waterman, described how that he had been twelve months and upwards on board ship with Thames water, obtained in the manner just mentioned, and that it remained good all the time: the heavy earthy matters settled firmly to the bottom of the casks; but on the bung being started, it was necessary to give the water "a wide berth," for the smell was almost unbearable – sometimes the force of the gas had burst out the bungs with a report like that of a pistol. A similar process, on a large scale, is going on daily on the Thames. The soil, put in motion by the action of the water, is now more considerable than formerly; and the amount of poisonous gases which is thrown off is proportionate to the increase of the sewage which is passed into the stream. Fifteen or sixteen years ago the Thames water was not so bad, and persons on the river did not hesitate at dipping in a vessel and drinking the contents. Such a thing now would be like an act of insanity; and yet we are told, on good authority, that in a part of Rotherhithe a number of poor persons, who have no proper water-supply, are obliged to use, for drinking and other purposes, the Thames water in its present abominable condition, unfiltered. This is a matter which should receive immediate attention.

George Godwin, *Town Swamps and Social Bridges*, 1859

SHOP ASSISTANTS

Saleswomen in shops. This is a good employment for a strong young person. A tall figure is considered an advantage, and the power of standing for many hours is requisite. A good deal of fatigue has to be undergone at first, but a shop girl told me that after a few weeks, they get so used to standing it seems as natural as sitting. The life is far more healthy to most persons than that of a dressmaker.

The power of making out a bill with great rapidity and perfect accuracy is also necessary, and this is the point where women usually fail. A poor half-educated girl keeps a customer waiting while she is trying to add up the bill, or perhaps does it wrong, and in either case excites reasonable displeasure. This displeasure is expressed to the master of the establishment, who dismisses the offender and engages a well-educated man in her place. He pays him double wages, but then feels sure that his assistant will not drive away customers by his incapacity.

Parents who intend their daughters to become saleswomen should take care that they are thoroughly proficient in arithmetic. Good manners are also requisite ... the higher the class of shop, the more obliging and polished the manners of the assistants are expected to be. The slightest want of politeness to customers, even if they are themselves unreasonable and rude, is a breach of honesty towards the owner of the establishment, for if customers are offended they are likely enough to withdraw to some other shop. No one, therefore, ought to enter on this employment who does not possess entire self-command.

Salaries from £20 to £50 a year, with board and lodging. These situations are usually obtained by private recommendation.

Emily Faithfull, *Choice of a Business for Girls*, 1864

There is another ceremony performed with much clattering solemnity of wooden panels, and iron bars, and stanchions, which occurs at eight o'clock in the morning. Tis then that the shop-shutters are taken down. The great "stores" and "magazines" of the principal thoroughfares gradually open their eyes; apprentices, light-porters, and where the staff of assistants is not very numerous, the shopmen, release the imprisoned wares, and bid the sun shine on good family souchong, "fresh Epping sausages," "Beaufort collars," "guinea capes," "Eureka shirts," and "Alexandre harmoniums." In the smaller throughfares, the proprietor often dispenses with the aid of apprentice, light-porter, and shopman – for the simple reason that he never possessed the services of any assistants at all – and unosten-tatiously takes down the shutters of his own chandler's, green-grocer's, tripe, or small stationery shop. In the magnificent linendrapery establishments of Oxford and Regent Streets, the vast shop-fronts, museums of fashion in plate-glass cases, offer a series of animated tableaux of poses plastiques in the shape of young ladies in morning costume, and young gentlemen in whiskers and white neckcloths, faultlessly complete as to costume, with the exception that they are yet in their shirt sleeves, who are accomplishing the difficult and mysterious feat known as "dressing" the shop window. By their nimble and practised hands the rich piled velvet mantles are displayed, the moire and glacé silks arranged in artful folds, the laces and gauzes, the innumerable whim-whams and fribble-frabble of fashion, elaborately shown, and to their best advantage.

George Augustus Sala, *Twice Round the Clock,* 1859

SIGHT-SEEING

Sight-seeing in the opinion of many experienced travellers, is best avoided altogether. It may well be, however, that this will be held to be a matter of opinion, and that sight-seeing will continue to flourish until the arrival of that traveller of Lord Macaulay's, who has found his way into so many books and newspapers, but whose nationality shall not be hinted at here. One piece of advice to the intending sight-seer is at all events sound. Never go to see anything by yourself. If the show be a good one, you will enjoy yourself all the more in company; and the solitary contemplation of anything that is dull and tedious is one of the most depressing experiences of human life. Furthermore, an excellent principle—said to be of American origin—is never to enquire how far you may go, but to go straight on until you are told to stop. The enterprising sight-seer who proceeds on this plan, and who understands the virtues of "palm oil," is sure to see everything he cares to see.

Charles Dickens (Jr.), *Dickens's Dictionary of London*, 1879

SLANG

Beak – A magistrate, a police magistrate ...

Banyan days – This phrase is employed by sailors to denote the days when no animal food is served out to them. ...

Bloke – This word has recently become popular to signify disrespectfully a man, a person, a party. ...

Boss – The master or chief person in a shop or factory. This word, recently introduced to England from the United States, was originally used by the American working classes to avoid the word master – a word which was only employed to signify the relation between a slave-owner and his human chattel. ...

Brick – This expression implies the highest commendation of a man's character. "He's a regular brick," ie. the best of good fellows. ...

Bumper – A full glass or goblet. ...

Cabbage – To steal; originally and still applied to tailors and milliners, who are supposed to cut off for their own use pieces of the cloth, silk, velvet or other materials entrusted to them to be made up. ...

Cagg – To abstain for a certain time from liquor. . . .

Corned – Drunk, intoxicated. . . .

Crib – A house, a lodging, a place of rest for the night. . . .

Cove – A man, a person. . . .

Dander – To have one's dander up; to be incensed, angry, resolute, fierce. . . .

Doss – A resting place, a bed; doss-ken, a tramp's lodging house . . .

Fawney-rig – The trick of dropping a ring. Fawney bouncing, selling rings for a pretended wager. . . .

Gammon – Deception. Gammy, ill-tempered, ill-natured. . . .

Gum – Loud abusive language. "Let us have no more of your gum" . . .

Hookem-snivey – To feign mortal sickness, disease and infirmity of the body in the streets in order to excite compassion and obtain alms. . . .

Hook it – be off! . . .

Kidney – Of the same kidney, ie. alike, resemblant. . . .

Rhino – Money; the portion or share of the proceeds of a robbery, divided among the robbers. . . .

Ran-tan – To be on the ran–tan, to be roaring drunk. . . .

Shine – A disturbance, a row; "don't kick up a shine;" shindy, a domestic disturbance; a quarrel. . . .

Slate – To beat, a good slating, a severe beating. . . .

Shandy-gaff – A mixture of ale and gin, and sometimes of ale and ginger-beer. . . .

Skilly – Workhouse gruel, or thin soup; sometimes called skilligolee . . .

Toke – Dry bread; toc (French argot or slang), false gold, anything ugly, deceptive, or of bad quality. . . .

Tantrums – Violent fits of bad temper. . . .

All the Year Round, October 17, 1874

SLAUGHTERHOUSES

I consider slaughtering within the City as both directly and indirectly prejudicial to the health of the population;—directly, because it loads the air with effluvia of decomposing animal matter, not only in the vicinity of each slaughter-house, but likewise along the line of drainage which conveys away its washings and fluid filth; indirectly, because many very offensive and noxious trades are in close dependence on the slaughtering of cattle, and round about the original nuisance of the slaughter-house you invariably find established the concomitant and still more grievous nuisances of gut-spinning, tripe-dressing, bone boiling, tallow-melting, paunch-cooking, etc.

Ready illustrations of this fact may be found in the gut-scraping sheds of Harrow Alley, adjoining Butchers' Row, Aldgate; or in the Leadenhall skin-market, contiguous to the slaughtering places, where the stinking hides of cattle lie for many hours together, spread out over a large area of ground, waiting for sale, to the great offence of the neighbourhood.

Dr John Simon, *Report of the Medical Officer of Health*, 1849

SLOPSELLERS

Accordingly I was led, by the gentleman whose advice I had sought, to a narrow court, the entrance to which was blocked up by stalls of fresh herrings. We had to pass sideways between the baskets with our coat-tails under our arms. At the end of the passage we entered a dirty-looking house by a side entrance. Though it was midday, the staircase was so dark that we were forced to grope our way by the wall up to the first floor. Here, in a small back room, about eight feet square, we found no fewer than seven workmen, with their coats and shoes off, seated cross-legged on the floor, busy stitching the different parts of different garments. The floor was strewn with sleeve-boards, irons, and snips of various coloured cloths. In one corner of the room was a turn-up bedstead, with the washed out chintz curtains drawn partly in front of it. Across a line which ran from one side of the apartment to the other were thrown the coats, jackets, and cravats of the workmen. Inside the rusty grate was a hat, and on one side of the hobs rested a pair of old cloth boots, while leaning against the bars in front there stood a sackful of cuttings. Beside the workmen on the floor sat two good-looking girls – one cross-legged like the men – engaged in tailoring.

My companion having acquainted the workmen with the object of my visit, they one and all expressed themselves ready to answer any questions that I might put to them. They made dress and frock coats, they told me, Chesterfields, fishing-coats, paletots, Buller's monkey jackets, beavers, shooting coats, trousers, vests, sacks, Codringtons, Trinity cloaks and coats, and indeed, every other kind of woollen garment. They worked for the ready-made houses, or "slopsellers." "One of us," said they, "gets work from the warehouse, and gives it out to others. The houses pay different prices. Dress coats, from 5s. 6d. to 6s. 9d.; frock coats the same; shooting coats, from 2s. 6d. to 2s. 9d. In summertime, when trade is busy, they pay 3s. Chesterfields, from 2s. 6d. to 3s.; some are made for 2s.; paletots, from 2s. 6d. to 3s. "Aye, and two days' work for any man," cried one of the tailors with a withered leg, "and buy his own trimmings, white and black cotton, gimp, and pipe-clay." "Yes," exclaimed another, "and we have to buy wadding for dress coats; and soon, I suppose, we shall have to buy cloth and all together. Trousers, from 1s. 6d. to 3s.; waistcoats, from 1*s*. 6*d*. to 1*s*. 9*d*. Dress and frock coats will take two days and a half to make each, calculating the day from six in the morning till seven at night; but three days is the regular time. Shooting coats will take two days; Chesterfields take the same as dress and frock coats; paletots, two days; trousers, one day."

Henry Mayhew, *'Labour and the Poor'*
(in the *Morning Chronicle*), 1849

SLUMS

Not far from the Tunnel there is a creek opening into the Thames. The entrance to this is screened by the tiers of colliers which lie before it. This creek bears the name of the Dock Head. Sometimes it is called St. Saviour's, or, in jocular allusion to the odour for which it is celebrated, Savory Dock. . . .

On entering the precincts of the pest island, the air has literally the smell of a graveyard, and a feeling of nausea and heaviness comes over any one unaccustomed to imbibe the musty atmosphere. It is not only the nose, but the stomach, that tells how heavily the air is loaded with sulphuretted hydrogen; and as soon as you cross one of the crazy and rotting bridges over the reeking ditch, you know, as surely as if you had chemically tested it, by the black colour of what was once the white-lead paint upon the door-posts and window-sills, that the air is thickly charged with this deadly gas. The heavy bubbles which now and then rise up in the water show you whence at least a portion of the mephitic compound comes, while the open doorless privies that hang over the water side on one of the banks, and the dark streaks of filth down the walls where the drains from each house discharge themselves into the ditch on the opposite side, tell you how the pollution of the ditch is supplied.

The water is covered with a scum almost like a cobweb, and prismatic with grease. In it float large masses of green rotting weed, and against the posts of the bridges are swollen carcasses of dead animals, almost bursting with the gases of putrefaction. Along its shores are heaps of indescribable filth, the phospho-retted smell from which tells you of the rotting fish there, while the oyster shells are like pieces of slate from their coating of mud and filth. In some parts the fluid is almost as red as blood from the colouring matter that pours into it from the reeking leather-dressers' close by.

The striking peculiarity of Jacob's Island consists in the wooden galleries and sleeping-rooms at the back of the houses which overhang the dark flood, and are built upon piles, so that the place has positively the air of a Flemish street, flanking a sewer instead of a canal; while the little ricketty bridges that span the ditches and connect court with court, give it the appearance of the Venice of drains, where channels before and behind the houses do duty for the ocean. Across some parts of the stream whole rooms have been built, so that house adjoins house; and here, with the very stench of death rising through the boards, human beings sleep night after night, until the last sleep of all comes upon them years before its time. Scarce a house but yellow linen is hanging to dry over the balustrade of staves, or else run out on a long oar where the sulphur-coloured clothes hang over the waters, and you are almost wonderstruck to see their form and colour unreflected in the putrid ditch beneath.

At the back of nearly every house that boasts a square foot or two of outlet – and the majority have none at all – are pig-sties. In front waddle ducks, while cocks and hens scratch at the cinderheaps. Indeed the creatures that fatten on offal are the only living things that seem to flourish here.

Henry Mayhew, *A Visit to the Cholera District of Bermondsey*, 1849

SMALL ADS, MYSTERIOUS

DEAR PEEPS. – Bib entreats you to COME HOME. Business is being most satisfactorily arranged.

LOVEY. – I find it Now impossible to carry out our intentions. Ruin and starvation would be the result.

TO GUSSIE – ANNIE has RETURNED from Calcutta, and is very anxious to see you. Address A.M., Mr. James Mason's, solcitors, 19, Maddox-street, Regent-street, W.

Write to me at uncle's. All forgiven. Everything will be settled immediately. My love unchangeable. – COSIE

LITTLE AMERICAN – I have been ill – ill almost to death. I have no daughter of my own; will you not come and see me once again. – R.B.

FORESTGATE. – If you really love me and do not wish to work out your own misery and my ruin, forget me. You know you would not be happy. It is no slight trial to me. The direction was right.

The Times, October 31st, 1868

SMITHFIELD MARKET

Surrounded by dirty streets, lanes, courts, and alleys, the haunts of poverty and crime, Smithfield is infested not only with fierce and savage cattle, but also with the still fiercer and more savage tribes of drivers and butchers. On market-days the passengers are in danger of being run over, trampled down, or tossed up by the drivers or "beasts"; at night, rapine and murder prowl in the lanes and alleys in the vicinity; and the police have more trouble with this part of the town than with the whole of Brompton, Kensington, and Bayswater. The crowding of cattle in the centre of the town is an inexhaustible source of accidents. Men are run down, women are tossed, children are trampled to death. But these men, women, and children, belong to the lower classes. Persons of rank or wealth do not generally come to Smithfield early in the morning, if indeed, they ever come there at all. The child is buried on the following Sunday, when its parents are free from work; the man is taken to the apothecary's shop close by, where the needful is done to his wound; the woman applies to some female quack for a plaister, and if she is in good luck she gets another plaister in the shape of a glass of gin from the owner of the cattle. The press takes notice of the accidents, people read the paragraph and are shocked; and the whole affair is forgotten even before the next market day.

For years Smithfield has been denounced by the press and in Parliament. The Tories came in and went out; so did the Whigs. But neither of the two great political parties could be induced to set their faces against the nuisance. The autonomy of the city, moreover, deprecated anything like government intervention, for Smithfield is a rich source of revenue; the market dues, the public-house rents, and the traffic generally, represent a heavy sum. In the last year only, the Lords and Commons of England have pronounced the doom of Smithfield. The cattle market is to be abolished. But when? That is the question—for its protectors are sure to come forward with claims of indemnity, and other means of temporisation; and the choice of a fitting locality, on the outskirts of the town, will most likely take some years. For we ought not to forget that in England everything moves slowly, with the exception of machinery and steam.

Max Schlesinger, *Saunterings in and about London*, 1853

SOUP KITCHENS

We cross the boundary of the labyrinth of which we speak, and a searching wind drives a cold rain against our legs as we turn down the Southwark Bridge-road, and stop before a large wooden gateway, like the entrance to a manufactory. It is too dark to see the words 'South-London Night-Refuge,' which are painted on a board above; and even the inscription on the gate itself, which announces that the manufacture going on inside is the concoction of soup for the benefit of the poor, is for the time obscured. There is no mistaking the place, however; for about fifty women are waiting – O how anxiously! – for six o'clock, when the gate will be opened, and as many of them admitted as can be provided for out of the funds already in hand for the purpose. Did you ever see more wistful faces as the flicker of the street-lamp falls on them for a moment? – faces wan with hunger, and many of them furrowed with the marks of suffering; but few of them bearing an impatient expression – not one with the defiant stare or the servile smirk of the regular pauper. One or two of them, with indistinct bundles, round which they wrap their scanty shawls so carefully that we know they have brought their babies with them to get the warmth and shelter for which they know not otherwise where to turn. Young women: here and there one with a damaged crumpled flower in her bonnet; only one or two without bonnets, and they are evidently unaccustomed to use the shawl as a covering for the head. None speaking except in a low tone, and then but little, as though the anxiety to be among the number chosen precluded much conversation. So they stand; and it is with a feeling of dismay that we learn how the want of necessary funds will forbid the admission of more than half the number of applicants that the place will hold. Fifty men and fifty women, instead of a hundred or more of each, are to be the guests to-night; and the rest, to whom the inviting finger of the keen-eyed manager does not point when he opens the gate, must wander other whither.

Thomas Archer, *The Terrible Sights of London*, 1870

"SPRING-HEELED JACK"

Many among the public have hitherto been incredulous as to the truth of various representations made to the Lord Mayor of the gambols of "Spring-heeled Jack," the suburban ghost ... The following authentic particulars, however, of a gross and violent outrage committed on a respectable young lady, and which might not only have caused her death, but that of both her sisters, by the unmanly brute, will remove all doubt on the subject. ...

Miss Jane Alsop, a young lady 18 years of age, stated that at about a quarter to 9 o'clock on the preceding night she heard a violent ringing at the gate in front of the house, and on going to the door to see what was the matter she saw a man standing outside, of whom she inquired what was the matter, and requested he would not ring so loud. The person instantly replied that he was a policeman, and said "For God's sake, bring me a light, for we have caught Spring-heeled Jack here in the lane." She returned into the house and brought a candle and handed it to the person, who appeared enveloped in a large cloak, and whom she at first really believed to be a policeman. The instant she had done so, however, he threw off his outer garment, and applying the lighted candle to his breast, presented a most hideous and frightful appearance, and vomited forth a quantity of blue and white flame from his mouth, and his eyes resembled red balls of fire. From the hasty glance which her fright enabled her to get at his person, she observed that he wore a large helmet, and his dress, which appeared to fit him very tight, seemed to her to resemble white oil skin. Without uttering a sentence, he darted at her, and catching her partly by her dress and the back part of her neck, placed her head under one of his arms, and commenced tearing her gown with his claws, which she was certain were of some metallic substance. She screamed out loud as she could for assistance, and by considerable exertion got away from him and ran towards the house to get it. Her assailant, however, followed her, and caught her on the steps leading to the hall-door, when he again used considerable violence, tore her neck and arms with his claws, as well as a quantity of hair from her head; but she was at length rescued from his grasp by one her sisters . . . .

Mr. HARDWICK expressed his surprise and abhorrence at the outrage, and said that no pains should be spared to bring its miscreant perpetrator to justice.

The Times, 1838

STEAMBOATS

We hurry along the bridge, with its pagoda-like piers, which serve to support the iron chains suspending the platform, and turn down a flight of winding steps, bearing a considerable resemblance to the entrance of a vault or cellar.

On the covered coal barges, that are dignified by the name of the floating pier, are officials in uniform, with bands round their hats, bearing mysterious inscriptions, such as L. and W. S. B. C., the meaning of which is in vain guessed at by persons who have only enough time to enable them to get off by the next boat, and who have had no previous acquaintance with the London and Westminster Steam Boat Company. The words "PAY HERE" are inscribed over little wooden houses, that remind one of the retreats generally found at the end of suburban gardens; and there arc men within to receive the money and dispense the "checks," who have so theatrical an air, that they appear like money-takers who have been removed in their boxes to Hungerford Stairs from some temple of the legitimate drama that has recently become insolvent.

We take our ticket amid cries of "Now then, mum, this way for Creemorne!" "Oo's for Ungerford?" "Any one for Lambeth or Chelsea?" and have just time to set foot on the boat before it shoots through the bridge, leaving behind the usual proportion of persons who have just taken their tickets in time to miss it.

Barges, black with coal, are moored in the roads in long parallel lines beside the bridge on one side the river, and on the other there are timber-yards at the water's edge, crowded with yellow stacks of deal. On the right bank, as we go, are seen the shabby-looking lawns at the back of Privy Gardens and Richmond Terrace, which run down to the river, and which might be let out at exorbitant rents if the dignity of the proprietors would only allow them to convert their strips of sooty grass into "eligible" coal wharves.

Westminster Bridge is latticed over with pile-work; the red signal-boards above the arches point out the few of which the passage is not closed. The parapets are removed, and replaced by a dingy hoarding, above which the tops of carts, and occasionally the driver of a Hansom cab may be seen passing along.

After a slight squeak, and a corresponding jerk, and amid the cries from a distracted boy of "Ease her!" "Stop her!" "Back her !" as if the poor boat were suffering some sudden pain, the steamer is brought to a temporary halt at Westminster pier.

> Henry Mayhew and John Binny, *The Criminal Prisons of London*, 1862

"STREET ARABS"

Any one who has had occasion to visit in, or even walk through, the narrow, evil-smelling courts and alleys where lodge the lowest and most destitute of the London poor cannot help having been struck with the number of tiny, dirty, half-clothed children who run about and play on the muddy pavements. What will be their future? Abandoned perhaps at an early age by their parents, or having parents who are worse than no parents, driven by hunger to steal, will not they soon pass from ignorance to vice?

Many people seem to think that London street arabs are naturally too bad to be reclaimed; but this is by no means the truth, as you will see when I tell you a few instances of their gratitude and affection.

Very often the ragged-school teacher—poor enough himself—has to give a piece of bread to one of his class, to keep the child from fainting, and there are 'refuges' attached to the schools, where some of the poorest of the scholars are fed and lodged until employment can be found for them. The late Lord Shaftesbury was the leader of the philanthropists who first recognised the need of rescuing ragged children from their terrible life. Many London arabs have been sent to the colonies, and there, finding good situations, have lived a healthy life of honest hard work. A group of these emigrants, well – behaved and fine lads, insisted on being known as 'Lord Shaftesbury's boys,' and by their loyalty and grateful remembrance of those who had helped them induced a wealthy Australian gentleman to aid, very substantially, the London ragged schools. One youth, who emigrated to South Africa, got on in life so well that he was able to send £12 to the refuge where he had been sheltered in his days of misfortune, and asked for a lad to be chosen from out of those in the institution, and sent to him as an apprentice. Equally good work is done by Dr. Stephenson's Children's Home in Bonner Road.

'Uncle Jonathan', *Walks in and Around London,* 1895

STREET FOOD

The street-sellers engaged in the sale of eatables and drinkables, are, summing the several items before given, altogether 6,347: of whom 300 sell pea-soup and hot eels; 150, pickled whelks; 300, fried fish; 300, sheeps trotters; 60, ham-sandwiches; 200, baked 'tatoes; 4, hot green peas; 150, meat; 25, bread; 1,000, cat and dogs' meat; 300, coffee and tea; 1,700, ginger-beer, lemonade, sherbet, &c.; 50, elderwine; 4, peppermint – water; 28, milk; 100, curds and whey and rice-milk; 60, water; 50, pies; 6, boiled pudding; 6, plum "duff"; 150, cakes and tarts; 4, plum-cakes; 30, other cheaper cakes; 150, gingerbread-nuts; 500, cross-buns; 500, muffins and crumpets; 200, sweet stuff; 6, cough-drops; 20, ice-creams. But many of the above are only temporary trades. The streetsale of hot cross-buns, for instance, lasts only for a day; that of muffins and crumpets, baked potatoes, plum-"duff," cough-drops, elder-wine, and rice-milk, are all purely winter trades, while the sale of ginger-beer, lemonade, ice-creams, and curds and whey, is carried on solely in the summer. By this means the number of the street-sellers of eatables and drink-ables, never at any one time reaches the amount before stated. In summer there are, in addition to the 10,000 costers before mentioned, about 3,000 people, and in winter between 4,000 and 5,000, engaged in the eatable and drinkable branch of the street-traffic.

Henry Mayhew, *London Labour and the London Poor*, 1851

SUBURBIA

The vastness of suburban London distinguishes the city emi-nently from the continental cities. A mile beyond Paris you are in a wilderness of sand hills, gypsum quarries, sterile rocks, and windmills; beyond the walls of Rome there is literally an immense expanse of desert; whereas London, if we may borrow a bull, surrounds itself, suburb clinging to suburb, like onions, fifty on a rope. The suburbs, which George Colman described emphatically as "regions of preparatory schools," have a character peculiarly their own; once seen, they cannot be mistaken. They are marvellously attached to gardening, and rejoice above all things in a tree in a tub. They delight in a uniformity of ugliness, staring you out of countenance with five windows in front, and a little green hall door at one side, giving to each house the appearance of having had a paralytic stroke; they stand upon their dignity at a distance from the road, and are carefully defended from intrusion by a bodyguard of spikes bristling on a low wall. They delight in outlandish and ridiculous names: a lot of tenements looking out upon a dead wall in front, and a madhouse in the rear club together and introduce themselves to your notice as OPTIC TERRACE; another regiment is baptized by the christian and surnames of PARADISE PROSPECT; while a third lot, standing together two and two, after the manner of the Siamese Twins, are called MOGG'S VILLAS, BUGSBY'S COTTAGES or GEMINI PLACE. The natives of these outlandish places are less wealthy than genteel … they are eloquent on the merits of an atmosphere surcharged with dust, which they earnestly recommend for inhalation, under the attractive title of "fresh air".

All shopkeepers, tradesmen, and others in these regions are insufferably bad and dear; every body is supplied with the staple of their consumables from town, and it is only on an emergency that the suburban dealers are applied to. Knowing that their articles are not required for the regular consumption, they take good care to make those pay well whose necessities compel them occasionally to have dealings with them.

John Murray, *The World of London*
[in Blackwoods Magazine], 1841

My dear wife Carrie and I have just been a week in our new house, 'The Laurels', Brickfield Terrace, Holloway – a new six- roomed residence, not counting basement, with a front breakfast-parlour. We have a little front garden; and there is a flight of ten steps up to the front door, which, by-the-by, we keep locked with the chain up. Cumming, Gowing, and our other intimate friends always come to the little side entrance, which saves the servant the trouble of going up to the front door, thereby taking her from her work. We have a nice little back garden which runs down to the railway. We were rather afraid of the noise of the trains at first, but the landlord said we should not notice them after a bit, and took £2 off the rent.

George and Weedon Grossmith, *The Diary of a Nobody*, 1892

SWIMMING

Swimming. —The principal Swimming Clubs in London are as follows

ALLIANCE, City of London Bath, Golden-lane, Barbican. 1*s*. per quarter.

AMATEUR, St. George's Bath, Buckingham-palace-road. 10*s* 6*d*. per annum.

CADOGAN, Chelsea Bath, 171, King's-road, Chelsea. 10*s*. 6*d*. per annum.

CAMDEN, St. Pancras Bath, King-street, Camden Town. 2*s*. per month.

CYGNUS, Addington-square Bath, Camberwell. 10*s*. per annum.

DREADNOUGHT, Victoria Bath, Peckham. 1*s*. 6*d*. per quarter.

EXCELSIOR, St. Pancras Bath, Tottenham-court-road. 2*s*. 6*d*. per quarter. ILEX. Lambeth Bath, Westminster-bridge-road. 5*s*. per annum.

NORTH LONDON, North London Bath, Pentonville. 2*s*. 6*d*. per quarter.

OTTER, Marylebone Bath, Marylebone. 10*s*. 6*d*. per annum.

REGENT, St. Pancras Bath, Ling-street, Camden Town. 1*s*. per month.

ST. PANCRAS, St. Pancras Bath, Tottenham-court-road. 2*s*. 6*d*. per quarter.

SERPENTINE St. George's Bath, Davies-street, Berkeley-square. 10*s*. per annum.

SOUTH LONDON, Lambeth Bath, Westminster-bridge-road. 1*s*. per month.

SOUTH EAST LONDON, Victoria Bath, Peckham. 2*s*. 6*d*. per annum.

WEST LONDON, St. Pancras Bath, Tottenham-court-road. 2*s*. per quarter.

Racing frequently takes place at the various baths, and, in the season, in the Thames and Serpentine; indeed, some enthusiasts even race in the latter unsavoury water at Christmas. There is a floating bath on the Thames at Charing-cross.

Charles Dickens (Jr.), *Dickens's Dictionary of London*, 1879

T is for Traffic Lights

The world's first traffic lights were erected in Westminster, near
the Houses of Parliament. Built in 1868, they were gas-lit, with
semaphore-like arms, manually operated by a policeman. The
lights exploded within six months of being erected, and a system
of lights was not attempted again in London for several decades.

TEA-SHOPS

AN invitation to contemplate a London without tea-shops may seem rather hopeless, but nevertheless, up to about 1875, such an institution was, in the modern sense, to the Cockney unknown. And when it came it was not an innovation that caught on with the speed of the Great Fire. Probably the advent of the girl clerk prompted its inauguration, and her ever-increasing numbers favoured its development.

Aerated bread was first heard of about 1860, and was the invention of Dr. Dauglish of Malvern, who aimed at the abolition of manual kneading with its associated nastiness and dangers to cleanliness and health. This he accomplished by means of yeast-less dough, mixed by machinery and impregnated with carbonic acid gas. Nothing but flour, water, a little salt and gas – no sweat! It was liked by many. For years the Company confined itself to the making and sale of its special bread and cakes.

The first ABC shop to sell tea, coffee, milk, etc., and provide sitting accommodation which I knew was in the courtyard of Fenchurch Street Station and about the date named had only recently been opened. I understood it was the initial attempt and was prompted by the fact that the sale of bread alone was not proving a dividend-earning proposition. Things have developed with the ABC and its imitators since then, but little is heard now of the mechanically mixed bread which was the Company's *raison d'être* and its employees know about as much of Dr. Dauglish as they do of St. Francis of Assisi.

Alfred Rosling-Bennett, *London and Londoners in the 1850s and 1860s*, 1924

TELEGRAPHY

The Electric Telegraphs throughout the Kingdom being now national property, are managed by the General Post Office: the head office being in St. Martin's-le-Grand, London. More than 300 branch offices are now distributed through London, so that no quarter or neighbourhood is far distant from one. By means of the London Postal Telegraph messages may be sent in a very short time from any part of London, through 400 or 500 miles of wires carried over the tops of the houses, and under the streets. The charge is 1*s.* for 20 words exclusive of addresses of sender and receiver – increasing at a rate of 3*d.* per 5 words beyond that number – to any part of the United Kingdom. Foreign telegrams are charged at various rates.

Murray's Handbook to London As It Is, 1879

THE submarine cable and the land telegraph have together equipped the earth with a complete and highly developed nervous system, sensitive to the slightest shock or jar. Fifty years ago the world's nerves were in a very primitive stage of development. Electricity, however, has annihilated space in its relation to time, and bound the nations of the earth together in a way which was inconceivable before the first submarine cable was laid. Last month we had two illustrations which strikingly indicated the transformation which the electric cable has brought about in our everyday life. The scene of the Spanish-American War is several thousand miles distant from our shores, but day by day we have followed its course with almost as full a knowledge of the events of the previous twenty-four hours as if we had been on the spot. The world-wide sorrow which found expression on the death of Mr. Gladstone was one of the most impressive events of modern times. But it was a tribute to the power of electricity no less than to the personality of the dead statesman.

The Review of Reviews, 1898

TERRORISM
THE DYNAMITE OUTRAGE IN LONDON

THE SCOTLAND-YARD EXPLOSION

The explosions in St. James's-square, combined with that at Scotland-yard, on Friday night, May 30, threw the West-End into a state of excitement such as probably has not been witnessed for many a year.

LIKE THE REPORT OF A CANNON

sounded the last explosion, which threw Scotland-yard into consternation. It took place shortly after half-past nine o'clock. Inspector Grainger was on duty inside the police station itself, and Inspector Robson of the Criminal Investigation Department, was in charge of the detective offices. Two police officers were stationed outside the police station, and two reserve men were with Inspector Robson in the detective office. Another policeman was on duty just outside the urinal on the north-east side of the building standing in the centre of the yard, the greater part of which is used as offices by the Criminal Investigation Department. This had been looked upon as a likely place to be fired upon if the Fenians should decide on attacking the chief police office, and special care was taken in watching it. It is certain that it was here the explosion originated, for the whole front of this portion of the building up to the second floor was found by Inspector Grainger and his men, when alarmed by the noise and the screams of people who had been hurt as they ran round to the scene of the catastrophe, to have been blown out.

THE CONSTABLE ON DUTY

near the spot was found to be severely injured, and had to be removed in a cab to Westminster Hospital. Just fronting this corner of the building stands a public-house with a wide frontage, known as

THE RISING SUN

The whole of the frontage of that house was also wrecked. Two carriages had been standing waiting at this house. One of them had been completely destroyed, and the driver, who was standing by it, seriously injured. He was taken to the Charing-cross Hospital. The driver of the other vehicle, which also had a wheel wrenched off it, and fell side-ways on to the pavement, was, it was understood, seated on his box at the time, and blown right off it. He was also severely injured, and taken to Charing-cross Hospital, but his wounds, although serious, were not so bad as those of his fellow-coachman, he having apparently been less in the direction which the flying masonry took.

The Penny Illustrated Paper, 1884

THAMES TUNNEL, THE

Life in the Thames Tunnel is a very strange sort of life. As we descend, stray bits and snatches of music greet our ears. Arrived at the bottom of the shaft, there is the double pathway opening before us, and looking altogether dry, comfortable, and civilised, for there are plenty of gas-lights; and the passages which communicate between the two roadways, are tenanted by a numerous race of small shop-keepers, offering views of the tunnel, and other penny wares for sale. These poor people never see the sun except on Sundays. The strangers in London are their best, and indeed I may almost say, they are their only customers.

As we proceed, the music becomes more clear and distinct, and here it is: a miniature exhibition of English industrial skill. It is an Italian organ, played by a perfect doll of a Lilliputian steam-engine. That engine grinds the organ from morning till night; it gives us various pieces without any compunction or political scruples. The Marseillaise, German waltzes, the Hungarian Rakowzy march, Rule Britannia, Yankee Doodle, etc., does this marvellous engine grind out of the organ. Those London organs are the most tolerant of musical instruments that I know of; they appeal to all nations and purses. And what is more marvelous still, they are not stopped by the police, as they would be in Vienna or Berlin, even though the cosmopolitan organ-grinder might descend tens of thousands of feet below the bed of the Spree or the Danube. In the present instance, the organ and the engine are mere decoy-birds. You stop, and are invited to look at "the panorama"—at the expense of "only one penny." You see Queen Victoria at that interesting moment in which she vows to "love, honour, and obey" Prince Albert. You also see a Spanish convent, which no panorama can be without; and the Emperor Napoleon in the act of being beaten at Waterloo—the chief scene of every London panorama.

Max Schlesinger, *Saunterings in and about London*, 1853

Thames Tunnel. – This great, but for many years comparatively useless, work of Sir Isambard Brunel was carried under the river from Wapping (left bank) to Rotherhithe (right bank) at a cost of nearly half a million of money. For about twenty years after its completion it was one of the recognised sights of London, and a kind of mouldy and poverty-stricken bazaar established itself at the entrance of the tunnel. The pence of the sightseers and the rent of the stalls proved wholly insufficient even to pay current expenses, and in 1865 the Tunnel Company were glad to get rid of their white elephant at a loss of about half its original cost. It now belongs to the East London Railway Company. NEAREST Steamboat Pier, Tunnel; Railway Stations, Wapping and Rotherhithe; Omnibus Routes, Blackwall and Rotherhithe.

Charles Dickens (Jr.), *Dickens's Dictionary of the Thames*, 1881

THEATRE AUDIENCES

The theatre is the most popular resort of pleasure-seeking workmen, and the gallery their favourite part of the house. Two or three mates generally go together, taking with them a joint-stock bottle of drink and a suitable supply of eatables. Or sometimes two or three married couples, who have "no encumbrance," or who have got some neighbours to look after their children, make up a party, the women carrying a plentiful supply of provisions. To the habituées of the stalls and boxes the eating and drinking that goes on in the gallery may appear to be mere gluttony, though the fact really is that it is a simple necessity. There is scarcely a theatre gallery in England from the back seats of which it is possible to see and hear with any degree of comfort, or in a manner that will enable you to comprehend the action of the piece without standing during the whole of the performance, and standing up in a gallery crowd is a thing to be contemplated with horror. In order to get a place in the gallery of a well attended theatre on a Saturday night from which you can witness the performance while seated, it is necessary to be at the entrance at least half an hour before the doors open, and when they do open you have to take part in a rush and struggle the fierceness of which can only be credited by those who have taken part in such encounters. And when you have at length fought your way up the narrow, inconvenient, vault-like staircase, and into a seat, and have recovered sufficiently to reconnoitre your position, you find yourself one of a perspiring crowd, closely packed in an ill-lighted, ill-ventilated, black hole of Calcutta-like pen, to which the fumes of gas in the lower parts of the house ascend. It is not unlikely, too, that you find yourself seated next to some individual who has been rendered ferociously quarrelsome by having been half strangled in the struggle at the doors, and who, upon your being unavoidably pressed against him, tells you in a significant manner, not to "scrouge" him whoever else you scrouge. To endure this martyrdom some substantial nourishment is absolutely necessary, and the refreshments of the gods provided by the theatrical purveyors of them, being of a sickly and poisonous, rather than an ambrosial character, consisting for the most part of ale and porter, originally bad, and shaken in being carried about until it has become muddy to the sight and abominable to the taste; rotten fruit, and biscuits stale to the degree of semi-putrefaction; those gods who take a supply of refreshments with them when they go to a theatre, display, not gluttony, but a wise regard for their health and comfort.

Thomas Wright, *Some Habits and Customs of the Working Classes*, 1867

THIEVES

The last of the criminal classes are the thieves, who admit of being classified as follows:-(1.) Those who plunder with violence; as "cracksmen," who break into houses; "rampsmen," who stop people on the highway; "bludgers" or "stick slingers," who rob in company with low women. (2.) Those who hocus or plunder persons by stupefying; as "drummers," who drug liquor; and "bug-hunters," who plunder drunken men. (3.) Those who plunder by stealth, as (i.) "mobsmen, or those who plunder by manual dexterity, like "buzzers," who pick gentlemen's pockets; "wires," who pick ladies' pockets; "prop-nailers," who steal pins or brooches; and "thumble screwers," who wrench off watches; and shoplifters, who purloin goods from shops; (ii.) "sneaks-men," or petty cowardly thieves, and of these there are two distinct varieties, according as they sneak off with either goods or animals. Belonging to the first variety, or those who sneak off with goods, are "drag-sneaks," who make off with goods from carts or coaches; "snoozers," who sleep at railway hotels, and make off with either apparel or luggage in the morning; "sawney-hunters," who purloin cheese or bacon from cheese-mongers' doors; "noisy racket men," who make off with china or crockery-ware from earthenware shops; "snow-gatherers," who make off with clean clothes from hedges; "cat and kitten hunters," who make off with quart or pint pots from area railings; "area sneaks," who steal from the area; "dead-lurkers," who steal from the passages of houses; "till friskers," who make off with the contents of tills; "bluey-hunters," who take lead from the tops of houses; "toshers," who purloin copper from ships and along shore; "star-glazers," who cut the panes of glass from windows; "skinners," or women and boys who strip children of their clothes; and mudlarks, who steal pieces of rope, coal, and wood from the barges at the wharves.

Those sneaks-men, on the other hand, who purloin animals, are either horse-stealers or "woolly bird" (sheep) stealers, or deer-stealers, or dog-stealers, or poachers, or "lady and gentlemen racket-men," who steal cocks and hens, or cat-stealers or body snatchers.

Henry Mayhew and John Binny, The Criminal Prisons of London, 1862

TOWER SUBWAY, THE

A curious feat of engineering skill, in the shape of an iron tube seven feet in diameter driven through the bed of the Thames between Great Tower-hill and Vine-street. The original intention was to have passengers drawn backwards and forwards in a small tram omnibus. This, however, was found unremunerative, and the rails having been taken up the tunnel has since been open as a footway. Unfortunately, however, after subtracting from its diameter the amount necessary to afford a sufficient width of platform, there is not much head-room left, and it is not advisable for any but the very briefest of Her Majesty's lieges to attempt the passage in high-heeled boots, or with a hat to which he attaches any particular value. It has, however, one admirable quality, that of having cost remarkably little in construction. NEAREST Railway Stations, Aldgate (Metrop.) and Cannon-street (S.E.); Omnibus Routes, Aldgate High-street and Fenchurch-street; Cab Rank, Great Tower-street.

Charles Dickens (Jr.), *Dickens's Dictionary of London*, 1879

But the need of a tunnel for foot passengers below bridge persisted and in 1869 the Thames Sub-way from Tower Hill to Tooley Street was inaugurated. It consisted of a cast-iron tube seven feet in diameter, put together in pieces, Mr. Barlow being the engineer. It was expeditiously constructed without a hitch, in that respect forming a remarkable contrast to its unlucky forerunner. This sub-way was closed for traffic on the opening of the adjacent Tower Bridge, but remains intact, and I believe was usefully employed during the Great War. Its entrance kiosk still stands near the Tower gates. The London County Council have since made several sub-river tunnels, one at Rotherhithe itself, so justifying the old idea, but now they have expeditious lifts instead of wearying stairs, and moreover charge nothing for all their trouble.

Alfred Rosling-Bennett, *London and Londoners in the 1850s and 1860s*, 1924

TOYS
A MERRY CHRISTMAS is nothing without DUGWELL and SON's GUINEA BOX of EVERLASTING AMUSEMENTS which contains

THE SULTANS VOLCANIC FOUNTAIN. A Chymical Wonder.

FIVE BUNDLES of STICKS, and How to Use Them

ELECTRIC SPIDERS that Resent being Trod Upon

A SNAKE in the GRASS, the Scientific Mystery. Caution – Not the L.S. Company's

FAIRY INCANTATIONS, or Transformation Scene

THE FUNNY WRESTLERS – The Lover Link – Wheel of Life – Optic Gyrator – Conjuring for Ladies – A Star to Puzzle Wise Men – &c. Most astounding guinea's worth (wide public press). Sent free on receipt of post office order payable to R. DUGWELL, toy importer, 97 New Road, Whitechapel, London. E. City depot, Steven's Model Dockyard, 22 Aldgate.

advertisement from The Times, 1869

I am very fond of buying toys for children; but I don't take them to the Pantheon for that purpose. I fear the price of the merchandise which the pretty and well-conducted female assistants at the stalls have to sell. I have been given to understand that incredible prices are charged for India-rubber balls, and that the quotations for drums, hares-and-tabors, and Noah's arks, are ruinously high. I have yet another reason for not patronising the Pantheon as a toy mart. It frequently happens that I feel slightly misanthropic and vicious in my toy-dealing excursions, and that my juvenile friends have sudden fits of naughtiness, and turn out to be anything but agreeable companions. Woe betide the ill-conditioned youngsters who cause me to assume the function of a vicarious "Bogey!" But I serve them out, I promise you. To use a transpontine colloquialism, ungenteel but expressive, I "warm them." Not by blows or pinches – I disdain that; not by taking them into shops where they sell unwholesome pastry or deleterious sweetstuff – I have no wish to impair their infantile powers of digestion; though both processes, I have been given to understand, are sometimes resorted to by child-quellers; but I "warm them" by taking them into toy shops and buying them ugly toys. Aha! my young friends! who bought you the old gentleman impaled on the area railing while in the act of knocking at his own street door, and who emitted a dismal groan when the pedestal on which he stood was compressed? Who purchased the monkey with the horrible visage, that ran up the stick? who the dreadful crawling serpent, made of the sluggishly elastic substance – a compound of glue and treacle, I believe – of which printers' rollers are made, and that unwound himself in a shudderingly, reptile, life-like manner on the parlour carpet? Who brought you the cold, flabby toad, and the centipede at the end of the India-rubber string, with his heavy chalk body and quivering limbs, the great-grandfather of all the irreverent daddy-long-legs who wouldn't say their prayers, and were taken, in consequence, by those elongated appendages, and thrown, with more or less violence, downstairs? This is about the best method I know for punishing a refractory child.

George Augustus Sala, *Twice Round the Clock*, 1859

TRAFFIC JAMS

ELEVEN AM. One of the wheelers of a four-horse omnibus slipped on the pavement and fell down at the foot of the Holborn-side obelisk, between Fleet-street and Ludgate-hill. There's a stoppage. The horse makes vain endeavours to get up; there is no help for it, they must undo reins, buckles and straps to free him. But a stoppage of five minutes in Fleet-street creates a stoppage in every direction to the distance of perhaps half a mile or a mile. Leaning as we do against the railings of the obelisk, we look forwards towards St. Paul's, and back to Chancery-lane, up to Holborn on our left, and down on our right to Blackfriar's-bridge; and this vast space presents the curious spectacle of scores of omnibuses, cabs, gigs, horses, carts, brewer's drays, coal waggons, all standing still, and jammed into an inextricable fix. Some madcap of a boy attempts the perilous passage from one side of the street to the other; he jumps over carts, creeps under the bellies of horses, and, in spite of the manifold dangers which beset him, he gains the opposite pavement. But those who can spare the time or who set some store by their lives, had better wait. Besides it is pleasant to look at all this turmoil and confusion. And how, in the name of all that is charitable, are the London pickpockets to live if people will never stand still on any account?

The difficulty is soon got over. Two policemen, a posse of idle cabmen and sporting amateurs, and a couple of ragged urchins, to whom the being allowed to touch a horse is happiness indeed, have come to the rescue, loosening chains and traces, getting the horse up and putting him to again. It's all right. The fall of a horse gives exciting occupation to a score of persons, and even those who cannot assist with their hands, have at least a piece of excellent advice to give to those who can, exactly as if this sort of thing happened only once in every century in the crowded streets of London.

Max Schlesinger, *Saunterings in and about London*, 1853

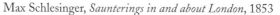

TRAFFIC LIGHTS

In the middle of the road, between Bridge-street and Great George-street, Westminster, Messrs. Saxby and Farmer, the well-known railway signalling engineers, have erected a column 20 feet high, with a spacious gas lamp near the top, the design of which is the application of the semaphore signal to the public streets at points where foot passengers have hitherto depended for their protection on the arm and gesticulations of a policeman – often a very inadequate defence against accident. The lamp will usually present to view a green light, which will serve to foot passengers by way of caution, and at the same time remind drivers of vehicles and equestrians that they ought at this point to slacken their speed. The effect of substituting the red light for the green one and raising the arms of the semaphore – a simultaneous operation – will be to arrest the traffic on each side. The signals when depressed will indicate that there is a regular foot crossing, and the signals will not interfere, it is thought, in the slightest degree with the ordinary use of the crossing. ... It is to be used for the first time at the assembling of the new Parliament on Thursday next. A more difficult crossing-place could scarcely be mentioned, and should the anticipations of the inventor be realised, similar structures will no doubt be speedily erected in many other parts of the metropolis.

The Express, 1868

TRAINING SHIPS

"Arethusa" and "Chichester," Office, 25, Great Queen-street, W.C. Two retired men-of-war, moored off Greenhithe; are lent by the Government to the Committee of the National Refuges for homeless and destitute children, the President of which is the Earl of Shaftesbury. The Chichester was opened in 1866, and the Arethusa in 1874. The two ships are fitted to accommodate together 400 boys, who are entered from fourteen to seventeen years of age, and to train them for a sea life either in the Royal Navy or merchant service. The ships are entirely supported by voluntary contributions, and a visit to either of them will afford ample proof that the funds are administered carefully, and with eminently satisfactory results.

Charles Dickens (Jr.), *Dickens's Dictionary of the Thames*, 1881

"Cornwall." – This reformatory training-ship of the School Ship Society is anchored off Purfleet. As a general rule the committee do not admit boys unless the three following conditions are satisfied:

1. That the boy be sentenced to not less than three years' detention.

2. That he be not less than 13 years of age nor more than than 15.

3. That he be certified as sound and healthy.

The comparative cost per head on ordinary maintenance and management is £23 5s. 8d. Funds are urgently needed, as "the amounts received on account of the Treasury allowance and the county and borough rates do little more than suffice for the maintenance of the boys and for the payments of the officers." Visitors are requested not to go on Saturday, which in cleaning day on board. The Cornwall was once the Wellesley, and was built in Bombay of teak in 1813.

Charles Dickens (Jr.), *Dickens's Dictionary of the Thames*, 1881

TRAMS

The tram came into existence to save the horse, it being shown clearly enough that the introduction of the rail meant the reduction of resistance and the easing of the horse's work; but, as a company for merely lightening a horse's labour would hardly be floatable, it was at once proposed to increase the weight and carrying capacity of the vehicle, so that the investor might share advantages with the horse. As a consequence, the poor horse is 20 per cent, worse off now than he was before the invention of the rail.

The average working life of a London omnibus horse is five years; that of a tram horse is only four. He is the same sort of horse; he comes to work at the same age; he costs about the same; and he works the same few hours; but so much greater is his effort that it costs a shilling a week more to feed him, and he is worked out in four-fifths of the time.

From the horse's point of view tramming, as we now have it, is by no means the perfect system of locomotion that some people imagine.

W.J.Gordon, *The Horse World of London*, 1893

TRANSVESTITES

At Bow-street, ERNEST BOULTON, 22, residing at 23, Shirland-road, FREDERICK WILLIAM PARK, 23, of 13, Bruton-street, Berkeley-square, law student, both of whom were in female costume, and HUGH ALEXANDER MUNDELL, 23, of 158, Buckingham Palace-road, were brought before Mr. Thomas, charged with frequenting the Strand Theatre with intent to commit felony. The prisoners Boulton and Park were defended by Mr. Abrams. When placed in the dock Boulton wore a cherry-coloured evening silk dress trimmed with white lace; his arms were bare, and he had on bracelets. He wore a wig and plaited chignon. Park's costume consisted of a dark green satin dress, low necked and trimmed with black lace, of which material he also had a shawl round his shoulders. His hair was flaxen and in curls. He had on a pair of white kid gloves. Mr. Superintendent Thomson, of the E Division was called, and stated that at half-past 10 o'clock on Thursday evening, he went to the Strand Theatre and saw the prisoners in a private box. Boulton and Park being in female costume. He noticed their conduct and saw one of them repeatedly smile and nod to gentlemen in the stalls. When they left the theatre all three prisoners got into a cab. They were then accosted and taken to Bow-street Police-station. . . .

Serjeant Kerley, detective, E Division, corroborated what had been stated, and added that while he was in the cab with the prisoners on their way to the station, Boulton and Park begged of him to let them go, as it could do him no good to take them to the station. If he would listen to them, he should have any sum he required. They never said anything about "having a lark" ... For the defence Mr. Abrams argued that the charge of felony was not made out, and that prisoners were only guilty of a "lark." Mr. Flowers said they had indulged in the so-called lark for a very long time. The question was were the prisoners without any other and more serious purpose? Did they entice gentlemen to their apartments to extort money from them? Mr. Abrams said he thought not.

The Times, 1870

Tuesday, 19 November. Went out to the Westminster Police Court, to the examination of Mary Newell, the maid of all work who robbed her master last week, went off in man's clothes, travelled down to Yarmouth, took lodgings there, smoked cigars, & made love to her landlady. Assuming that she had as I was told done it only for a lark, I admired her pluck skill and humour, and wished to observe her person & character. But the inspector who helped to catch her showed me that she was probably a practised thief and a dissolute girl ... At noon the court opened, with a great rush of people to see the prisoner. As a barrister, I had a reserved seat in front of her. She was led in and placed on high in the dock: a sullen but fairly good looking girt, of moderate height, and not unfeminine. Drest in shabby finery: her hair, which she had cut short, hanging over her forehead. Her hat, coat, trousers, and the rest of her male clothing were exhibited on a table ... After she had been committed for trial at the Sessions, I walked away with her master—a surveyor—and his pupil, the young man whose name & garments she assumed. She was a dirty and untidy servant, they said; was in the habit (they now found) of stealing out to low theatres alone, hiring cabs to go in and smoking cigars with the cabmen.

Arthur Munby, *Diary*, 1861

TREADMILL, PUNISHMENT BY

The tread-wheel, which was first brought into use at Brixton prison in 1817, is said to have been the invention of Mr. Cubitt, the engineer of Lowestoft, who, on being adjured by one of the magistrates of the county jail at Bury, to invent some mode of employing the idle prisoners, was suddenly struck with the notion of an elongated wheel, which resulted in the invention of the machine that has been the terror of idle scoundrels ever since, and is generally known among them as "the mill."

The wheel, which is, in fact, a cylinder extending the whole length of the building, contains twenty-four steps, something like those used to mount a paddle-box; the circumference of this cylinder is sixteen feet, and the steps are eight inches apart, so that a revolution of the "wheel" includes twenty-four steps. At every thirtieth revolution, that is to say, every fifteen minutes, a bell connected with the machine, announces that the "spell" of work, which lasts a quarter of an hour, is finished, and on the days that a prisoner is set to work at the "mill," he completes fifteen of these spells, or nearly four hours of the hardest labour to which any human being need be subjected. There are three tiers or galleries in front of this wheel, where the prisoners can never mount the terrible steps which sink beneath the tread of each unhappy Sisyphus, as he holds with the ends of his fingers the ledge which extends at about the height of his shoulders. Each prisoner is divided from his neighbour by a woodwork screen, shaped like the end of a "box" in a coffee-room, and as their backs are presented to me, I learn what I had long suspected, that the human back is as expressive of character under some circumstances as the human face. It is easy to see, too, that experience will enable the prisoner at the tread-wheel to avoid the labour to which the novice is subject by his endeavours to mount the steps, instead of allowing them to come down to the proper level, and sliding his foot easily upon each in succession. ... Whatever expedients they may adopt, however, there is no doubt that this at least is hard labour. If I ever had a doubt of it, that doubt is removed, as I see the men come down hot, panting, and bathed in perspiration, to sit on the benches at the bottom of the gallery; while others take their places in the vacant stalls to keep the relentless cylinder in motion. The amount of resistance of the wheel is regulated according to the number of men employed upon it, by a "governor" and a horizontal fan placed on a pedestal in the adjoining yard; but I am glad to learn that this exhausting labour is no longer useless, since it has been applied to the grinding of the prison flour, which is now pouring from the hopper in a neighbouring apartment, fitted like a mill, while the miller himself, with every appearance of that jollity proverbial to his calling, is sitting amidst his sacks reading a newspaper.

Thomas Archer, *The Pauper, The Thief and The Convict*, 1865

UVW

U is for Underground

'WELL I'M SURE NO WOMAN WITH THE LEAST
SENSE OF DECENCY WOULD THINK OF GOING
DOWN *THAT* WAY TO IT.' A joke from *Punch* of 1864.
The first underground line, the Metropolitan, between
Paddington and Farringdon Road, opened in 1863.

UNDERGROUND RAILWAYS

Yesterday the Metropolitan (underground) Railway was opened to the public, and many thousands were enabled to indulge their curiosity in reference to this mode of travelling under the streets of the metropolis.

The trains commenced running as early as six o'clock in the morning from the Paddington (Bishop's-road) station, and the Farringdon-street terminus, in order to accommodate work-men, and there was a goodly muster of that class of the public, who availed themselves of the advantages of the line in reaching their respective places of employment. At eight o'clock the desire to travel underground in the direction of the City began to manifest itself at the various stations along the line; and by nine it became equally evident to the authorities that neither the locomotive power nor the rolling stock at their disposal was at all in proportion to the requirements of the opening day. From this time, and throughout the morning, every station became crowded with anxious travellers who were admitted in sections; but poor were the chances of a place to those who ventured to take their tickets at any point below Baker-street, . . . Once in motion, all appeared to be right, the riding very easy, and a train which left Farringdon-street at 2:15 reached King's-cross station at 2:18 (a little over a mile), bringing up at the platform in three minutes. Gower-street was reached at 2:25, Portland-road at 2:30, Baker-street at 2:36, Edgware-road at 2:42, and the terminus at Paddington at 2:48; thus performing the journey in 33 minutes, including stoppages at the various stations. . . . Of the general comfort in travelling on the line there can be no doubt, and the novel introduction of gas into the carriages is calculated to dispel any unpleasant feelings which passengers, especially ladies, might entertain against riding for so long a distance through a tunnel. Yesterday, throughout every journey, the gas burnt brightly, and in some instances was turned on so strong in the first-class carriages, in each of which there were two burners, that when the carriages were stationary, newspapers might be read with facility; but, in motion, the draft through the apertures of the lamps, created so much flickering as to render such a feat exceedingly difficult. The second-class carriages are very nicely fitted with leathered seats, and are very commodious, and the compartments and arms in the first-class render overcrowding impossible.

There is one point to which attention was attracted as being adverse to the general expectation, and that was that it was understood that there was to be no steam or smoke from the engines used in working this tunnel railway. All we can say is, that on one of the journeys between Portland-road and Baker-street, not only were the passengers enveloped in steam, but it is extremely doubtful if they were not subjected to the unpleasantness of smoke also.

The Times, 1863

URINALS

At WORSHIP-STREET, Dr. JAMES CAMPBELL, residing at 6, Church-lane, Whitechapel, attended in answer to a summons which charged him with having unlawfully caused and procured one Richard Cleverley to affix certain posting bills upon a building without the consent of the owner. Richard Shirley, 286 A Reserve, deposed that on the morning of the 31st October, between 9 and 10 o'clock, he saw the man Cleverley in the act of posting four bills on a urinal situate in High-street, Shoreditch. The witness asked him who was his employer, and he replied "Dr. Campbell of 6, Church-lane, Whitechapel." In answer to a further question from the constable, he stated that he was paid 2*s.* a day for posting the bills. He had a can of paste and a number of bills with him at the time. The constable called on the defendant Campbell, and on inquiring as to whether he employed Cleverley to post bills he replied in the affirmative. He further said, "I have not been in the business long. I was not aware that I was doing wrong or that it was an offence. I only came into the profession in July last." One of the bills in question was produced and it was understood that in it the defendant had represented himself to be a legally qualified medical practitioner. ... They related to the defendant's ability to cure certain diseases. The magistrates convicted the defendant in the penalty of 40*s*. and costs.

The Times, 1867

George Williams, 21 years of age, was indicted for a robbery with violence... The prosecutor was Mr. Augustus Delany Smith, a solicitor in Great James-street, Bedford-row. On the night of the 18th of November, about a quarter to 10 o'clock, he was passing along King's-road, going towards his office. He turned into a urinal at the back of Bedford-row. There was a gas-lamp immediately over the urinal, and a boy was inside with lighted candles. He was leaving the place, when the prisoner entered, seized the gold guard chain of his watch, and attempted to take it from him.

The Times, 1869

VIGILANTES

LYNCH LAW IN ISLINGTON – Finding that the powers of the police are insufficient to check the rowdyism that has long been prevalent in Upper-street, Islington, on Sunday nights, a party of about twenty inhabitants, armed with canes, sallied out on the evening of the 6th and belaboured the roughs with so good an effect that the people returning from church were, to their agreeable surprise, allowed to walk home unmolested. The roughs were utterly astonished and beaten off by the unexpected attack, while the police were delighted with the vigorous display of civil force. A similar patrol is to be made on Sunday evening next. This vigorous action has apparently at length aroused Colonel Henderson, who has issued orders to his subordinates to adopt energetic measures for the preservation of the peace.

The Penny Illustrated Paper, 1870

VITRIOL ATTACKS

Anne Baker, a respectable looking young woman, was charged with having thrown a quantity of vitriol upon the dresses of two young females.

Ellen Seaton, a well-dressed girl, said that she was returning home through St. James's-park on the previous evening, with another female, when hearing a footstep behind them, they turned round and saw the defendant with a bottle in her hand, from which she was throwing something on her shawl and silk dress. On examining the shawl, which was fourfold thick on her shoulders, she found it was eaten quite into holes some by liquid, which she afterwards discovered to be vitriol; her silk dress was similarly damaged. The value of the shawl and dress was 4*l*.

In answer to an inquiry from the magistrate, complainant assigned as a reason for the act, that she had given evidence some time against a friend of the defendant's.

Complainant's friend proved that some vitriol had also gone upon her dress, and that the amount of damage was 10*s*.

Defendant denied the charge, and called a witness who swore she was not guilty of the offence.

Mr. GREGORIE said, he had no doubt the offence had been committed as described by complainant and her friend. He then ordered defendant to pay 4*l*. 10*s*., the amount of wilful damage, or in default to be imprisoned two months.

The Times, 1842

WASHING MACHINES

BRADFORD'S Patent "Vowel" WASHING MACHINES, Wringers and Mangles

EXPERIENCE OF USERS.

"The Washing Machine we had of you has been in constant use for ten years, and has done the washing for our family of seven ever since, without the aid of a washer-woman."

"The Machine ('Vowel' E) saves labour, soap, and fire, and my family are delighted with it. I can safely recommend it to anyone. I wish I had bought one before."

"Your 'Vowel' A has been in constant use for seven years, and Mrs. W. saye it has repaid original cost many times over."

"Many thanks for the excellent washer-woman' ('Vowel' I Machine) you provided for us – she is a treasure. In a few hours yesterday, two boys worked off the washing of the whole institution, containing nearly two hundred inmates."

"My servants wash more clothes and much better in one day with your Machine than they used to do in three days without it."

advertisement from *Dickens's Dictionary of London*, 1879

With regard to the first of these the question has to be answered, is it better to put linen out to wash or to wash it at home? Experience replies that it is more economical to wash it at home; very much pleasanter to send it out. The economy of washing at home is found not so much in the immediate saving of laundry bills (though that is considerable) but in the fact that clothes washed at home wear very much longer than those which are put out to wash. Laundresses as a class decry the use of lime and deleterious powders which save labour but destroy fabric; individual laundresses appear invariably to make use of them, and it is a very unusual thing to meet with one who does not use "just a little." The consequence is that linen washed carefully at home lasts three times as long as that which is put out to wash.

At the same time every one knows how disagreeable it is to have washing about. Modern improvements and machinery, washing machines, wringing machines, drying machines, &c. &c., lessen the unpleasantness connected with it, but they do not abolish it altogether. Of course a good deal depends upon the construction of the house and the appliances at command. Where the wash-house is built apart from the house, for example, and where there is space for drying out of the sight of the family, the business may be got through without a general sense of discomfort being experienced, but when the clothes have to be washed in a kitchen not very far away from the living-rooms occupied by the family, there is no hiding matters. Doors may be closed, copper-lids kept down, but the secret escapes. The pervading sense of warm flat irons described by Mr. Weller as being typical of the "kilybeate taste of mineral water," is typical also of soapy water; facts proclaim themselves, do what we will to keep them quiet, and every one in the house has a consciousness that the laundress is at the centre of the situation.

Cassell's Household Guide, c.1880

WYLD'S GREAT GLOBE

The gigantic Globe of Mr. James Wyld, Mr., now opened in Leicester-square, is modelled on a scale of ten geographical miles to an inch horizontal, or six inches to a degree, and it is one mile to an inch vertical, the diameter being sixty feet. By means of a gradual ascent at different stages this colossal figure of the earth, with its mountain and valley, sea and river, may be viewed from a moderate distance. The objects just mentioned are represented by numberless raised blocks, and castings in plaster, figured on the interior concave of the sphere, the fittings up of which must have been both difficult and expensive. The President of the Royal Geographical Society, in his late address, stated that Mr. Wyld was good enough to show and explain to him the whole of his undertaking, with which he was both surprised and pleased. "Recollecting that only a limited part of a sphere can meet the eye at once, it occurred to Mr. Wyld, that, by figuring the earth's surface on the interior instead of the exterior of his globe, the observer would be enabled to embrace the distribution of land and water, with the physical features of the Globe, at one view. And in this," added the president, "he has succeeded; from the great size, the examiner of details is hardly aware that he is gazing on a concavity. The attempt is well worthy of the projector and of the spirit of the age."

Little need be added to such high authority; but the last phrase reminds us that Mr. Wyld has himself recorded, that, "but for the Industrial Exhibition, his work would never have been undertaken. The congregation in London of the different nations and races of our empire and of the world was deemed the proper moment for the completion of a great model of the Earth's Surface, and the realisation of a thought which had for many years occupied his mind." We are also informed, that, had time or the occasion permitted, and had obstructions not been offered by some of the inhabitants of Leicester-square, Mr. Wyld would have endeavoured, by the formation of attached galleries, class-rooms, and museums, to render the institution still more available for the allied studies of geology and ethnology; nor does he yet abandon the hope of being able to do so. What is already realised, however, is an important boon, and calculated to supersede to a great extent the inefficient use of maps.

Illustrated London News, 1851

WORKHOUSES

Of the regulation which prohibits the visits to the workhouse of the friends of the inmates, I have hitherto said nothing. It is one which is of a piece with the general harshness of the administration of the law. In what way must the mind of the man be constituted, who first conceived the idea of refusing to the wretched pauper the meagre consolation of a visit of any remaining friend he had when he flung himself, as a last resource, into a workhouse? In his nature, there must, indeed, be little of the milk of human kindness. There exists not the shadow of a pretext for this heartless severity. Are we to be told, that if permission were conceded to the friends of paupers to visit them in the workhouse, the regulation would be attended with inconvenience? That has been said; but it has not, to use the mildest language the slightest foundation in fact. Alas! by the time a poor wretch has been compelled to seek a refuge in the workhouse, the number of his friends has been sadly reduced. Fortunate, indeed, may he consider himself, if there be a single individual among his former acquaintances, even where their name was legion, who feels for and sympathises with him to such a degree as to prompt that individual to pay him an occasional visit in the workhouse. Reverses have a wonderful effect in lessening the number of one's friends. In how many instances does adversity scatter one's friends to the four winds of heaven? In how many instances do they all vanish as suddenly as if they had, by some magical influence, been spirited up to some other planet? How many paupers are

315

therein every workhouse, who, were the doors open at all times to the visits of friends, would never be inquired about by a single human being in the world? How miserable and groundless, then, the pretext that inconvenience would result from admitting the few persons who might feel disposed to pay an occasional visit to those in the workhouse whom they had known in other and better days? Surely so poor and cheap a consolation, as the sight of one who commiserated them in their unhappy condition, might be allowed the inmates. But no: they must needs be shut up from every manifestation of the sympathy of their fellow-creatures, as if they had committed some atrocious crime, by which they had forfeited all claim to the kindly consideration of mankind. ... An instance occurred a few months since in a workhouse in the suburbs of the metropolis, in which intelligence was accidentally conveyed to a daughter that her father was on his death-bed: she hurried that moment to the workhouse, but was refused admission. With tears in her eyes, and a heart that was ready to break, she pleaded the urgency of the case: the functionary was deaf to her entreaties: as soon might she have addressed them to the brick wall before her. His answer was, "It is contrary to the regulations of the place: come again at a certain hour." She applied to the medical gentleman who attended the workhouse, and through his exertions obtained admission. She flew to the ward in which her father was confined: he lay cold, motionless, and unconscious before her—his spirit was gone: he had breathed his last five minutes before. Well may we exclaim, when we hear of such things, "Do we live in a christian country? Is this a civilised land?"

James Grant, *Sketches in London*, 1838

Z is for Zazel

The extraordinary success of Zazel's performances attracted
large audiences at the Royal Aquarium. Zazel was a 14 year old
girl named Rosa Matilda Richte. One of the first 'human
cannonballs', she delighted the crowd with her death-defying act.
She would later tour with PT Barnum, unfortunately
breaking her back in one of her elaborate stunts.

X-RAYS

THE RONTGEN X RAYS – St. JAMES'S-HALL. – PRACTICAL DEMONSTRATIONS of the X RAYS (Rontgen's Marvellous New Light Discovery) DAILY at 2.30 and 4.0 by T.C.HEPWORTH, F.C.S., F.R.P.S., Admission, 2s. 6d. Schools and parties at reduced terms by arrangement. Mr. Hepworth's entertainment includes illustrations by the aid of the new Electric Lantern of the wonders of Up to Date Photography. St. James's-hall, Piccadilly entrance. Mr. Hepworth will photograph the hand of any of the audience. Engagements booked for evening at homes at Tree's Ticket Office, St. James's-hall.

advertisement from *The Times*, 1896

At WEST HAM, JOHN JOLLY, 46, Lansdowne-road, East Ham, a builder was charged on remand, with shooting Constable George Hill, 146 K, and with attempting to shoot Constable Edward Bateman, 697 K, with intent to murder them on January 25, outside the Stratford Police-court. . . . The circumstances have been reported. Hill, after being shot, was put under chloroform with the object of tracing the bulet, which, however, was not discovered till the Rontgen rays were employed. It was then seen to be in a cavity of the jaw, and up to the present it has not been considered advisable to attempt to remove it.

The Times, 1898

RONTGEN RAYS CASE AT HASTINGS. The Hastings coroner yesterday resumed the inquiry into the circumstances attending the death of Catherine Fanny Wilson, widow. Evidence was given to the effect that the deceased woman fractured her thigh when bicycle riding. On one occasion, the Rontgen rays were applied to the thigh for two hours to locate the fracture, and on the second occasion for two hours and 20 minutes. The woman wrote, a month before she died, a letter in which she alleged that her blood rested upon the two men – the medical man and photographer – who were the cause of all her suffering. Dr. Roberts said he considered the wound attributable to the Rontgen rays. In his opinion the cause of death was exhaustion from the effects of a shock caused by the fracture of the thigh and the Rontgen rays. Dr. Harry Mansell, who ordered the application of the rays, denied the allegation as to the time occupied. The jury ultimately found a verdict of "Death from shock and exhaustion," and stated that no blame was attached to the doctor or photographer.

*The Times,*1900

YACHTING

Yachting.—The magnates of the Royal Yacht Squadron or of the Royal Victoria Yacht Club are apt to allude in somewhat disparaging terms to Thames yachting, but there is no doubt that the Royal Thames and the Royal London Clubs have exercised a great deal of influence over yachting in English waters. Thames sailing is peculiar, and it requires a skilful pilot to grapple with the curious difficulties of sands and tide which are to be met with on the voyage from Gravesend round the Mouse. Those who have seen the Lower Hope or Sea Reach in bad weather, with a gale of wind blowing and the tides running-against it, will not be slow to admit that, especially on board one of the smaller craft, the Thames yachtsman wants skill and pluck as much as his brother who sails the open waters of the southern coasts. The principal London yacht clubs are the Royal Thames, which has a club-house in Albemarle-street. ... Among the features of the London yachting season are the races from Southend to Harwich and vice versa and the

Royal Harwich may also be classed among Thames yacht clubs. The head-quarters are naturally at Harwich. Entrance fee, £1 1*s*.; subscription £1 1*s*. The burgees of the above clubs are as follows: Royal Thames, blue and white cross with crown; Royal London, blue with City arms and crown; New Thames, dark blue with phoenix; Junior Thames, white with blue cross; Corinthian, blue with wreath; Nore, blue with cross and anchor; Royal Harwich, blue lion rampant. The matches of the larger clubs take place in May or June, and if a stranger wishes to see Thames yachting at its best, he should endeavour to obtain a ticket for the club steamer accompanying one of the races for cutters, or schooners and yawls. Tickets for these steamers can only be obtained through members of the respective clubs, but, a reference to the advertising columns of the newspapers will generally discover one or more boats chartered on these occasions for the accommodation of the general public.

Charles Dickens (Jr.), *Dickens's Dictionary of London*, 1879

ZOOLOGICAL GARDENS, THE

We were always at the Zoological Gardens; we not only had friends who gave us the green tickets, but we knew the keepers, one of whom lived in a lodge where we sometimes had tea, which always smelt of lion, and which now and then contained baby lions or other beasts, very small, very soft; which were being warmed and fed in front of his fire, and which I distinctly remember being allowed to nurse. I further recollect the feel of the rough tongues which licked our fingers, and being solemnly warned not to allow them to draw blood, for we were given to understand that, if they once tasted blood, the soft little kitteny things would become violent and gobble us up on the spot. Once I was in very real peril in these same gardens; I did not know that the horrible creature advancing towards me dragging a bit of chain and waving a stick was an escaped ourang-outang – the one specimen, I believe, then in any civilised country – and I was about to try and make friends when a white-faced keeper, followed by two or three other men, sprang out of the bushes and seized the chain; afterwards I heard the nurse tell my mother of the dreadful risk I had run, for our keeper friend had told her if they had not caught the beast when they did, he would have torn me limb from limb. . . . Yet another monkey obtained my undying hatred by stretching out a long lean arm, and grabbing a beautiful long feather out of my best hat, and when I stamped and raved with rage the beast ran up to the top of the cage, and tore it into the smallest of atoms . . . But much as I loved the gardens then, I love them a thousand times more now, when the animals are decently housed and treated, called by their names and looked after by their keepers, who really understand and care for their charges. The only thing that remains to be done is to teach the public to behave, to cease to prod the beasts with "swagger sticks," and to realise that monkeys don't eat sardine-tin lids or orange peel; and that the beautiful tame squirrels that now run fearlessly about the place, will soon lose their confidence in humanity if they are teased as they are at present, and not made friends with as they are in the Central Park in New York. I do not recollect such tiresome teasing on Sundays in the Zoo in old days, but I fancy the Fellows were more particular about to whom they gave their tickets; I know we used to be greatly envied because we had so many; now it seems to me that most of the Council School children, and brats of that ilk, disport themselves in the sacred spot on Sundays.

Mrs. J.E. Panton, *Leaves from a Life*, 1908

Appendices

APPENDIX I

A Note on Sources

DIARISTS AND LETTER-WRITERS

Arthur Munby (1828–1910), a middle-class diarist, famous for his obsession with the lives of working women, and his clandestine relationship with the servant Hannah Cullwick, whom he married in secret in 1873.

George Gissing (1857–1903), novelist, also wrote a fascinating diary, which chronicles, amongst other matters, the chaos of his domestic life ('Nothing could be more difficult than my position as regards the boy Walter. All but every statement made to him he answers with a blunt contradiction: to all but every bidding he replies "I shan't." . . . What a terrible lesson is the existence of this child, born of a loveless and utterly unsuitable marriage.').

Jane Welsh Carlyle (1801–1866), wife of Thomas Carlyle, described by the Oxford Dictionary of National Bibliography "the greatest woman letter writer in English".

Nathaniel Hawthorne (1804–1864), celebrated American author, stayed in London in the 1850s and published his journal of the period.

FICTION

Excerpts have been taken from three works of fiction: George and Weedon Grossmith's *The Diary of a Nobody* (1892), orginally a *Punch* serial in 1888/89, an affectionate satire of the suburban middle-class clerk, Mr. Pooter; George Reynolds, *The Mysteries of London* (1844), one of the most (in)famous examples of the "penny dreadful" serial; and Wilkie Collins's novel, *Basil* (1852) which happens to include an engrossing description of a mid-Victorian drawing-room, (albeit one of a nouveau riche linendraper, who follows the interior-design fashions of the day a little too closely).

GUIDEBOOKS

The tourist guidebooks referenced include *Black's Guide to London and Its Environs*, *Cruchley's London in 1865: A Handbook for Strangers*, Herbert Fry's *London*, *Mogg's New Picture of London and Visitor's Guide to its Sights*, *Murray's Handbook to London As It Is* and *Routledge's Popular Guide to London*. *Dickens's Dictionary* has already been mentioned in the Preface, and there is also an extract from the companion *Dictionary of the Thames*. Other specialist Victorian guides used include the historical guides for antiquaries and tourists, *Knight's London*, John Timbs's *Curiosities of London* and Peter Cunningham's *Hand-Book of London*, as well as a children's guide by 'Uncle Jonathan' *Walks in and Around London* and a coffee-table book of photographs by George Birch, *The Descriptive Album of London*.

JOURNALS

Diverse articles in journals have been cited, including items from the *Illustrated London News*, *Manufacturer and Builder*, *Municipal Journal and London*, *Penny Illustrated Paper*, *Punch*, *The Express*, *The Graphic*, and *The Leisure Hour*.

LIFESTYLE GUIDES

The Victorian publishing industry thrived on giving helpful hints to readers. I have, therefore, drawn upon *London at Dinner*, a guide to the best eateries in 1850s London, and Lieut. Col. Newnham-Davies's *Dinners and Diners*, a compilation of a pioneering set of restaurant reviews that first appeared in the *Pall Mall Gazette*. I hope the reader will indulge me in a handful of more general pieces, from *Cassells Household Guide*, Emily Faithfull's *Choice of a Business for Girls*, Mrs. Beeton's *Book of Household Management* and, not least, *The Ladies' and Gentleman's Model Letter Writer*, an excellent guide on etiquette, in even the most trying of circumstances ('I scarcely know how to reply to your letter or to express what I feel at finding that you have given me your affection. I am not worthy of you in any way, but if you really think that I could make you happy. I will gladly try my best to do so.')

MEMOIR WRITERS

Alfred Rosling-Bennett (1850–1928), a talented electrical engineer involved in early telephony.

Edmund Yates (1831–1894), a journalist and author who also worked for General Post Office; a close acquaintance of Charles Dickens.

Edward Owen, a policeman in Hyde Park between 1874 and 1896.

Mrs. J.E. Panton (1847–1923), writer, daughter of the celebrated painter William Frith.

'*One of the Old Brigade*', an anonymous chronicle of 1860s London night-life.

T.H.S Escott (1844–1924), a journalist and editor of the *Fortnightly Review.*

MISCELLANEOUS

Advertisements filled Victorian London, whether in print, upon billboards, flyposters, or displayed upon *advertising vans* and upon the backs (and fronts) of *sandwich-board men*; hence the reader will find various advertisements herein.

Factual sources referenced include the *Report of the Commissioners of the Great Exhibition* and I have reprinted several complaining letters to *The Times*, which perhaps deserve their own category as a historical resource, ranging from tales of pickpockets to the nuisance of perambulators.

SOCIAL INVESTIGATION

The richest seam for mining Victorian London's social history is undoubtedly the various works published by 'social investigators'. In the main, such works fall into three categories.

The first category are exposés of the conditions of life amongst the poor, often containing both vivid description and statistical information. The most famous work in this area is that by the journalist and writer Henry Mayhew, including *The Criminal Prisons of London*, *Labour and the Poor* (in the *Morning Chronicle*) and his masterpiece *London Labour and the London Poor*. Others in this book include Charles Booth's *Life and Labour of the People in London*; Arthur Sherwell's *Life in West London*; Friedrich Engels's *The Condition of the Working Class in England*; George Godwin's *London Shadows* and *Town Swamps and Social Bridges*; George R. Sims's *How the Poor Live* and Dr John Simon's official report, as Medical Officer, on health in the City of London.

The second category are more character studies and reportage, often chronicling the poor, but also showing the weird and wonderful diversity of London life. I have drawn liberally upon Albert Smith's *Sketches of London Life and Character*; Charles Dickens's *Sketches by Boz*; Charles Manby Smith's *Curiosities of London Life* and *The Little World Of London*; Daniel Joseph Kirwan's *Palace and Hovel: Phases of London Life*; David W. Bartlett's *London by Day and Night* (a rather dubiously inaccurate work in places, cobbled together by an American author, but with some interesting passages); Edmund Yates compliation of journal articles, *The Business of Pleasure* George R. Sims's *Living London*; Gustave Doré and Blanchard Jerrold's *London: A Pilgrimage*; J.Thomson and Adolphe Smith's *Street Life in London* (combinding tales of the London poor with photographs of the individuals in question); James Grant's *Sketches in London*; James Greenwood's collected journalism, including *In Strange Company, The Mysteries of Modern London, The Wilds of London, Unsentimental Journeys* and *Toilers in London*; John Murray's *The World of London*; Max Schlesinger's *Saunterings in and about London* (a fascinating account by a German visitor to the metropolis); Montagu Williams's *Round London: Down East and Up West*; Thomas Wright's *Some Habits and Customs of the Working Classes*; Watts Phillips's *The Wild Tribes of London*; Richard Rowe's *Life in the London Streets* and, last but not least, W.J.Gordon's *The Horse World of London* (chronicling every category of working horse and the men who manage them).

The third category are moralistic pieces, often written to high-light the work of charities, or draw attention to particular moral issues. The reader will find extracts, therefore, from the twin anonymous works *Tempted London: Young Men*, and *Toilers in London; or Inquiries concerning Female Labour in the Metropolis*; plus 'The Riverside Visitor's' *The Pinch of Poverty*. I have also referred to Thomas Archers's *The Pauper, The Thief and The Convict* and *The Terrible Sights of London*; J. Ewing Ritchie's *The Night Side of London*; Rev. J. Garwood's, *The Million-Peopled City* and, finally, an obscure, rather vigorously written pamphlet by one Henry Vigar-Harris, *London at Midnight* which very much portrays the nocturnal city as a 'Modern Babylon'.

Further reading can be found on my web-site: *www.victorianlondon.org*.

Victorian Currency

The basics of Victorian coinage:-

- *one pound* (£1, but also shown as 1*l.*) contained 20 shillings.
- 1 *shilling* (1*s.*) contained 12 *pence*.
- thus there were 240 *pence* (20 x 12) to every pound.

Victorian words to do with currency:-

- 1 *guinea* was £1 1*s.* (or 21 shillings) - ie. a pound with an additional shilling.
- 1 *crown* was five shillings (and a half-crown, naturally, two and a half shillings).
- a *sovereign* was a gold pound coin (as opposed to a note); a *half-sovereign* was, of course, ten shillings.
- a *florin* was a two shilling coin (introduced in 1849).
- 1 *farthing* was a ¼ penny.

Victorian currency slang, most of which predates the 19th century in origin

- a *yellow George* was a guinea; also a *shiner*.
- a *dollar* was a crown (5*s.*) piece; also a *bull*.
- a *George* was a half-crown.
- a shilling was also a *bob*, when specifying a number (as in "I paid six bob for this"); also a *hog* (rare).
- a *fiddler* was a sixpence; also a *grunter*; also a *kick*.
- a *flag* was fourpence.
- a *deuce* was twopence.

- a *brown* was a copper coin, either the penny, happenny or farthing; also simply a *copper*.
- a *mag* was a halfpenny (nb. also often written as the more slangy *happenny*).
- a *fadge* was a farthing (rare).

APPENDIX III

Victorian Wages

CLOTHING

A garter-maker doing piece-work at home could earn 1s. 2d. to 1s. 7d. a day; ("but then I have silk to find, and that costs me 6d. a dozen ... I think I burn half a pound of candles extra when I am at work. ... Half a pound of candles is 2½d. ... at the 1s. 7d. I can get 1s. 0½d. clear."). A skilled seamstress, employed on 'best class of work', could earn 22s. to 26s. per week. However, many were forced to rely on sweatshops, where 7-8s. per week was the going rate.

(sources: Arthur Sherwell, *Life in West London,* 1897; Henry Mayhew, *Labour and the Poor*, 1849; *Tempted London*, 1889)

MANUAL LABOUR

It was common to hire labourers on a daily basis, making regular income uncertain. Typically wages would be £40–£60 pa. Skills and specialisation helped: Henry Mayhew tells of a sewer-flusher earning a regular income of £1 4s. per week (£65 pa.). A skilled workshop employee could expect £75 pa.

(sources: Thomas Wright, *Some Habits and Customs of the Working Classes*, 1867; Henry Mayhew, *Labour and the Poor*, 1849)

OFFICE WORK

A Bank of England clerk's wages ranged from a starting salary of £75–£500 pa, according to seniority and time served. A clerk in the civil service could expect a similar progression; likewise a clerk in the Post Office, with senior posts earning £350–£500 pa. Bank clerks generally earned £20–£50 pa at the start (aged 18), rising £5–£10 per year. A cashier could expect about £150 pa after thirteen or so years service. A suburban bank manager, however, could only expect £100 pa.

(sources: James Grant, *The Great Metropolis*, 1837; *Tempted London*, 1889; Edmund Yates, *His Recollections and Experiences*, 1885)

SERVANTS

Butlers were the top earners, at £40–£100 pa., followed by cooks (£18–£50 pa) and footmen (£20–£40 pa), often chosen more for their decorative looks than skills. A nursery governess could receive from £20–£40 pa, parlour-maids from £12–£30 pa and a mere maid-of-all-work, anything from £6–£15 pa. Servants who 'lived-in' received free board and lodging.

(sources: Charles Dickens (Jnr), *Dickens's Dictionary of London*, 1879; *Cassell's Household Guide*, 1880s)

SHOPS

A female shop assistant might expect between £20 and £50 pa. A male shop worker in a large store might only receive £25 pa after apprenticeship, but could hope for a £10 annual rise up to about £120 pa. The "first men" or "buyers" in big department stores could earn anything from £300–£1000 pa.

(sources: Emily Faithfull, *Choice of a Business for Girls*,1864; Henry Mayhew, *Labour and the Poor*, 1849; *Tempted London*, 1889)

TECHNOLOGY

A female telegraphist could earn £40–£100 pa, depending on her skill. A head telegraphist could rise to £150 pa.

(source: *Cassell's Household Guide*, 1880s)

APPENDIX IV

Family Budgets

A middle-class annual budget (£500 pa) from *Cassell's Household Guide*:

	£	s.	d.
Rent, rates, taxes, and cost of locomotion	72	10	0
Housekeeping (provisions, coal, gas, servants' wages, laundry, and wear-and-tear)	250	0	0
Clothing	62	10	0
Education	32	10	0
Insurance, medical attendance, and savings	62	10	0
Incidental expenses	20	0	0
	£500	0	0

. . . . FROM the housekeeping, taken at £250, for an income of £500 a year, the following deductions may be taken as a pretty fair allowance:

	£	s.	d.
Servants' wages. £14 per annum, or £1 3s. 4d. per month, for a general servant; and £12 per annum, or £1 per month, for nurse or housemaid	26	0	0
Gas	8	0	0
Coals and Coke	12	0	0
	£46	0	0

A working-class weekly budget, for a tailor's family in 1890s Soho, from Arthur Sherwell's *Life in West London*, 1897:

	£	s.	d.
Rent (including 2/- off arrears)		13	0
Baker's a/c for bread (including 1/- off arrears)		3	9
Groceries for week		2	6½
Paid for washing (in consequence of wife working at trade)		2	9
Joint of meat (to last three days)		2	7½
Meat, for remaining 4 days		2	3
Vegetables for week		3	0
1½ cwt. coals (at 1/4 per *cwt.*)		2	0
Butter for the week (1 *lb*)		1	0
Sundry household requisites, soap, soda, etc.		1	0
Oil			8
Insurance and Club money		1	4
Hire of machine		1	6
Fair of boots for child		2	11
Total expenditure (for six persons)	£2	0s.	4d.
Balance of income over expenditure		3s.	5d.
Total	£2	3s.	9d.

The absence of any item of expenditure for beer or other alcoholic drinks is noteworthy. Moreover, with the exception of one item of 2/11 for boots for one of the children, there is no mention made of clothes, the cost of which, for a family of six persons would necessarily be great.*

APPENDIX V

Housing

	Cost (weekly)
A furnished house in the West End	5 to 25 guineas
'Elegantly furnished rooms' in the West End	4 to 15 guineas
An unfurnished house in Holland Park (wealthy suburb, Kensington area)	7 to 10 guineas
A sitting room and bedroom in Pimlico (well-to-do suburb)	1 to 4 guineas
A house in suburban Walthamstow (a railway commuter suburb, NE London)	10 to 40s.
Three rooms in Soho (relatively poor but central London district)	14 to 20s.
House on Shaftesbury-park model housing estate, built for working men and their families in Battersea (varied with size of house, from five rooms through to eight)	7s. 6d. to 11s.
Single room in Soho (relatively poor but central London district)	6 to 8s.
Single room for "mechanic" (manual labourer) in lodgings	3 to 6s.
Two rooms in Peabody Model Housing	4s. 9d.
Society for Improving the Condition of the Labouring Classes model housing estate, two room cottage	3s. 6d.

HOTELS   (per night)

Bed & Breakfast, with Dinner and 'attendance' at the Midland Grand Hotel	14*s.*
Bed & Breakfast at a City boarding-house	3*s.*
Bed in shared room in 'low lodging house'	1–4*d.*

(sources: *Murray's Handbook to London As It is*, 1879; *The Surburban Homes of London*, 1881; *Dickens's Dictionary of London*, 1879; *Cruchley's London*, 1865; Henry Mayhew, *London Labour and the London Poor*, 1851; Arthur Sherwell, *Life in West London*, 1897; *Illustrated London News* on "Model Lodging", 1846).